A LIGHT AMONG THE GENTILES

A LIGHT AMONG THE GENTILES

*Jewish Missionary Activity in
the Second Temple Period*

Scot McKnight

Fortress Press
Minneapolis

A LIGHT AMONG THE GENTILES
Jewish Missionary Activity in the Second Temple Period

Library of Congress Cataloging-in-Publication Data

McKnight, Scot.
   A light among the gentiles : Jewish missionary activity in the
Second Temple period / Scot McKnight.
     p.   cm.
   Includes bibliographical references and index.
   ISBN 0-8006-2452-1 (alk. paper)
   1. Judaism–History–Postexilic period, 586 B.C.–210 A.D.–
Historiography. 2. Proselytes and proselyting, Jewish. 3. Jews–
History–586 B.C.–70 A.D.–Historiography. 4. Christianity–
Origin. I. Title.
BM176.M38 1991   90-14063
296–dc20   CIP

The paper used in this publication meets the minimum requirements of American National Standard for Information Sciences—Permanence of Paper for Printed Library Materials, ANSI Z329.48–1984.

Manufactured in the U.S.A.   AF 1-2452
95   94   93   92   91   1   2   3   4   5   6   7   8   9   10

Day Dowman
In memoriam

and

Jimmy Dunn

Contents

Acknowledgments

THIS BOOK HAS ITS ORIGINS in a side interest of mine in Jewish literature of the first-century period that began during my doctoral work on the missionary discourse in Matthew 9:35–11:1 at the University of Nottingham. Because of the kind graces of the administration of Trinity Evangelical Divinity School, I was able to devote part of a sabbatical in the fall of 1987 to writing up the results of my previous work. I express my gratitude to President K. M. Meyer and Deans W. C. Kaiser, Jr., and B. J. Beitzel for their continuing support of academic scholarship.

Since that first draft, many colleagues, some of whom have become my friends as a result of this work, have read portions or the entirety of the manuscript. I wish to express my thanks to these critics: B. D. Chilton (Bard College), D. Senior and C. Osiek (Catholic Theological Union), S. J. D. Cohen (Jewish Theological Seminary), L. H. Feldman (Yeshiva University), A.-J. Levine (Swarthmore College), D. E. Aune (St. Xavier College), and M. Wise (University of Chicago). I am grateful especially to Larry Hurtado (University of Manitoba) for making detailed comments on the entire work. His comments have often found their way into the book without specific documentation, and he will surely detect his own ideas at places. I am also grateful to Norman Golb (University of Chicago) for inviting me to read a paper to his seminar and to R. D. Chesnutt (Pepperdine University), A. T. Kraabel (Luther College), and R. Riesner (Tübingen) for making available to me copies of articles that I could not otherwise obtain.

The librarians of many collections have shown their customary expertise in locating difficult-to-find materials: I mention especially Eleanor Warner (Rolfing Library, Trinity Evangelical Divinity School), C. C. Broyles (Tyndale House), and the wonderful staff at the University of Nottingham, especially Tony Barker and Glenis Pickering. Other libraries that have been most helpful are Garrett Evangelical Theological Seminary, Seabury-Western, Northwestern University, and St. Mary of the Lake. Such a trail of assistance makes one aware of the community that is needed to do scholarly work.

My community has at its center a supporting family. I express my gratitude to my wife, Kristen, for her patience during a decade while

I lived at times among ancient synagogues and curious authors. Our children, Laura and Lukas, have kept us sane and tied to tasks other than our research. During that time they came to love the charitable wife of Tom Dowman, the president of the Carlton Rotary Chapter, a philanthropic organization that looked after our family during our first year in Nottingham. Day Dowman adopted our children as a surrogate grandmother and taught them how to speak English properly, while their other grandmothers missed them for two years. Tragically, at the end of our stay in England, Day passed away because of cancer. We miss her but remember her with the utmost of affection.

Further, I express my deepest appreciation to Professor James D. G. Dunn, formerly of the University of Nottingham, who even after a relocation to Durham University, continued to supervise my work and offer his incisive observations. In making this work public I am again reminded of the debt I owe him, and, as a small token of that debt, I dedicate this book to him along with Day Dowman.

Finally, I am deeply grateful to Mr. Timothy Staveteig, of Fortress Press, for his painstaking carefulness in handling the details of this book. He and the editorial team at Fortress impressed me time and again with their precision and attention to detail. Their work has improved the quality of this book in no small measure. In addition, I express my thanks to my graduate assistants who have chased down bibliography and helped with the indexes; in particular, I am thankful to D. Scott Wagoner and Matt Williams.

Scot McKnight

Introduction

THE REVISER OF E. Schürer's *magnum opus, The History of the Jewish People in the Age of Jesus Christ,* states: "No full and satisfactory study of proselytism in the Graeco-Roman period has yet been written, and fundamental uncertainties remain as to both the numerical scale and the conditions of acceptance of both proselytes proper and 'God-fearers.'"[1] It is my purpose to present an inductive examination and to propose a theory that may throw some light on one area of this dark corner of Second Temple Judaism, namely, the nature and extent of Jewish missionary activity. Thus, although this monograph surveys the evidence from the ancient world on Jewish missionary activity, it does so to elucidate only one aspect of those data.

Scholars agree that earliest Christianity was a missionary movement of major proportions, but the question of the origin of the missionary impulse in earliest Christianity remains unsettled. In particular, did this later movement derive its missionary zeal from its parent religion, Second Temple Judaism? Many have concluded so. According to D. Georgi, "The spread of Judaism . . . thus compares quite favorably with the missionary successes of the early church. This is especially true when one considers that the mission of the Jesus-believers, unlike that of Jews before them, received a soil already prepared. Indeed, the church came to inherit the successes of Judaism."[2] A survey of some approaches may indicate the context of the present inquiry.

Previous Approaches

Discussions of Jewish missionary activity have been neither plentiful nor comprehensive, although many scholars have expressed judgments regarding such matters as "God-fearers," baptism, and the abundance of proselytes.

The dominant research into the question of Jewish missionary activity has emerged from the *Religionsgeschichtliche Schule* and perhaps finds its most poignant expression in one of the earliest works on the subject, A. Bertholet's *Die Stellung der Israeliten und der Juden zu den Fremden* (1896). Among the most important and influential works after Bertholet (given here in shortened titles) are A. von Harnack, *Mission* (1904–5);

K. Axenfeld, "Die jüdische Propaganda" (1904); S. Bialoblocki, *Die Beziehungen des Judentums zu Proselyten* (1930); F. M. Derwacter, *Preparing the Way* (1930); G. F. Moore, *Judaism* (1927–1930); B. J. Bamberger, *Proselytism* (1939); P. Dalbert, *Die Theologie der hellenistisch-jüdischen Missionsliteratur* (1954); J. Jeremias, *Jesus' Promise* (1956); K. G. Kuhn, "*prosēlytos*," in *Theologisches Wörterbuch zum Neuen Testament* (1959); D. Bosch, *Die Heidenmission* (1959); E. Lerle, *Proselytenwerbung* (1960); F. Hahn, *Mission* (1963); D. Georgi, *The Opponents of Paul* (1964, 1986 rev.); and F. Millar, "Gentiles and Judaism: 'God-Fearers' and Proselytes," in E. Schürer, *History* 3.1: 150–77. Others could be mentioned, but this list represents the more important treatments.

The general consensus of this literature is that Judaism was, in varying degrees, undoubtedly a missionary religion. Individual Jews, and Judaism in general, endeavored to reach out with the message of monotheism, national privilege, and spiritual morality to those who were not Jews, regardless of the manner of their outreach. Studies of this topic, however, have different emphases.

Classic treatments, which do little more than "restate" the (uninterpreted?) data themselves, can be found in G. F. Moore's chapter "Conversion of Gentiles" and Fergus Millar's revision of E. Schürer's *History of the Jewish People.* Most studies, however, seek to explain the development of the Israelite missionary impulse in the context of an emerging universalism in Judaism itself, especially Diaspora Judaism. Some of these studies, unfortunately, are bent on showing this development as a movement toward the superiority of Christianity. Noteworthy treatments include those of A. Bertholet, A. von Harnack, W. Bousset (*Religion*), A. Oepke, O. Michel, J. Jeremias, F. Hahn, K. G. Kuhn and H. Stegemann, H. J. Schoeps (*Paul*), M. Simon, J. J. Collins (*Between*), and D. Georgi's frequently ignored chapter "Missionary Activity in New Testament Times."

Since the late 1930s, Jewish scholars have responded to the customary polemical assertion of late nineteenth- and early twentieth-century German scholarship on Judaism, that (post–Bar Kokhba, talmudic) Judaism was largely unconcerned with proselytes and was, in fact, often hostile to them or to the charge that modern Judaism proves itself inferior to modern Christianity because of the former's disinterest in missions. These countertreatments either explain the noninvolvement or seek to show the inherent missionary nature of Judaism. The more notable apologetical studies hailing from Jewish scholars are B. J. Bamberger; W. G. Braude, *Jewish Proselytizing* (1940); J. S. Raisin,

Gentile Reactions (1953); and J. R. Rosenbloom, *Conversion to Judaism* (1978).

Although these important treatments come at our subject from different angles, the consensus is that Judaism (usually seen in monolithic terms) of the Second Temple period was a missionary religion. In fact, it is regularly contended that Judaism of the period was an aggressive missionary movement and sought out converts with religious zeal. K. G. Kuhn has bequeathed to a generation or two of students the comment that there was in the Jewish Diaspora "a lively Jewish mission,"[3] and Dieter Georgi, agreeing with G. Rosen and G. Bertram, states, "there existed among the Jews a widespread missionary awareness and a corresponding missionary activity."[4] G. F. Moore, whose work on Judaism is singularly accurate for its time, stated that "the belief in the future universality of the true religion ... led to efforts to convert the Gentiles to the worship of the one true God and to faith and obedience according to the revelation he had given, and made Judaism the first great missionary religion of the Mediterranean world."[5]

Perhaps the classic statement of this is by J. Jeremias, and, because of his stature and erudition in New Testament scholarship, his conclusion has been handed down as an "assured result." He stated: "At the time of Jesus' appearance an unparalleled period of missionary activity was in progress in Israel" and "Jesus thus came upon the scene in the midst of what was *par excellence* the missionary age of Jewish history." Finally, he concludes, "Jesus grew up in the midst of a people actively engaged, both by the spoken and written word, in a Gentile mission, whose impelling force was a profound sense of their obligation to glorify their God in the Gentile world."[6] Apart from the problem this conclusion creates for Jesus' own inactivity in a Gentile mission, the evidence Jeremias cites either is late, or is from the Diaspora (which then works against his own point about Jesus), or proves something else. Further, his conclusions here can hardly be squared with his later conclusion that Jesus and Judaism looked entirely to God and the future for the conversion of Gentiles.[7] It is the purpose of this study to challenge the consensus of these scholars.[8] It may seem foolhardy to question the conclusions of scholars of such sapience, but this consensus seems to be shifting. Leading the revision of contemporary scholarship on Judaism is A. T. Kraabel, who has recently surveyed six questionable assumptions about ancient Judaism. One of these is the missionary nature of Judaism. His characterization of much of the scholarship on this point goes like this: "Proper Judaism became contaminated because Jews were too eager to speak the religious language of gentile piety, to make their religion appealing to their neighbours, in order to gain converts or *proselytoi*, proselytes."[9] I am seeking to establish Kraabel's criticism in this monograph.

Finally, a cursory examination of scholarship on Jewish missionary activity reveals that there has not been a serious reappraisal of the evidence and an inductive explanation of that data within two generations. In the last generation we find only Georgi's monograph and the revision of Schürer. The present work will bring to bear on this topic some of the more recent developments in our understanding of Judaism of this time.[10]

The Focus of This Study

This study is an attempt to set out the facts about the nature and extent of Jewish missionary activity in Second Temple Judaism from the data that can be retrieved from and about this period. However valuable study of the Old Testament view of mission may be, such an analysis remains outside the boundaries of this study. Further, the rabbinical literature could be examined as a separate study, but I am here concerned primarily with Second Temple Judaism, the alleged context of earliest Christianity's missionary practices and theories. In addition, this study is an attempt at historiography. I am neither insensitive to nor unaware of other approaches to ancient literature, including the tradition-critical analyses of the various layers of a given document as well as the more recent developments in literary and narrative criticism; however, this essay is concerned with facts about Judaism and its practices in the Second Temple period insofar as they can be discerned. I am aware also of the implications of heuristic emphases (e.g., levels of adherence in Judaism), but I am convinced that these emphases are in fact the questions of the historian. They enable us to understand issues not often directly discussed in the ancient evidence. Accordingly, although the text of *Joseph and Aseneth* may not directly say anything about Jewish missionary activity, what it says (in idealistic terms) about conversion may shed light on Jewish missionary activity.

Defining Terms

One of the notable deficiencies of this advancing area of study is the lack of consistency in the use of terms. I define a "missionary religion" as a religion that self-consciously defines itself as a religion, one aspect of whose "self-definition" is a mission to the rest of the world, or at least a large portion of that world. This religion at the same time practices its mission through behavior that intends to evangelize nonmembers so that these nonmembers will convert to the religion. There may be a vast chasm between one's belief system (e.g., we are a missionary religion) and one's actual practice (e.g., but we do not behave in such a way that one sees that we are a missionary religion).[11]

In our day we might easily identify certain well-defined groups of American religion as a "missionary religion." Thus, few will doubt that the Church of Latter-day Saints (the Mormons) is a missionary religion. Mission is written into the fabric of the religion, and it is consistently practiced by adherents to the religion. A significant portion of evangelicalism can also be characterized as missionary religion, from local evangelistic pastors to larger programs like the Billy Graham crusades. These groups can be properly called missionary religions because they define themselves as such and behave accordingly. Examples of the reverse might be the Amish or portions of mainline Protestantism. Whereas each of these movements adheres to the foundational documents of Christianity, which inculcate missionary behavior, rarely do the individual members of these movements actually participate in the process of "converting others" to their faith. Whatever one thinks of these movements, the point remains the same: A missionary religion is one that both defines itself as a missionary movement and behaves in a missionary manner. This is how I will use the expression "missionary religion," and I shall ask whether it is historically accurate to describe Judaism as a "missionary religion." My conclusion will be that the evidence does not support such a description.

Another term in need of definition is "conversion,"[12] a classic definition of which was offered by A. D. Nock: "By conversion we mean the reorientation of the soul of an individual, his deliberate turning from indifference or from an earlier form of piety to another, a turning which implies a consciousness that a great change is involved, that the old was wrong and the new is right." He continues:

> Judaism said in effect to a man who was thinking of becoming a proselyte: "You are in your sins. Make a new start, put aside idolatry and the immoral practices which go with it, become a naturalized member of the Chosen People by a threefold rite of baptism, circumcision, and offering, live as God's Law commands, and you will have every hope of a share in the life of the world to come."[13]

Nock further contended that Judaism and Christianity had no rivals in conversion because the other religions of antiquity expected only adherence; the only true rival was a philosophical school. He stated: "The Jew and the Christian offered religions as we understand religion; the others offered cults...."[14]

Modifying the view of Nock, S. J. D. Cohen argues that conversion "entailed not only recognition of Judaism's truth but also incorporation into the Jewish community."[15] This community aspect of conversion is highly significant and has been brought out especially by recent sociological analyses. Although the definitions of Nock and Cohen are useful, some recent research in the field of religious sociology has given added nuance to the nature of conversion. Accordingly, the use of these studies for antiquity is promising, and, in fact, a few scholars have already begun to apply the results. Before discussing these scholars, however, we need to look at the work of D. A. Snow and R. Machalek.[16]

Snow and Machalek point out that there are various degrees in the conversion process, from simple alternation to a radical change such as the conversions of Augustine and Paul. They suggest, therefore, that change is not the best device for detecting conversion, but that a crucial element is the changing of "one's universe of discourse." They state: "Viewed in this light, conversion concerns not only a change in values, beliefs, and identities, but more fundamentally and significantly, it entails the displacement of one universe of discourse by another or the ascendance of a formerly peripheral universe of discourse to the status of a primary authority."[17] They survey the scholarship, then, for the empirical factors indicating conversion: (1) membership status, (2) demonstration events, and (3) rhetorical indicators. Snow and Machalek contend for the third empirical factor, the presence of rhetorical indicators. These rhetorical indicators, discerned through a study on the Nichiren Shoshu Buddhist movement, are fourfold: (1) reconstructing one's biography, (2) adopting a master attribution scheme, (3) suspending analogical reasoning, and (4) embracing the role of a convert.

Snow and Machalek's work has become influential, although it is not without its critics. In particular, C. L. Staples and A. L. Mauss have argued that the determining feature of conversion is the convert's own self-reconceptualization. The rhetorical features of Snow and Machalek are the convert's own tools and methods for self-transformation. The essence of conversion is redefining the self, because conversion is inherently subjective. Their conclusion is worth quoting: "We propose that conversion be viewed as a process; that this process is fundamentally one of self-transformation; that self-transformation is achieved primarily through language . . . ; and that the convert plays an active role in his or her own self-transformation."[18]

The results of these and many other studies have been applied recently to antiquity by B. R. Gaventa and A. F. Segal.[19] Gaventa, in particular, has clarified the issues well, stating: "To ask about conversion is to ask what attracts people to a faith, what changes in their understanding of themselves and of the world, and what supports them in the new faith. It is also to ask about a community of believers, its self-understanding, and its attitudes toward outsiders, seekers, and newcomers."[20] She sees three different categories of personal change: (1) alternation, (2) conversion, and (3) transformation. "Alternation is a relatively limited form of change that develops from one's previous behavior; conversion is a radical change in which past affiliations are rejected for some new commitment and identity; transformation is also radical change, but one in which an altered perception reinterprets both present and past."[21]

In my opinion, Gaventa's work is insightful, especially for New Testament students. Although I tend to agree with her work on the nature of conversion, particularly the varieties of conversion-like changes in life, the evidence for conversion to Judaism does not permit these kinds of subtle differences. The subjective perception of conversion is almost completely unavailable to modern historians. Nonetheless, in this study I shall try to use the terms that have been established in the discussions surveyed above. "Conversion," for us, involves three features: (1) cognitive agreement with the religion to which one is turning,[22] (2) socialization into that group, and (3) a restructuring of oneself, involving at least a biographical reconstruction.

But even here the historian must be careful. Ancient Judaism is a diverse movement, and conversion is a local factor. One does not, in effect, convert to Judaism so much as one converts to a local display of Judaism (say, Sardisian or Alexandrian Judaism with its own diversities). Furthermore, different groups no doubt had different perceptions of what constituted conversion. What counted as conversion for one group of Jews may not have been seen as conversion for another.[23]

The Context

The challenge of this short monograph could be taken in several ways, and at this point I wish to give to my reader a few hints at how I prefer this study *not* to be read. My central thesis that Second Temple Judaism was largely unconcerned with missionary activity and that it was not a missionary religion, even though conversion did take place, does not at all mean that Judaism lacked compassion or that it was confined to ghettos and concerned only with obedience to the Torah by God's elect.

Instead, I find Judaism of this period to be both compassionate and amazingly compliant with the cultural forces within which it developed. Statements on separation in ancient literature, as I will argue below, are best understood as reflecting religious convictions, not social and racial relations. Martin Hengel, J. J. Collins, and especially A. T. Kraabel have demonstrated this clearly. Nor do I want to be understood as saying that Christianity is a superior religion to Judaism because it is a missionary religion. I do not think that the superiority of a religion ought to (or can) be measured by its evangelistic behavior any more than that the superiority of modern Christian or Jewish groups ought to be assessed by their successes in evangelism. Some of the world's most notorious figures have been alarmingly and inexplicably adept in forms of "evangelism," whether we think politically, in the case of Adolf Hitler, or religiously, in the case of Jim and Tammy Bakker. Consequently, the conclusions of this work ought not to be set in an apologetical *Sitz im Leben,* and the reader is asked to bear this in mind. I am not urging a particular set of beliefs through this monograph.

The Procedure

In presenting this material I have proceeded topically. An option would be to describe the missionary orientation of various sociological groups, examining also the distinctive aspects of different social classes. In the end I decided against this approach because I am not convinced that we can assign all the data of the ancient world to various sociological and theological groups with sufficient rigor to warrant such an approach. Moreover, this would leave much of the evidence in undefined categories and therefore almost useless. To be sure, such a typology could be useful. Furthermore, I sensed that such an approach would require a running dialogue with all those scholars who have assigned various documents to different groups. The book would be perforce lengthened beyond the desired confines.

Another approach would be geographical. One could investigate how Jews in Alexandria believed and behaved over against how Jews in Asia Minor did the same. Again, the positive implications of this approach are outweighed by its major problem: How sure can one be about assigning all the evidence to various geographical locations? Thus, we might know now enough to say something intelligent and accurate about Sardis and Alexandria, but what do we do with a text like *Joseph and Aseneth?* Would we put it in Alexandria? What about the rabbinic evidence? Is it Palestinian, or Galilean, or something else? Furthermore, to give but one example, what does one do with evidence from Josephus when he is describing something in Palestine? Does such evidence reflect more what Josephus sees in Rome than what actually occurs in Palestine? The difficulty of finding secure answers to such questions led me away from this approach. It would be good to have information about Jewish missionary activity in various geographical locations, but I doubt that we can locate enough of the data to make a survey of the material for our question sufficient.

A different procedure would be to trace the history of the missionary movement during the Second Temple period, but a similar form of ignorance arose. Can one date the documents of this period so securely that one can be confident enough to provide a developmental scheme? I doubt it. Any glance at the introductions to the ancient literature makes clear that scholarship has not yet arrived at secure conclusions regarding the dating of these books.[24] Another factor complicates this chronological scheme, namely, the problem of various sociological movements in diverse locations operating in different fashions at different periods of history. Is there not an a priori presumption against any neat developmental scheme? This bewildering confusion, in my opinion, makes any chronological descriptions of Jewish missionary movements suspect from the outset.

A final approach would be to proceed author by author, allowing the historian to place each text carefully in its context and in the larger theological patterns of the ancient author, but the problems with this approach are too numerous. For one, few would want to read a list of authors and what they think about proselytism. Moreover, it is impossible to determine the authorship of many books of ancient Judaism, including such documents as the Qumran writings and the rabbinic works. Contextual study is paramount, but synthesis determined by legitimate heuristic devices is the tool of the historian.

Consequently, the approach here will be synthetic. By this I mean that I shall attempt to cut a cross section through the ancient evidence around a certain theme—Jewish attitudes toward proselytism. I shall not simply list a multitude of ancient authors and then proceed, from their own particular theological viewpoint, to state that author's views on the various notions associated with missionary activity. In opting for this synthetic approach, I do not want to misconstrue the evidence by giving the impression that there is a unified pattern or orthodox system of thought about the Gentiles, nor do I want to suggest that Judaism was monolithic and uniform.[25] In fact, one of the conclusions to which I shall point is the diversity of Jewish authors over Gentile questions. However, in order to avoid a tedious and protracted presentation, I have chosen not to atomize the evidence into single authors, although I do not doubt that such a study could be useful to historians.[26]

In examining the evidence found in the ancient world, I shall proceed in roughly chronological order. Since many ancient books went through a series of redactions, extending even into the Middle Ages, it is simply impossible to be precise concerning the date and audience. Further, by most accounts, the dates of many ancient documents and inscriptions can be estimated only by century. Consequently, I shall begin with the so-called apocryphal and pseudepigraphical literature, move to the Dead Sea Scrolls, Philo, Josephus, and the rabbinic writings. Supplementing each of these presentations will be comments on inscriptions and epigraphical data, along with Greco-Roman authors and Jewish historians. Following this I shall round off the picture by examining the New Testament evidence to see if it also sheds light on the picture we have framed from non-Christian sources. I shall abandon a chronological approach with respect to the New Testament data. Instead, this literature has been isolated for separate examination simply to avoid prejudging the case with literature that arose in direct, polemical contrast to the Jewish literature. An interesting study in itself, of course, is how the various authors of the New Testament viewed Judaism.

A few comments are in order here regarding how I, as a nonexpert, will utilize rabbinic literature. To begin, I am concerned almost exclusively with tannaitic literature, although a few references will be made to the Amoraim.[27] In our concern with the Tannaim, however, we shall be utilizing all the evidence that is attributed to them in order to gain a maximum of data. Some of this material, as Jacob Neusner has demonstrated, is undoubtedly later, but the dating of this material will not be our primary concern.[28] Further, I am more particularly concerned with pre-Ushan or Jamnian masters and their traditions.[29] In focusing on these traditions, in the context of the tannaitic literature, we can gain the most that can be gleaned from these sources pertaining to missionary ideas and activity. For stratifying the material I am debted to Jacob Neusner's many works, especially his *Rabbinic Traditions.*

The following questions will be asked of the data: What can we discern from the sources regarding Jewish attitudes to Gentiles? What attitudes did the Jews have regarding proselytes and proselytism? How did Jews convert Gentiles? Did Jewish "missionaries" have a set message that was preached? What were the requirements expected of a convert? What are the various levels of adherence to Judaism?

It is my hope that this work will contribute to the Jewish–Christian dialogue, perhaps shedding light on our common but diverse roots and perhaps also aid in the present debate regarding the origins and "background" of Christian missionary activity.

1

Judaism and the Gentile

PERHAPS AT NO POINT has Christian and Jewish propaganda been more visible in biblical scholarship than in the discussion of Jewish missionary activity. One notices slanted treatments particularly in the late nineteenth and the early twentieth century in authors from Germany, most notably in their attempts to assert the superiority of Christianity over Judaism through demonstrations of active universalism and individualism on the part of the earliest Christians as opposed to legalism, nationalism, and separatism on the part of ancient Judaism. These apologetical treatments were met in kind with counter-apologetics that attempted to prove that Judaism was not misanthropic in nature but was instead a universalistic and missionary religion. The topic of this chapter is a noteworthy example of this propaganda. However interesting such debate might be, this form of historiography is, in reality, propagandistic apologetics. This chapter will attempt to present the evidence as evenly as possible and, I hope, will avoid the pitfalls of many who have construed history as an exercise in apologetics.[1] In this chapter I am concerned with evidence of attitudes and beliefs along with data that speak of Jewish practices. Admittedly, this is a broad topic, but I contend that this is the proper starting place for any discussion of proselytism among Jews.

Jewish Attitudes toward Gentiles

There can be no doubt that Jewish attitudes to Gentiles were often dictated by such factors as local self-consciousness, historical circumstances, and individual vision.[2] The discoveries at Sardis, for instance, have now established the importance of local conditions. It is no longer accurate—nor ever was it—to speak of "*the* Jewish attitude toward Gentiles." It is now necessary to address local conditions and, as a result of studying local conditions, to see if we might discover common features of Jewish attitudes toward Gentiles. Even here it is surely important to distinguish between Palestinian and Diaspora Judaism.

We shall begin with the evidence found in the apocryphal and pseudepigraphical writings. I shall try to isolate some solid evidence and make observations. There are, broadly speaking, two kinds of evidence: that which speaks of Jews assimilating to or integrating with the cultures and religions of their environment and that which speaks of resisting various cultures and religions. A word of caution is in order. The various "integrating" features are not here used to define a sociological group in contrast to those with "resisting" features. The facts now support clearly the grid that most Jewish groups (the Essenes seem more bent than any other group on consistent anti-Hellenism) both resisted non-Jewish culture and also integrated themselves into that culture. Resistance to and assimilation to were concurrent dispositions of most Jews. In general, however, we may describe some features that move from normal, even unsuspecting integration with non-Jewish environments to some outright hostility and separation.

Integrating Tendencies

The work of Martin Hengel has demonstrated beyond doubt that Palestine in general, and Judaism in particular, at least in the period from Alexander the Great until about 150 B.C., was markedly influenced by Hellenism in such areas as theology, economics, philosophy, education, and language.[3] Furthermore, the influence of Hellenism was pervasive, however subtle. When Jews resisted various elements of Hellenization, for example, the profanation of the temple system, that resistance was at the same time being countered by subtle workings of the Hellenistic way of life in literature and commerce to which the Jews were apparently open. As J. J. Collins has stated, this favorable openness to, and therefore influence by, Hellenism during this period is directly related to the elimination of social dissonance. The influence of Hellenism, then, is as much a part of social relations and boundaries as it is ideological toleration.[4]

More than sixty years ago I. Heinemann stated that "among all of the ancient people none learned as much from the Greeks as the Jews."[5] K. L. Schmidt has demonstrated how an innate openness is ideologically grounded in the history of Israel and Yahweh's command to be kind to the gēr tôšāb, the resident alien.[6] Abundant evidence can be marshaled to demonstrate the positions of Heinemann and Schmidt. I have isolated eight aspects of the integrating tendency of Second Temple Judaism and to these I now turn.

Eight Aspects of the Integrating Tendency

These are universalism, friendliness, gentile participation in Judaism, citizenship, Hellenistic education, intermarriage, assimilation, and apostasy. It is impossible to do justice to each of these topics in this format, but we can gain an impression for our larger question about proselytism.

Universalism. The notion of God's reign over the whole world and the consequent international solidarity which that notion suggests have their origin in Scripture (e.g., Gen. 12:1–3; Isa. 42; 49; 56),[7] but they are further developed in the literature of our period, and sometimes with a "pluralistic" twist.[8] In bringing up the matter of universalism, I do not suggest that universalism by itself is assimilation or syncretism. Rather, I am concerned with the logical foundation that this plays in Jewish attitudes toward Gentiles and how this foundation expresses itself in the evidence we survey.

Undoubtedly, the foundation of a favorable attitude toward Gentiles is a recognition that God is creator of all and that humanity is, at some level, a unity. Ben Sira speaks of the universal brotherhood of humanity (Ecclus. 13:15), and 18:13 reads: "Human compassion extends to neighbours, but the Lord's compassion extends to everyone" (NJB). For Philo, God has a providential concern for the whole world and its inhabitants (*Decal.* 178; *Spec.* 1:169, 308; *Praem.* 9; *Cher.* 109; *Prov.* 2:6).[9] Thus, "created things . . . are brothers, since they have all one Father, the Maker of the universe" (*Decal.* 64), "every man being a partaker of mortal nature" (*thnētēs physeōs metechōn* [*Decal.* 99]). Again, "they can claim to be children of the one common mother of mankind, nature . . ." (*Decal.* 41).

Josephus discovers a genetic connection between all people (*Ag. Ap.* 2.94) and that God presides over all (*Ag. Ap.* 2.122)[10] and is "father of all" (*Ag. Ap.* 2.152). Thus, in his polemics with Apion, Josephus asserts that Jews are open to all men: that we have a code that urges "friendly relations with each other, and humanity towards the world at large" (*Ag. Ap.* 2.146). It can be inferred from Josephus that universalism leads to kindness to other nations; it is possible that this is a logical foundation for proselytism or at least his positive attitude toward Gentiles and conversion.

The impact of universalism can be felt in the rabbis as well. Observe *m. Yad.* 4:4; *t. Yad.* 2.17; *b. Ber.* 28a, where Judah, the Ammonite proselyte, approaches the sages in Beth Hamidrash. From Deut. 23:3 it is known that Ammonites are never to enter the assembly, which led Rabban Gamaliel II to prohibit Judah's marriage to a Jew. But Rabbi Joshua b. Hananiah, a contemporary, by exegeting Isa. 10:13 and Jer. 30:3, convinced Rabban that the distinction was no longer ascertainable. Ammonites, therefore, were no longer banned.[11] This tendency toward relaxation—and many others could be cited (e.g., *t. Sanh.* 13.2)—may be attributed to the development of universalism, other political and social forces notwithstanding.

Friendliness. Philo contended that Jews were "peacefully inclined to all" (*Flacc.* 94), even naturally so (*hōs eirēnikous tas physeis* [*Leg.* 161]), and "prayed for all mankind" (*Leg.* 306; *Spec.* 1.97; *Virt.* 141). Even one's enemies were to be treated kindly (*Virt.* 109–15). Thus, he says, "we should do no wrong to men of other nations, if we can accuse them of nothing save difference of race, which is no matter for accusation" (*Virt.* 147). It ought to be observed here that Philo makes these kinds of comments at the same time that he argues vigorously for the election of Israel (see below). There can be little doubt that the Jews were generally friendly with their neighbors—in spite of doubts raised by some of the Greco-Roman authors.

Friendliness, even complete integration, can be illustrated by the evidence from Sardis in its implications for how the Jews, who had been permanent residents probably from the end of the third century B.C. (but see Obad. 20), interacted with their Gentile neighbors (see Josephus *Ant.* 14.235, 259–61; 16.171).[12] Even if the massive building now known was clearly not a part of Second Temple Jewish life, and even if earlier synagogues were not as diverse in actual functions performed within, the synagogue layout and its implications will be used here to illustrate Jewish integration.[13]

The building used by the Jews here is a massive, artistic community center and was used apparently for religious, educational, and social services. The south end of the building, which is 100 m. long, included a synagogue connected to a gymnasium[14] and comprised approximately two dozen Roman shops that faced "Main Street." This building was integrated into, or a part of, the city's gymnasium-bath complex and the synagogue was able to hold as many as one thousand people.

Here we see a Judaism that is "a minority, but a powerful, perhaps even wealthy one, of great antiquity in a major city of the Diaspora, controlling a huge and lavishly decorated structure on 'Main Street' and able to retain control of it as long as the city existed."[15] The architecture itself shows us a Judaism that is friendly, assimilated, integrated, and powerful—however, still Jewish.[16] Judaism should not be seen as an insular sect or a segregated ghetto.[17]

Other pieces of evidence suggest similar friendliness and integration. One inscription reads: "Aurelius Olympias, of the tribe of Leontioi, with my wife and children, I have fulfilled my vow."[18] The "tribe of Leontioi," probably a version of "the tribe of Judah" (Gen. 49:9), also associates these Jews with the Lydian and Persian Sardis connection with the lion, which was a mythic symbol of power in Sardis. Thus, these Jews belonged to two worlds, which, in effect, were but one unified world.[19] The evidence we now have suggests also that Jews had the same kinds of jobs their Gentile neighbors had and that Jews were members of the city council, holding positions of considerable influence.[20] In addition, some scholars are now putting forward the theory that Jews acclimated to their various cultures by enabling women to become religious and social leaders.[21]

If this evidence from Sardis, confirmed by evidence from other locations in Asia Minor, is anywhere near the picture of Judaism in the first century, we have compelling evidence for revising how Judaism has been described in its relation with Gentiles and, for our point, significant evidence for Jewish integration and friendliness.

Gentile participation in the Jewish religion. Perhaps rooted in Old Testament law (Lev. 22:25) and aspiration (1 Kings 8:41-43), friendship penetrated behind the veiled curtains of religious rites.[22] This can be observed with respect to the Jewish temple and other holy things in Judaism, including the building of synagogues for Jews.

Whether it is seen in the general permission of others, including potentates, to worship in the temple, to offer sacrifices (Josephus *J.W.* 2.412-16)[23] or to donate gifts (*J.W.* 5.563; *Ant.* 13.145-47, 168, 242), or in the reading of their Scriptures (*Ant.* 1.11; cf. Pseudo-Longinus *De Sublimitate* 9.9),[24] Judaism seems to have been flexible with respect to its holy things. In fact, Josephus says that Jesus, the high priest, pleaded with the Idumaeans, speaking of Jerusalem as "the spot which is revered by the world and honoured by aliens" (*J.W.* 4.262). The temple, he continues, is a place "which flung wide its gates to every foreigner for worship" (4.275). Whatever may be said of Jewish particularism, that particularism emerged from a context that permitted Gentiles to worship, at some level, with Jews in the temple. This permission was extended to Jewish customs as well (Josephus *Ag. Ap.* 1.162-67; 2.281-84), such as the Sabbath (*CPJ* 3.43-87).[25] It is most likely that those who did participate in these Jewish customs and rituals would have been perceived in different categories by different groups of Jews.[26]

Citizenship and official recognition. Even the most ardent of nationalists valued legal protection in the political assembly (*politeuma*) and fought for it when under threat.[27] It was, according to Philo, "the sole mooring on which our life was secured" (*Flacc.* 74; see also *Leg.* 155, 157). In Palestine there was a continual pursuit of treaties (Josephus *Ant.* 8.50-54; 12.160-224, 414-19;[28] 13.33, 37-42, 43-57, 83-85, 124-29, 134, 145-47, 163-70,[29] 227; cf. 1 Macc. 15:16-24[30]). Aristobulus was even dubbed a "philhellene" (13.318), but neither citizenship nor official recognition should be perceived as apostasy. Jews were tolerated probably because they proved themselves tolerable and tolerating of others.

Adjacent to this literary evidence are the epigraphical and papyrological data that evince a Jewish name being followed by a (more acceptable?) Greek or Latin name. This widespread phenomenon is almost certainly to be explained as integration, whether the motives are political, commercial, or cultural.[31]

Hellenistic education. If there was demand to move up the social ladder in the Hellenistic world, one method made the move much easier—education in Hellenistic schools.[32] Accordingly, it is apparent that many Jewish scholars arose from Hellenistic cities in Palestine. The best evidence of this development in Judaism, so far as I am aware, is found in Philo.

Education, according to Philo, was good for all (*Spec.* 2.21-22; *Cher.* 129; *Sacr.* 47-48; *Migr.* 72; *Mut.* 229; *Prob.* 4, 13-15, 98; *Virt.* 40-44), and so, like other Alexandrians, some Jews educated their children in the encyclical (*Mos.* 1.23-24; *Spec.* 2.228-30; *L.A.* 3.244; *Migr.* 72; *Her.* 274; *Prob.* 143), even if Torah wisdom had to be added to Hellenistic education (*CPJ* 1:39 n. 99; Philo *Leg.* 115, 210, 230, 314; *Spec.* 2.88, 228-30, 233, 236; 4.16, 149; *L.A.* 1.99; 3.244; *Ebr.* 80-81; *Congr.* 79; *Virt.* 141; *Praem.* 162).[33] According to Josephus, Herod's path to influence was paved by a Roman education (*Ant.* 15.373).[34] Archelaus and Philip had the same privilege (*J.W.* 1.602; not in *Ant.* 17.79-82).[35]

The impact of this education is predictable (and surely intended): the spirit of Hellenism was absorbed. Indeed, as is said of one of Herod's sons, "The offspring of Alexander abandoned from birth the observances of the ways of the Jewish land and ranged themselves with the Greek tradition (*pros ta hellēsi patria*)" (*Ant.* 18.141).

Education was so crucial that a rewriting of Jewish history took place: Joseph, the patriarch, was educated in Alexandria with a "liberal education" (*kai paideian te tēn eleutherion epaideue*) at the tutelage of Egyptians (*Ant.* 2.39); Moses experienced the same (*Ant.* 2.216). Education, however geographically widespread we are unable to tell, was surely one of the securist ways of integrating into non-Jewish society. The path, we suppose, was probably taken by many.

Intermarriage. Marrying a Gentile illustrates integration. Ezra's reforms were not permanent in Jewish society, and, in fact, intermarriage began early (Deut. 7:3) and remained a constant factor—even if it was problematic to some.[36] Josephus tells us, without condemnation, that Joseph married a foreigner (*Ant*. 2.91–92), that Antipater married Cypros, a lady of an illustrious Arabian family (*J.W*. 1.181), and through such a relation gained influence with the Idumaeans (*Ant*. 14.121). Esther's story was not a cause of pride, because she had premarital intercourse and hid her nationality (*Ant*. 11.198–204). The marriage of Herod to a Samaritan, Malthace, and their daughter Olympias (*Ant*. 17.20) brought Herod no favor among the Jews (see also *J.W*. 1.446; *Ant*. 5.319, 335; 8.21; 11.302–3, 311–12; 13.228; 18.109, 340–52).[37]

Various other forms of integration. Friendliness and openness at times surrender to a deeper assimilation, the erosion of the Jewish faith through adaptation. However true this assimilation may have been, it is not always possible for us to detect when "caving in" occurred. In the *Letter of Aristeas* we find such assimilation and observe a blurring of national distinctions. Aristeas's notion that "these people worship God the overseer and creator of all, whom all men worship including ourselves, O King, except that we have a different name. Their name for him is Zeus and Jove" (16) would have found immediate rejoinder in many, if not most, Jewish circles, even if there was some agreement that their God was universal lord because he was creator (17, 19).

Similar assimilation may be seen with respect to the Jewish rite of circumcision, the mark of covenantal adherence. The attempts to hellenize Jerusalem, and so all of Judaism, are found throughout the literature (3 Macc. 2:29–33; 1 Macc. 1:10–15, 42, 52–53; 6:21; 7:5–50; 9:23, 25–31, 58, 69, 73; 10:61; 11:21, 25), and *epispasm*, the attempt to cover up circumcision, is surely the ultimate act for repudiating Judaism (e.g., 1 Macc. 1:15; *T. Moses* 8:1–5).[38] It may be that this act is apostasy itself (see below). It might be noted, in rejoinder, that not all Jews perceived circumcision as essential, and this is probably the case. I would contend that the removal of the signs of circumcision is frequently, if not always, a symbolic act demonstrating a disavowal of Judaism and the covenant circumcision expresses. Not circumcising a newborn Jewish boy, however, would need to be treated separately.

Even a casual reading of the Wisdom of Solomon confronts the reader with integration, ideological adaptation, and assimilation to Hellenism (1:14–15; 2:2, 6; 8:4, 7; 18:4),[39] but the text that reveals a greater amount of integration and assimilation is 4 Maccabees. 4 Macc. 1:1–35 queries "whether devout reason is absolute master of the passions" (1:1) and contends that "reason is the guide of the virtues and the supreme master of the passions" (1:30)(*OTP* 1:544, 545). Whatever one may think of the ideas, one cannot deny that these notions of "autocontrol of the passions" are not found in many other forms of Judaism.[40] It may be argued that these ideas are actually foreign to Judaism and betray an assimilation to the anthropology and ethics of the foreigners. However, even here we must be cautious; what we find here may have been entirely acceptable to the Jewry from which it emerged.

A further instance of integration, in the religious dimension, can be seen in the use of Theos Hypsistos as a title for God in various areas of Asia Minor.[41]

In modern Philonic studies there is an overwhelming consensus that Philo is a typical case of what may be termed "Hellenistic Judaism." Thus, V. Tcherikover has said of Philo that he is "the embodiment of the ideal towards which the Jewish Hellenistic literature had been striving from the 2nd century BCE—the creation of a synthesis between Hellenism and Judaism."[42] E. F. Ferguson says that Philo "presents the modern reader with the concrete phenomenon of a person who apparently fully assimilated Hellenistic culture while remaining immovably loyal to his Jewish heritage."[43] I contend that this dual embodiment of Philo is precisely the problem: Philo represents both Judaism and Hellenism, and he is as much Jew as Greek. It is nearly impossible, and certainly a distortion, to argue that Philo's Judaism is a departure. Rather, it expands what we have grown to see as Judaism.

Without getting into the texts and details here, one might point out Philo's Platonic epistemology (*L.A.* 3.91-93; *Virt.* 176; *Congr.* 41-43)[44] and his intimate acquaintance with athletics.[45] In H. A. Harris's masterful presentation of Greek athletics, he says of Philo: "There is no other writer in Greek who so often and so vividly conjures up before his reader's eyes a picture of what went on in a sports stadium at the beginning of the Christian era."[46] I can agree with Harris that "if a Jewish writer . . . uses illustrations drawn from athletics, both he and his Jewish readers had some familiarity with these sports."[47] In light of modern archaeological discoveries, this inference makes sense: if there were athletics in the culture, it is more than likely that Jews were involved.

Apostasy. There is a fine line between integration, adaptation, and assimilation, on the one hand, and assimilation and apostasy, on the other. Every religion has its taboos and its boundary lines.[48] Although it would be foolhardy to define for Judaism those taboos with a fixed certainty beyond which would constitute sure apostasy, it remains a fact that such lines were drawn. I would agree that those lines would have been drawn by different people in different places. For most Jews, however, those lines existed, whether they were drawn fairly tightly (as with the Essenes at Qumran or with the instigators of the Maccabean rebellions) or more loosely (with someone like Philo or some tolerable Jews in Sardis). We suggest that the following were, for most Jews, examples of going too far.

At times, Jews compromised monotheism and, in effect, ceased to be Jews—at least in some religious sense.[49] Some women (see, e.g., *Spec.* 3.169-77; *Flacc.* 89; *Hyp.* 7.3; *Virt.* 1-50; *Sacr.* 32) succumbed under the pressure of Flaccus's persecution to eat pork (*Flacc.* 96), and, according to some perceptions, such a practice amounted to apostasy.[50] Further, the language of *Spec.* 1.56-57 may reflect the apostasy of some during Philo's time: "spurning their ancestral customs and seeking admission to the rites of a fabulous religion." This, according to Philo, is "backsliding" (*paranomia*; see also *Virt.* 182; *Ebr.* 51; *Mos.* 2.193-208).

Josephus records evidence for apostasy as well. Antiochus of Antioch converted to Hellenism, detested Jewish customs, and sacrificed in the manner of the Greeks—and exhorted others to do the same (*J.W.* 7.50-53). Menelaus and the Tobiads abandoned Judaism "to follow the king's laws and adopt the Greek way of life" (*Ant.* 12.240-41). One of Herod's sons, Alexander, and his children forsook Judaism (18.141). According to Clearchus, Aristotle met a Jew who "not only spoke Greek, but had the soul of a Greek (*hellēnikos ēn . . . tē psychē*)"(*Ag. Ap.* 1.180).[51] These examples indicate that the influence of Hellenism during the Second Temple period at times generated overt apostasy from Judaism. Though this area is in need of further study, I suspect that the number of apostasies was not sufficient to be a major concern, except for perhaps at the time of Maccabean wars. Furthermore, the records of this period were preserved by those who had a rather fixed view of what was tolerable behavior for Jews—a view that no doubt would have had many detractors.

These eight examples of various kinds of integration and assimilation, from an innocent universalism to blatant apostasy, demonstrate the serious level of interaction with Hellenistic culture by Judaism. We turn now to the opposite trend in Judaism. Further, the resistance of Judaism is found at the same time as traces of assimilation, illustrating the complexity of Jewish-Gentile interaction.

Resistance Tendencies

The positive attitude seen so frequently in Jewish literature by no means exhausts the evidence. There is just as much evidence of a different nature altogether.[52] Consequently, it must be asked, how can these authors maintain a marked integration into gentile society and, at the same time, offer comments that appear to be prejudicial and condemnatory? Before we attempt an answer to this question, we need to survey the evidence.

To begin with, the origins of potential hostilities and prejudices are to be found in the Hebrew Scriptures. The author of Judges had little appreciation for the children of Israel when they did not drive out the foreigners from the land that Yahweh had given them (1:27–2:5), and idolatry is the foundation for most of the condemnations of the Scriptures (see, e.g., Exod. 20:4-6; Deut. 4:15-24; 27:15). To name but one example, intermarriage was prohibited because it was especially dangerous both to purity in worship and nation (Exod. 34:15-16; 1 Kings 11:1-4; Ezra 9-10; Prov. 5:3-23). Other evidence could be cited, but the texts are well known.

Misanthropy among the Jews?

Some Gentiles accused Jews of misanthropy. It seems probable that this charge had some (even if mostly misunderstood) foundation in the attitudes and practices of Jews.[53] Thus, according to Josephus, Haman can say "both by its customs and practices it [the Jewish nation] is the enemy of your people and of all mankind" (*Ant.* 11.212), and it is "an unfriendly nation mingled with all mankind, which has peculiar laws, is insubordinate to kings, is different in its customs, hates monarchy and is disloyal to our government" (11.217). This text may be historically accurate, even if embellished, or it may reflect conditions at the time of Josephus. Nonetheless, it expresses a common observation of Jews by Gentiles in the ancient world: Jews did not always seem to regard social compatibility as top priority. Integration took place; sometimes, however, it was expected to occur in the other direction.

Further, it is very probable that the negative evaluations of Gentiles by Jews that gave rise to Gentile aspersions sprang directly from personal experience and historical circumstances. One is not surprised to find vehement remarks following the attempt to hellenize Jerusalem or the sackings of Jerusalem under Pompey and Titus, or to find appreciatory attitudes expressed following times of protection, as found for instance in Philo, Josephus, and the rabbis.

Be that as it may, Jews regularly expressed exclusivistic notions that reveal anything but universalism (e.g., 4 Ezra 3:32-36; 6:55-59).[54] As M. Goodman states in his revision of Schürer, "This theoretical and practical *amixia* (separation), which ran counter to the whole tendency of Hellenistic times, was a constant and particular reproach against the Jews."[55]

In the following I shall survey six different forms of Jewish resistance to assimilation: separation, temple circumscription, warnings of idolatry, prohibition of intermarriage, revolting against reforms, and vindictive judgment scenes. Because this chapter is introductory, I shall simply touch on the topics and cite some relevant evidence.

(1) *Separation, nationalism, and sinners.* Drawing upon levitical codes and Ezra-like exhortations, some Jews consciously *separated* themselves from Gentiles, whether for self-identification, nationalistic, or ceremonial reasons. That this concept of separation frequently takes place in the midst of an active integration demonstrates, however, that separation may often be religious exclusivity, rather than social division. Even the *Letter of Aristeas,* which glories at times in accommodation, shares a separatistic attitude: God gave the Law "that we [i.e., the Jews] might not mingle at all with any of the other nations but remain pure in body and soul, free from all vain imaginations, worshipping the one Almighty God above the whole creation" (139; *APOT*). Thus, because all humanity is sinful (277), Israel is to remain "distinct" (151; *OTP*). This evidence is significant because of its juxtaposition with favorable attitudes, as noted previously. Separation from sin is found also in *Jubilees* (1:9, 19; 6:35; 15:34; 23:23, 24; 24:28),[56] and a clear actual life setting may be seen in *Joseph and Aseneth* 7:1–8:11.

Separation often expresses itself in nationalism, the consciousness of being both a national body and the elect of God (2 *Bar.* 29:2; 48:24; 72:1–6). The author of 2 *Baruch* can say, "And concerning the nations much could be said: how they acted unrighteously and wickedly, and how they never proved themselves to be righteous" (62:7; *APOT*). Thus, Israel has no equal in holiness or obedience (4 Ezra 3:32–36; see also 5:23–30; 6:55–59). Only Israel, Philo says, recognized the truth (*Spec.* 2.166), and so "Israel," by etymology, means "seeing God" (*Leg.* 3–4).[57] Israel is the "chosen race" (*Post.* 92) and the "best of races" (*Congr.* 51). Some form of nationalism is at the heart of many Jewish documents and so need not be cited in full here.[58]

The Essenes of Qumran are known for sectarian nationalism and social separation,[59] not only from Gentiles but also from unfaithful Israelites (CD 6:14, 15; 7:13; 8:4, 8, 16; 11:4–5; 12:6–11; 13:14; 16:9; 19:17–29; 1QS 1:4; 5:1–2, 10–11; 6:15; 9:5, 8–9, 20–21; 1QH 14:21–22; 11QTemple 48:7–13; 60:16–21). Separation emerges as a sociological rule in order to avoid sin and idolatry (CD 11:15; 12:6, 9). The scrolls, especially the *War Scroll,* seem to assign the Gentiles to the wrath of God (1QM 2:7; 4:12; 6:6; 9:9; 11:9, 15; 12:11, 14; 14:5, 7, *et passim;* 1QpHab 5:4; 1QSa 1:21).[60]

If Jews spoke with admiration of their own nation, the same cannot be said of other nations. The list of derogatory comments about other nations is almost as long as there are nations. Evidence is found in many ancient writers, particularly Philo, Josephus, and the rabbis. It ought not to be doubted, however, that many of these comments are socially accepted rhetoric.[61] Furthermore, it is almost certainly true that derogatory comments about other nations express as much ideology and elective consciousness as they do social realities.

One example can be taken from Philo and his expressions about Egyptians, admittedly an evocative group of people for Philo.[62] The Torah was given to Moses because of the corruption of the cities, especially those in Egypt (*Dec.* 2–13, esp. 7–9). Egyptians, Philo states, are naturally excited about minute matters (*Flacc.* 17), they are jealous (29), oppressive (96), and are prone to flattery, hypocrisy, and idolatry (*Leg.* 162; *Vita* 8–9; *Jos.* 254; *Dec.* 76–80; *Post.* 165; *Ebr.* 95; *Conf.* 173). In fact, Egypt is "a seed bed of evil" (*Leg.* 166). It ought to be added that this castigation of Egyptians works itself out in criticisms of Joseph (*Som.* 2.10–154).[63] In sum, Egyptians love their passions and sense-perceptions—particularly objectionable traits for Philo (*Sacr.* 51; *Post.* 96, 113; *Migr.* 160; *Congr.* 83, 85; *Fug.* 18). At the bottom of Philo's comments is probably his repulsion toward paganism and sinful deeds (*Vita* 40–63), where the concern is entirely for pleasure (*Vita* 58; cf. *Agr.* 23–25; *Spec.* 3.113) and materialism (*Som.* 2.48–64; see also *Leg.* 200; *Spec.* 4.16, 157–59; *Sacr.* 44). Moreover, he detested, as he ought to have, pagan infanticide, which he says was done "through their ingrained inhumanity" (*heneka tēs physikēs apanthrōpias; Spec.* 3.110; *Virt.* 131–33).

This is evidence of a consciousness of Jewish separation and its consequence: nationalism. Again, however, it is not demonstrable that such attitudes reflect the realities of social interaction. In fact, as we saw earlier in this chapter, we have more evidence suggesting full integration than separation. Nonetheless, these data do speak of a concept of exclusivity, a separation that is rooted in God's election and Jewish solidarity.

(2) This notion of separation extended to the *temple precinct circumscribing foreign intrusion,* a restriction not uncommon in ancient religions.[64] "Death without appeal" is the sentence for a Gentile entering the inner areas of the temple (Philo *Leg.* 212). Josephus speaks frequently of a gentile restriction in this regard (*J. W.* 1.152, 354; *Ant.* 3.318–22;[65] 11.101; 14.482–83; *Ag. Ap.* 2.209–10; cf. 2.257–61). The clearest social symbol, "set in concrete," is of course the temple inscription: "No foreigner may proceed inside the wall around the holy place and the enclosure. Whoever does will have himself to blame for the death that

ensues" (*mēthena allogenē eisporeuesthai entos tou peri to hieron tro-
phaktou kai peribolou. hos d'an lēphthē heautō aitios estai dia to exako-
louthein thanaton*). Inscribed on the wall of the second court about
2.5–4.5 feet high, this warning was found, in Greek and/or Latin, at
regular intervals around the temple wall.[66] Before we move on we need
to pause to ask why Jews made this prohibition. There is some evidence
that Jews saw Gentiles as necessarily unclean[67] and, therefore, unfit for
the temple (*J.W.* 1.229; 2.150; 6.427; *Ant.* 19.332; *m. Pes.* 8:8; *m. 'Ed.*
5:2; see also *m. Šabb.* 1:7–9[68]). In spite of arguments to the contrary, this
proposal remains the best explanation.

At any rate, this social symbol regulating movements in and out of
the temple demonstrates the point at hand: Gentiles, although welcome
to worship with Jews, could only penetrate so far into Judaism. In the
case of conversion to Judaism, no doubt, full participation was probably granted. But until that point there was both a beckoning and a
warning hand.

(3) *Idolatry* is repudiated throughout the Scriptures, and this polemic
appears throughout Jewish literature (Wisdom of Solomon 14:12–31;
Joseph and Aseneth 8:5–7) and need not be surveyed here. Philo, for
instance, reports Gaius's attempt to foist emperor worship on the
Jewish nation, which met stiff resistance (*Flacc.* 41–53; *Leg.* 132–37).
Repudiation of idolatry is probably the most common form of resistance to gentile culture in Judaism.[69]

(4) A leitmotif of Tobit is the *prohibition of intermarriage* with the
nations (1:9; 3:10; 5:11, 13; 6:12; 7:13).[70] Thus, Tobit exhorts his son
Tobias with the following words:

> My child, avoid all loose conduct (*porneia*). Choose a wife of your father's
> stock. Do not take a foreign wife outside your father's tribe, because we
> are the children of the prophets. Remember Noah, Abraham, Isaac and
> Jacob, our ancestors from the beginning. All of them took wives from
> their own kindred, and they were blessed in their children, and their race
> will inherit the earth. (4:12; NJB)

Philo repeats the prohibition but offers a fuller (and significant)
rationale:

> But also, he [the Lawgiver] says, do not enter into the partnership of
> marriage with a member of a foreign nation (*mēde alloethnei . . . koi-
> nōnian gamou syntitheso*), lest some day conquered by the forces of
> opposing customs you surrender and stray unawares from the path that
> leads to piety and turn aside into a pathless wild. And though perhaps
> you yourself will hold your ground steadied from your earliest years by

the admirable instructions instilled into you by your parents, with the holy laws always as their key-note, there is much to be feared for your sons and daughters. It may well be that they, enticed by spurious customs which they prefer to the genuine, are likely to unlearn the honour due to the one God, and that is the first and the last stage of supreme misery. (*Spec.* 3.29; see also *Praem.* 152)

This same prohibition is found throughout Jewish literature (see *Jub.* 30:7–17; *T. Levi* 9:10; 14:6; Josephus *Ant.* 1.192; 11.70–71, 139–53, 307; 12.187; 17.20; 18.345, 347; *m. Qidd.* 4:3; *b. Qidd.* 74b–76a). However, as scholars have observed, an explicit prohibition of marrying any Gentile is not in the Pentateuch (see Exod. 34:11–17; Deut. 7:3–4; 23:2–9); on the other hand, Ezra 9–10 is more universal in scope.

The dominating motivations for this restriction appears to have been both moral and socioreligious: Jews may fall into idolatry and so damage their ethnic and religious identity. In spite of some sweeping restrictions, as for instance are found in Ezra 9–10, it is most probable that such restrictions were raised in particularly dangerous situations. The consistent warning about intermarriage (from biblical to later rabbinic times) occurs within the regular evidence of intermarriage. Again, social forces are probably to be called in to explain this ideological dissonance.

(5) *Revolting against politico-religious reforms.* A consciousness of being God's chosen people and the exclusiveness and separation unto God that unfolded from that consciousness are the primary factors at work in Jewish resistance to Hellenization.

Evidence for resistance is found especially in the Maccabean literature, which often depicts the attempted reformers as sinful, godless apostates (3 Macc. 2:32–33; 3:21–30; 1 Macc. 1:10–15, 43; 6:21, 52–53; 7:5–50; 9:23, 25–31, 58, 69, 73; 10:61; 11:21, 25; 2 Macc. 4:7–6:31; 11:24; 14:3). "It is no small thing to violate the divine laws, as the period that followed will demonstrate" (2 Macc. 4:17; NJB). As E. Bickermann stated, "The maccabean movement was above all a civil war, a religious war between the orthodox and the reformers."[72] The marvelous legends of 4 Maccabees are conceived in a similar womb. The Jews hated the reform attempts by Jason (4:19–21). This purified hatred for sin and unflinching commitment to God's law erupt into heroism when the boys, in the presence of their mother, are forced to decide. "Share in the Greek style (*metalabontes hellēnikou biou*), change your mode of living, and enjoy your youth" (8:8) is the offer of the Hellenizers. But the boys decide one by one, along with their mother (14:11–17:6), for death and therefore are promised eternal life with God (8:5–12:19). Antiochus's end, narrated for contrast, was ignominious (18:5). However ideologic-ally oriented the Maccabean literature may be, it nonetheless expresses a historical kernel of Jewish revolt against outsiders seeking to impose rule (with some religious connotations) on the elect of God.

Josephus also tells these stories of freedom fighting with some inter-esting detail (see, e.g., *J.W.* 1.36–53). In the teeth of another revolt, Pilate was shocked at the power of the Jewish resistance to his attempt to introduce busts of the emperor into the court (*J.W.* 2.169–74; *Ant.* 18.55–59, 60–62, 263–64).[73]

Resisting Hellenism, then, is more than cultural denial. It reflects a religious conviction about paganism and must be seen in that light. Any notion of misanthropy in this regard falls wide of the mark.

(6) *Vindictiveness.* A final aspect to which we point regarding resist-ance is the consistent expectation of a final judgment, earthly or not, in which God vindicates his people by punishing the wicked. Ben Sira, speaking from the context of oppression, expresses the common Jewish notion that God will display his power over the nations and Gentiles will consequently admit the sovereignty of the Jewish God (Ecclus. 36:1–17). His prayer request is this (Ecclus. 36:6–8 [NJB]; see also 50:25–26):

> Rouse your fury,
> pour out your rage,
> destroy the opponent,
> annihilate the enemy,
> hasten the day,
> remember the oath,
> and let people tell of your mighty deeds.
> Let fiery wrath swallow up the survivor,
> and destruction overtake those who oppress your people.

In spite of the conversion of Achior, which is probably more accurately seen as a nationalistic (and ideological) triumph than a per-sonal conversion, Judith remains "polemical, anti-Hellenistic, [and] tendentious."[74] Evidence for imprecations against, and condemnation of, Gentiles abounds in the literature from this period (see *1 Enoch* 48:7–10; 50:1; 56:5–8; 62:9–13; 63:1–12; 65:11; 90:19; 99:1–16; *Pss. Sol.* 17:3, 7, 22–25, 28;[75] *T. Moses* 10:7; *4 Ezra* 7:37–39; *2 Bar.* 67:2; 83:5–7).

Conclusions

What conclusions can we then draw from this presentation? First, Jews had a firm conviction, in the period of history with which we are concerned, that just as Yahweh was the creator, so Yahweh was also the sovereign lord of all humanity. The Jewish God was universally God. The older positions of I. Heinemann and K. L. Schmidt, mentioned at the outset of this chapter, are essentially correct: Jewish theology had a built-in, universal thrust. It begins with Gen. 1:1–2:3 and 12:3, reverberates throughout Jewish history, and is still found in the rabbis: as God created and therefore loved the world, so Jews, who took seriously obedience to God's designs, also loved the gentile world (see Ecclus. 18:13; Philo *Dec.* 41, 64; Josephus *Ant.* 2.94, 122, 152; 3.281; *Ag. Ap.* 2.146; *b. Ber.* 28a). The God of Israel is the God of all humanity.

Second, the evidence from this period of Jewish history and from virtually every sect and author (except perhaps the Qumran community at various periods in its history) demonstrates unequivocally that Jews were generally tolerant of, and kind to, Gentiles. For Palestine it needs to be remembered that, although Gentiles may not have been the focus of Jewish legal concerns, they were most probably pervasively present and fully integrated into Jewish life.[76] If negative comments are made, such evaluations are almost always found in writings in which there are also some positive attitudes expressed. Failure to take the entire context into account has often led scholars into inaccurate judgments regarding the attitude of Jews to Gentiles. It is the case that virtually every document that speaks negatively of Gentiles also speaks positively of the same group. It thus remains important to offer an explanation that considers both phenomena.

Inherent in Jewish theology is kind treatment of the *gēr tôšāb*, the resident alien, because, after all, that was at one time the plight of Israel (Exod. 20:2; Deut. 7:8). There is abundant evidence that Jews were indeed kind to other nations, both in Palestine and the Diaspora (Philo *Flacc.* 94; *Leg.* 161; *Virt.* 105–8; Josephus, *Ant.* 7.330; 13.85). The evidence found in pagan writers that Jews were misanthropists, although it has perhaps an individual or two for support, is contrary to overwhelming evidence of a different stripe. It must be noted that Jews, as a whole, appear in all the evidence to be a people that dwelled peaceably and apparently willingly among the Gentiles.

Third, and here we begin to touch on the next chapter, Jewish kindness extended to gentile participation in the Jewish religion, whether it was reading Israel's holy writings, using the synagogue, or giving gifts to the temple—even if the latter had some reasonable restrictions (Josephus *J.W.* 2.412–16; 4.275; *Ant.* 1.11; 16.43–44). This is, of course, supported by the presence of Gentiles in Jewish synagogues throughout the ancient world. The evidence of Sardis discussed above makes this abundantly clear. Here there is not a sharp segregation of synagogue from society; in fact, the Jewish synagogue is at the heart of the society in a fully integrated form.

Fourth, from the reverse angle, Jewish kindness was demonstrated in various forms and degrees of Jewish participation in Gentile society. Philo is one who particularly provides evidence in this regard (*Flacc.* 74; *Leg.* 155, 157) but Josephus's long list of treaties between Jews and non-Jews is not without import for understanding Jewish relations to Gentiles in Palestine–they were the foundation of peace (*Ant.* 13.334–37, 352–55, 376–78; 14:90, 122, 127–39, 144–55, 164, 186–267, 268, 307–8; 15:316–17, 387; 16:372). Herod's kindness to Gentiles, even if it caused problems at times, surely set the stage for a great deal of tranquillity (*Ant.* 15.326–30; 18.329). The education of Jewish boys in Hellenistic schools prepared for such peaceful interaction (Josephus *J.W.* 1.435; *Ant.* 16.6). There is no doubt that participation, through education and intermarriage, eventually led to deeper assimilation and apostasy, but integration shows quite clearly that Judaism was permeated with Hellenism and that Jews were an integral part of the fabric of Gentile culture.[77] The evidence of the list for the so-called soup kitchen at Aphrodisias (perhaps more accurately a burial society) shows the various positions of Jews in gentile society.[78]

How then do we explain the negative attitudes that consistently emerge? I believe the primary reason for criticism of the Gentiles was not nationalism, even if that appears at times as the form of expression; rather, the predominant reason for negative attitudes by Jews toward Gentiles is an expression of religious and social conviction, arising undoubtedly from the Jewish consciousness of being God's chosen and holy people. In other words, the evidence consistently bears out the view that Jews criticized Gentiles for basically one reason: pagan religion led to ethical practices that were unacceptable for those who were members of the covenant of Abraham and Moses. It is this which gives the statement of Tacitus the "ring of truth": Jews "despise gods, deplore their fatherland, and regard parents, children and kin as nothing" (*Histories* 5.5). This despising is not misanthropy or a lack of love; rather, it is a reflection of zeal for God, his Torah, his land, and his people.

This religious conviction is at the same time a sociological affirmation, as stated by G. G. Porton: "In whatever ways they interacted or remained apart, the point of the Mishnah-Tosefta is that Israelites constantly had to be aware of the fact that they were different from Gentiles. This was not a value judgment. It was what it meant to be an Israelite. . . ."[79]

The decision by Jews to separate from and condemn those who were immoral was not based on racial nationalism; rather, nationalism was an expression of a religious, social, and ethical orientation. The accusations against Jews for misanthropy were by and large ill-informed or misconstrued accusations (e.g., Josephus *Ant.* 11.212, 217; 18.257–60; 19.284–85).

It ought to be noted how the *Letter of Aristeas*, in one of its strongest separatistic comments, ties that separation into moral purity: God gave the laws to us so "that we might not mingle at all with any of the other nations but remain pure in body and soul, free from all vain imaginations, worshipping the one Almighty God above the whole creation" (139; *APOT*). Notice here that "not mingling" is defined as "living according to Jewish covenantal stipulations." Separation, therefore, is construed positively, as living a holy life. In *Jubilees*, a strongly separatistic book, the reason for separation is not nationalism or conceit (though at times the author may give that impression), but rather because Gentiles are sinners (1:19; 6:35; 15:34; *et passim*). In other words, the negative attitudes are religious convictions in social clothing. Even Philo's harsh comments about the Egyptians seem to be based on religious convictions (cf. *Leg.* 162; *Vita* 8–9; *Jos.* 254; *Dec.* 76–80; *Post.* 165; *Ebr.* 95; *Conf.* 173). I could go on, citing the foundations for such an argument, but enough has been said to illustrate the point that Jewish convictions that express themselves in negative attitudes toward Gentiles, like refusing intermarriage, resisting reforms, strong attacks against idolatry, and even predictions of judgment by God, are founded in the religious and sociological consciousness that Israel is elect, has participated in God's covenant, and consequently must live within the bounds of the covenant—and all those who do not live within this framework are not God's chosen and so will experience his wrath.

On the other hand, ideas rooted in theology are not exempt from the criteria of goodness and love. Rather, I want to say that these Jewish expressions against Gentiles are not misanthropic, nor are they arrogant. Jews sometimes saw themselves as God's people, left in a world that was often hostile to those with that conviction and struggling to explain their existence. Convinced of these truths, Jews often expressed themselves in condemnatory tones—just as Yahweh had taught them. Separation, then, is a religious conviction expressing itself in social boundaries.

If I can be granted my point that negative expressions are not necessarily fueled by misanthropy and hate, I must also admit that certain fringe elements of Jewish society did perhaps have less of a religious basis and probably more of a hateful, nationalistic disposition toward the Gentiles. One gains this impression, for instance, at times from the Qumran sect, especially as it expresses itself in 1QM. Again, although there is a very strong conviction of being God's elect, which forms the basis for this, I am not yet persuaded that this conviction was not also tainted with a degree of misanthropy. Whatever the reasons, such a view is not typical of Judaism and ought not to be cited to explain, for instance, Jesus restricting his followers to Israel (Matt. 10:5-6).

To sum up: I think one can say that the general orientation toward Gentiles was twofold: Jews were convinced that they were God's chosen people, formed under the covenant of Abraham and Moses, and therefore they detested and guarded themselves from sinful contamination found in the gentile world. However, Jews, throughout their history, were convinced that God was the ruler of the universe, that Yahweh had created the world, and that they were expected to be kind to the world. In my view, apart from an odd exception here and there, Jews lived up to both ends of this conviction: they were generally holy and kind. They were, in effect, Yahweh's light among the Gentiles.

But I must add that this picture paints Judaism in general colors. To be sure, there was considerable diversity within Judaism, and there were probably divisions over these very issues. My goal, however, is to explain what I found to be a general pattern, if not a "consensus." I do not want to suggest that this sketch is a description of some orthodox establishment, but I would like to contend that the ideas are found throughout the period in question and in a wide array of Jewish groups. To that extent it makes sense to me to speak of a general picture, much as E. P. Sanders has done with respect to a "pattern of religion" in Judaism.[80]

2

Judaism and Proselytes

IT HAS NOW BEEN established that the members of the covenant of Israel, although at times expressing themselves in separatistic categories, were not isolationists. Rather, Jews of the Second Temple period lived among the Gentiles and normally were integrated fully into gentile society. If Jews, then, lived among Gentiles, to what degree did Jews seek to convert these Gentiles to the covenant of Abraham? We can now narrow the topic further to the matter of how Jews regarded proselytism. This discussion must take its root in Jewish attitudes to Gentiles, because the Jewish attitude to proselytes is a direct growth from their attitude to Gentiles in general. Put differently, if the Jews lived among the Gentiles in peaceable terms, how did the Jews relate their religious beliefs to the Gentiles? Did they seek out converts?

Some rabbis revised history so that proselytizing was the activity of the patriarchs, like Abraham, and some modern scholars (e.g., A. Bertholet) contend that "every true religious experience carries within itself *a drive to expand to the largest extent possible.* "[1] W. G. Braude stated:

> After examining both the Halakah and the Haggadah bearing on pros-
> elytes and proselytizing I can definitely say that all the rabbis spoke
> enthusiastically of proselytizing and idealized converts and their makers.
> They were motivated by a profound desire to bring all creatures under
> the wings of the Shekinah—a mystically universal concept. Their
> methods in gaining converts were scrupulously ethical. I am prepared to
> affirm that in Palestine and in Babylonia there were no compromises on
> the observance of Jewish precepts by newcomers. If they were to qualify
> as Jews they had to observe the whole law.... There appears to be no
> evidence that Jews sent missionaries into *partes infidelium* to bring about
> mass conversions. Here and there isolated propagandists may have set out
> on their own initiative. But they approached individuals and not bodies
> of men and women.... I am inclined to regard mass propaganda as a
> Christian invention. In the main Jews secured converts through upright-
> ness of conduct, preaching in the synagogue, religious conversations with
> Tannaim and Amoraim and, probably, the influence of the Greek Bible.[2]

But B. J. Bamberger stated: "The idea of making converts only emerges gradually in the history of the Jewish religion; and organized

activity for this purpose does not appear to have started until the Maccabean period."[3] Still others, by far the majority, have charged Judaism
with a disinterest in evangelism and proselytizing.[4] My purpose is to
examine the evidence that has been cited and other data that I have
found to see which of these positions is closest to the facts.

Favorable Attitudes toward Proselytes

A significant amount of evidence confirms the positions of Bamberger
and Braude on the Jewish apologetical tradition.[5] Thus, we need to
examine such matters as named proselytes and the presence of Jews
throughout the Roman world to see if these factors demonstrate an
active missionary movement among Jews.

From the sources of the ancient world scholars have become accus-
tomed to hearing the names of many Gentiles and proselytes. As in the
Christian world today where the note of triumph is sounded for a
famous convert, so in the ancient world among the Jews.[6] The names
I mention here are "proselytes" only in the loosest senses of the term,
from honorable Gentiles to full converts. I mention them here to ask
what can be inferred from such a list. Further, it ought to be noted at
the outset that many of these names reflect legendary material rather
than reliable information about the persons. For whatever reasons, the
names of these individuals have been preserved, largely through the
efforts of ancient Jewish authors, because of their special relationship
to Judaism.

After Ruth, Achior the Ammonite is one of the earliest converts
known (Jth. 14:10). Artaxerxes is pictured as one who worshiped the
God of the Jews (Rest of Esther E 1-24, esp. 16, 18, 21-24),[7] and so
Ptolemy II also becomes a patron (*Ep. Arist.* 37, 40, 177, 179, 187-202,
203-94, 312, 317). In Bel and the Dragon we find the king of Babylon
cast similarly (28, 41). Aseneth is the most glorious convert of all (*Joseph
and Aseneth*).

Philo mentions Hagar (*Abr.* 251) and Tamar (*Virt.* 221-22) as proselytes to Judaism, but for Philo Abraham is the proselyte *par excellence.*
He is the prototype for abandoning all to go up to God (*Cher.* 31; *Mut.*
76; *Som.* 1:161).[8] Philo's use of Abraham certainly tells us more about
Philo's point of view than about history.

Josephus's list is full and varied: Raguel (*Ant.* 3.63-65, 69-72), Ruth
(5.318-37), Nebuchadnezzar (10.139), Darius (10.263), Artaxerxes
(11.268), Alexander the Great (11.330-31), Ptolemy II (12.52), Antiochus Eusebes (12.241-48), Fulvia (18.82), Petronius (18.279-83), the
royal family of Adiabene (*Ant.* 20.17-53; *J.W.* 2.520; 5.474-75;

6.356-57; cf. also *Gen. Rab.* 46:11),[9] Poppaea (*Ant.* 20.195) and the women of Damascus (*J.W.* 2.559-61).[10] One ought also to mention Simon ben Giora (*J.W.* 2.521, 652; 5.11; 7.154; 4.503), whose father was evidently a proselyte.[11]

Of the many who appear on inscriptions, two who can be mentioned are Felicitas (*CIJ* 462) and Veturia Paulla (*CIJ* 523).[12]

Names of proselytes from the rabbinic writings, even if one looks only at the Tannaim, are abundant:[13] apart from "proselyting exegesis," which included such names as Abraham (*b. Hag.* 3a), Jethro (*b. Sanh.* 94a), and Job (*b. B. Bat.* 15b), we find Shemaiah and Abtalion, two pretannaitic teachers of Hillel. The "chain of tradition" in *m. 'Abot* has them following hard on the heels of Judah b. Tabbai and Simeon b. Shetah (1:8-9) and are the tradents for Hillel and Shammai (1:10-15). Shemaiah lined up with the Hillelite tradition (*m. Hag.* 2:2).[14] Later traditions suggest that these two teachers were descendants of proselytes (*b. Sanh.* 96b; *b. Git* 57b; *Sifre Num.* 7 on 5:12). *'Abot de Rabbi Nathan* contains the famous story regarding the different reactions of Shammai and Hillel to those "would-be" proselytes (*'Abot R. Nat.* 15.3, 24ab, pp. 91-92; see also *b. Šabb.* 31a).

Rabbis also mentioned Judah the Ammonite (*m. Yad.* 4:4; *b. Ber.* 28a; *t. Yad.* 2.17) and the royal family of Adiabene (*Gen. Rab.* 46:10; *m. Nazîr* 3:6; *t. Sukk.* 1.1; *b. Menah.* 32b; *b. Nid.* 17a; *b. B. Bat.* 11a), and, even more spectacular, Nero is portrayed as a convert (*b. Git* 56a). It seems probable that *t. Pesah.* 7.13 (cf. *y. Pesah.* 36b on 8:8) refers to proselyte temple guards of the gates who took ritual baths and ate Passover. This supports the view of Beth Shammai (*m. 'Ed.* 5:2; *m. Pesah.* 8:8), because proselytes were not required to be circumcised before Passover.[15]

Many other names could be given, but these suffice to point out that there was a sustained interest in recounting before readers those who had converted to Judaism from paganism and idolatry, whether that conversion was complete or not.

It is also clear, as discussed in the preceding chapter, from the evidence left to us that there was the Diaspora presence of Jews throughout the world and that Jews lived among the Gentiles (e.g., Josephus *J.W.* 3.57; 5.43; *Ant.* 5.318; 7.330, 335; 8.50; 13.85).[16] From existing texts and records, whether the data are in papyri, inscriptions, or texts,[17] it appears that Jews resided in most locations throughout the world.[18] Strabo states: "This people has already made its way into every city, and it is not easy to find any place in the habitable world which has not received this nation and in which it has not made its power felt" (*apud* Josephus *Ant.* 14.115). Philo further states that "so populous are the

Jews that no one country can hold them, and therefore they settle in very many of the most prosperous countries in Europe and Asia" (*Flacc.* 45–46).

From this rather extensive list of names and the worldwide presence of Jews, historians can infer many things. Adolf von Harnack and Joachim Jeremias, for instance, infer from this kind of data that there was an intensive missionary zeal on the part of Jews. A multitude of scholars have followed the lead of Harnack here, and this position has influenced a great deal of scholarship.[19] However, a list of names throughout several centuries of Judaism may be nothing more than accident, or it might suggest that converts were so few in number that names were remembered. I doubt that anything secure can be inferred from the presence of long lists of names from Jewish literature.

Further, very little can be made, so it seems to me, of the widespread presence of Jews throughout the Roman world. By itself, evidence that Jews were everywhere proves only that; such data say nothing conclusive about how many of these had become converts to Judaism. To infer results from demographics is a hazardous undertaking in historical work. For the demographical argument to work, secure population statistics at a given location at a given date are required, including the percentage of mothers, a secure birth rate and survival figure, and a secure population statistic two or three generations later. If the latter figure is significantly larger than the former, and if we can document that no large immigrations took place, and if the numbers are greater than what would be normal population growth, *then* we might have some evidence for growth by way of proselytizing. But the question that needs to be asked is, Has anyone such confidence regarding studies in population statistics for the ancient Jewish world? I, for one, am quite doubtful about these statistics and think that, until more careful and reliable data are available, this entire argument ought to be laid to rest.[20]

The point I wish to make is simple: In the history of scholarship on Jewish missionary activity these two data have been utilized over and over to prove aggressive Jewish missionary activity, and it ought to be noted that the evidence does not necessarily lend itself to such an explanation and can, in fact, be explained in any number of ways. Because so little can be known from names and demographics, it is needful to turn to the evidence that speaks directly about proselytes and missionary activity to see if the data here throw more light on our subject. Do the texts that speak about proselytism lead to firm conclusions about the nature of Jewish missionary activity?

Judaism and the Proselyte

It is a consistent feature of the ancient evidence, both Jewish and Gentile and both literary and nonliterary, that the Jews favored non-Jews' joining their religion – although it is surprising to me that no proselyting notions appear in *Corpus Papyrorum Judaicarum,* unless one finds such in names.[21] Some contend that proselytizing began in the Diaspora,[22] and others argue that it had its origins in Palestine.[23] Wherever it began, it is contended that "within the Graeco-Roman world, the Jewish religion had a strong power to attract, to the effect that a notable movement of conversion was produced."[24] Does the evidence suggest this inference? Was there really a missionary impulse in Judaism? Did it lead to a missionary movement?

Apocrypha and Pseudepigrapha

Tobit, when visiting Jerusalem, gave his second tithe in money to needy people (1:7), among whom were "proselytes who attached themselves to the sons of Israel" (1:8: *prosēlytois tois proskeimenois tois huiois Israēl*). Tobit 13:6 and 13:8 probably do not indicate non-Jews; however, 13:11 definitely sees gentile conversions in a positive light. Rooted in the aspirations of Isa. 9:1–2, the text reads: "A bright light will shine over all the regions of the earth; many nations will come from far away, from all the ends of the earth, to dwell close to the holy name of the Lord God, with gifts in their hands for the King of heaven." Here we have positive attitudes expressed about conversion to Judaism, although the attitudes may be little more than nationalistic aspirations. Whether or not this reflects a conversion movement is difficult to know.

In Ecclus. 10:22 the vast majority of manuscripts read "the rich, the noble, the poor" (NJB) but W. E. Oesterley and G. H. Box read "sojourner and stranger, alien and poor man" for which the Hebrew *Vorlage* would be *gr wzr nkry wrsh.* The latter text would indicate proselytes (in "sojourner" and "alien"; i.e., *nkry* and *gr*).[25] Such a rendering could be supported by "fearers of God" in 10:24; the passage is concerned with those among the people of earth with whom God is pleased and is undeniably universalistic.[26] Further, as a result of God's display of power (36:2–4, 6), Ben Sira speaks of a "strange people" (Ecclus. 36:2: *ethnē allotria*) which knows, as Israel does, the God of Israel (36:4).[27] These texts then may speak of a favorable attitude toward proselytes; however, the first text is textually suspect and the second only sees conversion in the future when God acts. This is hardly sufficient for inferring a missionary movement.

In the Song of the Three Children (LXX Dan. 3:82) we might ask to whom "the sons of men" refers? The context mentions Israel, priests, servants, spirits of the righteous, saints and meek, and Ananias-Azariah-Misael. It is possible that the phrase refers to Gentiles, even proselytes. The NJB has "all the human race." In Jth. 4:10 we discover that even "resident aliens" (*pas paroikos*) petitioned God in sackcloth when disaster appeared on the horizon. Apart from the legendary nature of these sources, the question has to be asked to what degree these texts reflect practice and to what degree they reflect aspiration (Dan. 3:82). The most that can be safely inferred here, so it seems to me, is that Jth. 4:10 might speak of some "partial conversions." To say more infers too much from the evidence.

The messiah would be the "light of the Gentiles" according to the Similitudes of Enoch (48:4; cf. also 50:2). On the day of affliction (50:1), when Jews will be victorious, God will cause some to repent and barely escape condemnation (50:3). At the last judgment, people from the whole earth will bring gifts to God (53:1). Similarly, *1 Enoch* 90:30–33 speaks of gentile conversions at the Last Day, Gentiles paying homage to Israel, and, following God's acts of power, the nations directing "their sight to the path of uprightness" (91:14). What ought to be noticed about 1 Enoch is that, although the Similitudes are probably from the first century A.D., there is a noticeable juxtaposition of conversion of Gentiles at the Last Day with no traces of missionary activity on the part of Jews. Conversion, for this author, was entirely an apocalyptic act of God wherein God subjugated Gentiles and drove them to admit the superiority of the Jewish nation. In fact, it may be accurate to frame this apocalyptic orientation sociologically: conversion may be the symbol for an oppressing group's being conquered.

In the Rest of Esther we find a similar picture: Artaxerxes is praised because he seems to have converted to Judaism to some degree (E 1–24, esp. 16, 18, 21–24), but such conversion is set within nationalistic and sociological categories (F 7–9; 8:17). The historical reliability of this material is suspect, although it does probably reflect the hopes of a later generation.

Similarly, the *Letter of Aristeas* presents Ptolemy II as one who worships the God of the Jews (37, 40, 177, 179, 187–294, esp. 187–202, 312, 317), which worship can be explained in terms of conversion or in terms of toleration of Hellenism. At any rate, Ptolemy has become the religious patron of Judaism. Even more propagandistic is the following statement:

> It is a man's duty . . . (to be generous) toward those who are amicably disposed to us. That is the general opinion. My belief is that we must

(also) show liberal charity to our opponents so that in this manner we may convert them to what is proper and fitting to them. You must pray God that these things be brought to pass, for he rules the minds of all. (*Ep. Arist.* 227; cf. 266–77)

In the *Testaments of the Twelve Patriarchs* we find the legendary story that Rotheos, the father of Bilhah the mother of Naphtali, was a Chaldean and God-fearing (*theosebēs; T. Naph.* 1:10). Further, at the Last Time, a priest-king of Levi will rise and "save the nations" (*sōsei panta ethnē; T. Sim.* 7:2; *T. Levi* 18:2–9). In addition, Levi and Judah will be God's agents in saving every race (*T. Levi* 2:10–11), because God will visit "all the Gentiles in His tender mercies forever" (4:4–6).[28] When the author states that the third portion of Levi's posterity will "be granted a new name, because from Judah a king will arise and shall found a new priesthood in accord with the gentile model and for all nations," one can infer that gentile salvation is in view under a new, more secularized leadership.[29] That this prophetic utterance reflects aspiration and not reality is a given.

The author asks about the potential danger to the Gentile world if Israel becomes impious, and he also speaks favorably about proselytizing, even if it appears to be future. He queries: "For what will all the nations do if you become darkened with impiety? You will bring down a curse on our nation, because you want to destroy the light of the Law which was granted to you for the enlightenment of every man (*eis phōtismon pantos anthrōpou*)" (*T. Levi* 14:4). This motif of a future conversion is more explicitly stated in *T. Jud.* 24:6; 25:5; *T. Dan.* 5:11; 6:7;[30] *T. Ash.* 7:3[31] and also in *T. Zeb.* 9:8: "And thereafter the Lord himself . . . will liberate every captive of the sons of men from Beliar, and every spirit of error will be trampled down. He will turn all nations to being zealous for him." In fact, *Testament of Benjamin* depicts the Jews as "missionaries through good deeds" (5:1–5) and, on the Last Day, some Gentiles will be delivered (9:2; 10:5) whereas some Israelites will not (10:6–10) because the former are elect.[32] We find then in these *Testaments,* however textually conflated and historically difficult, some evidence for undeniably positive attitudes about proselytes and proselytism, but the major emphasis is unquestionably on a conversion of Gentiles to Judaism at the end of history—when God acts. Apart from the legend about Rotheos (*T. Naph.* 1:10) we find no converts, and even here we find no traces of Jewish missionary activity. If we recognize that the *Testaments* may not reflect the historical realities of Second Temple Judaism, then it is even more clearly the case that the texts do not evince missionary activity.

According to Bel and the Dragon, another legend, "the king of Babylon became a Jew" (*Ioudaios gegonen ho basileus*) after Daniel overcame the Dragon (cf. 26–28, esp. 28), and later the king proclaimed the God of the Jews as the only God (41).[33] This is significant evidence for the desire of Judaism to gain converts to monotheism, but its legendary nature makes historical inferences about missionary activity suspect. Although the theme of gentile conversion appears clearly only once in the Wisdom of Solomon, it does so in a most emphatic manner. The Egyptians imprisoned the Jews "by whom the incorruptible light of the Law was to be given to the world" (18:4: *di' hōn ēmellen to aphtharton nomou phōs to aiōni didosthai*). This consciousness of mediation is a most startling notion for Jewish literature, one that has few, if any, parallels.[34] In other words, we have here unambiguous evidence for Jewish consciousness of a role in the world but, it must be emphasized, little evidence that such a conviction spurred missionary activity. It may be that the best explanation is a sociological consciousness on the part of Israel as being the people of God who have the truth and through whom all truth must be mediated.

Pseudo-Phocylides (39), commenting on levitical legislation regarding "resident aliens" (see Lev 19:33–34; 24:22), states that "strangers (*epēlys*) should be held in equal honor among citizens." The term *epēlys* often refers to a gentile convert,[35] but little historical inference can be drawn from this about social realities because so little is said.

The Sibyl construes a converting process that revolves around repentance and a confession of monotheism (*Sib. Or.* 3:247, 547, 550, 558–61, 624–31, 732–40, 762–65; 4:24–34, 162–78) and it is the Sibyl's duty to proclaim this monotheistic message to all (3:5–10, 811–12) because Israel alone has the true religion through the prophets (3:194–95, 582–83, 772–79). All nations will come to Israel (5:330–32), even Greeks (5:265). This message and conviction are buttressed by appeals to God's discriminating, just judgment (3:34–35, 56, 60–62, 71–92, 93–95, 97, 156, 174, 303–6, 556–61, 570–72, 601–6, 632–51, 669–97; 4:40–44, 162–92; 5:298–305, 414–33). Thus the climactic appeal:

> Then a man clad in linen, one of the priests, will say, "Come, let us change the terrible custom we have received from our ancestors on account of which they performed processions and rites to gods of stone and earthenware, and were devoid of sense. Let us turn our souls, singing out the praises of the imperishable God himself, the begetter who is eternal, the ruler of all, the true one, the king, the begetter who nourishes souls, the great eternal God." (5:493–500)

Noticeably, the next line speaks of a temple in Egypt—tying this hope for conversion to national election—and the general emphasis here is a future conversion.

The note that we hear so frequently about a future conversion of Gentiles is found also in 4 Ezra: "and the heart of the earth's inhabitants shall be changed and converted to a different spirit" (6:26). Again, 2 *Baruch* demonstrates similar ideas. Gentile conversion is in the future (68:5) but only for the nations that spared Israel (72:1–6). In fact, the Jews have been dispersed to "do good to the Gentiles" (1:4; 41:4; 42:5), and those who convert must separate themselves from Gentiles and mingle only with Jews (42:1-8). The Lord, it is said, will save all who draw nigh to him (41:4; 42:3; 48:19).[36]

Before examining further evidence of a positive sort, a preliminary conclusion may be drawn, namely, that positive attitudes toward proselytes and expectations of a future conversion of hordes of Gentiles do not necessarily mean that missionary activity is actually taking place. I believe that Judaism of the Second Temple period was largely favorable about proselytes, but to cite evidence for this as evidence for missionary activity is to run beyond the evidence. What a religion aspires to may be different from what that same religion practices.

Qumran Literature

In the scrolls of Qumran we find very little firm data about proselytism. If *gēr* means "proselyte," there were proselytes in the sect (CD 14:5-6; 15:5-6), even if ranked at the bottom of the sect (CD 9:1; 11:15; 12:6, 9, 11). There appear to be traces of proselytes, therefore, in the earliest stages of the community,[37] but as the sect ages there are fewer and fewer until we find such alarming statements as that proselytes will be excluded from the community (4QFlor 1:4). G. Vermes, although apparently without evidence so far as I can see (CD 12:11?), suggested that these proselytes were formerly slaves.[38] It is fair (but hardly surprising!) to say that there is no evidence that the Qumran sect had any interest in converting Gentiles.

Philo

An interesting comment of Philo is found when he relates Petronius's deliberating over the Jewish case (*Leg.* 211): "And those of other races who pay homage (*timētikōs echontas*) to them they welcome (*apodechontai*) no less than their own countrymen. . . ." We can only infer from this general statement that it was the Jewish custom, as far as Philo knew, to accept any who would respect Mosaic Torah—although this is far short of becoming a proselyte (a distinction Philo knows). In fact, there is evidence for a more relaxed attitude toward proselytism, or a different basis for accepting Gentiles, in Philo.[39] Some of the evidence I now discuss is broader than the discussion of "proselytes" in the stricter definition of that term.

Thus, Israel is depicted as a nation destined to pray for the world so that the world might "be delivered from evil and participate in what is good" (*Mos.* 1.149; cf. *Abr.* 98; *Spec.* 1.97). Nations are approved that respect Jewish customs (*Mos.* 2:17-25).[40] Philo's comment that all who pursue wisdom, truth, and the law of nature are acceptable seems either to equalize all nations or to denationalize Judaism. At any rate, such a view expresses a marked degree of openness to Gentiles.[41] This openness on the part of Philo probably reflects the realities of his social world, a world that knew of social integration with Gentiles. The translation of the Torah was done with the hope "that the greater part, or even the whole, of the human race might be profited and led to a better life by continuing to observe such wise and truly admirable ordinances" (*Mos.* 2.36; cf. also *Dec.* 81; *Spec.* 1.52).

This rather relaxed view of accepting Gentiles, however, is not the only view found in Philo. Philo does see the proselyte as a religious convert in a much fuller sense. God approves those who embrace the truth, whether through training or conversion (*ek tou metaballesthai*) "because their judgment led them to make the passage to piety" (*methormisasthai pros eusebeian*).[42] In the same place he says of the proselyte, "These last he calls proselytes in that they have approached (or drawn nigh) the new, God-loving commonwealth" (*Spec.* 1.51).[43] In fact, converts are those who, like Abraham, "have left . . . their country, their kinsfolk and their friends for the sake of virtue and religion" (*Spec.* 1:52).[44] They are "refugees to the camp of piety" and are given equal rank and love (*Spec.* 1.52). Again, converts have "denounced (*kategnōskosi*) the vain imaginings of their fathers and ancestors" (*Spec.* 1.53; see also 1.309; 4.176-78; *Virt.* 219; *Praem.* 27, 58, 152; *Cher.* 4-8, 31; *Som.* 2:273; *Mos.* 1.147) and have repented (*Spec.* 1.102-4; 2.73; *Virt.* 175-86, 220-27; *Cher.* 71; *Som.* 2.292, 299).[45] Further, conversion is not only moral; it is also enlightenment, the path to true wisdom. For instance, conversion seems to be essentially a movement from "ignorance" to "knowledge" (*amathia* to *epistēmē*; *Praem.* 61; see also *Post.* 18-21; *Migr.* 2, 184-95; *Heres* 239), but this experience comes to the unexpected and may never come to the seeker (*Deus* 92-93).

Perhaps the most intense enthusiasm expressed by Philo for proselytes is seen in his vision of the potential results of translating the Torah (*Mos.* 2.44):[46] "I believe that each nation would abandon its peculiar ways, and, throwing overboard their ancestral customs, turn to honouring our laws alone." In sum, for Philo a true proselyte is like Hagar (*Abr.* 251), one who has been enlightened as to the law and has chosen a new mode of life (cf. *Jos.* 87; *Praem.* 27, 114–17). In addition, as seen above at *Spec.* 1.51, this proselyte becomes a part of God's people.

Philo's enthusiasm for proselytes seems, however, to have a three-generation restriction: "if any of them [i.e., settlers] should wish to pass over into the Jewish community, they must not be spurned with an unconditional refusal . . . , but be so far favoured that the third generation is invited (*kalein*) to the congregation and made partakers (*metadidonai*) in the divine revelations" (*Virt.* 108). Two comments are in order: (1) the passage underlying this is Deut. 23:7–8 and refers to Edomites and Egyptians; (2) this section begins with "if any of them [i.e., settlers] should wish," where the partitive expression refers unquestionably to §107, that is, to the Egyptians. This suggests that in Alexandria it may have been only the Egyptians who had to wait three generations. Such a restriction would not be surprising in light of Philo's attitudes to Egyptians, as described previously.

A second issue pertains to initiates in the Philonic corpus.[47] One could take Philo's injunctions to plunge into the mysteries as exhortations to Gentiles (*L.A.* 3.219; *Cher.* 48; *Fug.* 85) but, as far as I can tell, there is no evidence which suggests that Philo has Gentiles in mind. Rather, Philo has Jews in mind who need to travel the vertical path to God. It is the mind that is initiated (*L.A.* 3.71, 100), and only Jews are mentioned as having been initiated (Jeremiah in *Cher.* 49; Sarah in *Sacr.* 60; Moses in *Gig.* 54). Thus, initiation terminology appears to be reserved for an exhortation to those "within the fold" to pursue the higher life. However, in light of Philo's universalism, even in the face of the absence of evidence for initiation of Gentiles, I can only conclude that Philo would be in agreement with the use of these terms for Gentiles who had found enlightenment.

Philo, then, appears to be open to any Gentile who wishes to join Judaism, to follow the Torah of Moses, and to pursue wisdom. In fact, for Philo the issue was one of truth and virtue, and he was concerned primarily with the true cosmopolitan.[48] Whether these aspirations of Philo are founded upon practice is impossible to tell, because he does not speak of conversions of Gentiles to Judaism. I think that there were conversions in Alexandria, and Philo may have been part of these conversions. However, almost nothing can be inferred from Philo about a missionary movement among Gentiles. His own obvious integration, however, tends to suggest Gentile conversions.

Josephus

Like most of the Jewish literature we have so far examined, Josephus's writings show essentially a positive attitude toward Gentile participation in Judaism.[49] In general, Josephus was happy about, indeed proud of, foreigners who praised the Jewish religion and Jerusalem, which was "revered by the world and honoured by aliens from the ends of the earth" (*J.W.* 4.262; see also 4.275, 327; 5.17; *Ag. Ap.* 2.280, 293). Thus, Roman gifts to the temple were a particular source of pride to the Jews (*J.W.* 5.563). It is hard, however, to see this as evidence about proselytes.[50]

On the other hand, Josephus relates with pride that "they [i.e., Antiochenes] were constantly (*aei*) attracting (*prosagomenoi*) to their religious ceremonies multitudes of Greeks, and these they had in some measure incorporated with themselves" (*J.W.* 7.45). In *J.W.* 2.560 we learn that great numbers of women in Damascus were converts.[51] Just how much can be made of these statements needs to be examined, but these are two pieces of evidence that clearly suggest that Judaism did carry on some kind of missionary activity and that Josephus, for one, was in favor of it.[52]

More particularly, Josephus later states that the legislator wanted to throw the customs "open ungrudgingly to any who elect to share them. To all who desire to come and live under the same laws with us, he gives a gracious welcome, holding that it is not family ties alone which constitute relationship, but agreement in the principles of conduct. On the other hand, it was not his pleasure that casual visitors should be admitted to the intimacies of our daily life" (*Ag. Ap.* 2.209–10).[53] Again, "while we have no desire to emulate the customs of others, yet [we] gladly welcome any who wish to share our own" (*Ag. Ap.* 2.261).[54] Without minimizing the favorability expressed, one ought not forget the historical context or the propagandistic and apologetical approach of our author.[55] It should be noted that the direction found here is the Gentile approaching the Jew and the attitude is positive. But a positive attitude is not identical to active missions, nor is the same to be construed as planned mission without further evidence. In other words, an enthusiastic openness to Gentile conversion is hardly evidence for missionary activity.

Rabbinic Literature

When we turn to the rabbis regarding proselytism, we encounter rabbis of various persuasions. This variety is unlike the fairly uniformly positive attitude of the apocryphal and pseudepigraphal writings as well as the works of Josephus and Philo. But there are plenty of assertions of a positive nature.[56] We ought to begin with the several legends that grew up around Hillel vis-à-vis Shammai over proselytes, in particular, the well-known stories involving the rejection of the would-be disciple (cf. Matt. 8:18–22) by the impatient Shammai in contrast to the subsequent acceptance by the gentle Hillel.[57]

The earliest account of this story is found in *b. Šabb.* 31a (cf. *m. Šabb.* 2:5), which is later expanded in *'Abot R. Nat.* 15:3 (24ab, p. 91). The incident involves a heathen who wants the whole Torah taught to him while he stands on one foot. Shammai repulses him, but Hillel, by crystallizing the law in a negative form of the golden rule, accepts him. Finally, a heathen desires to wear the high priestly garments, expresses it to Shammai, and is rejected; Hillel, however, makes him a proselyte and teaches him the law. The proselyte then realizes his status, abandons his power goals, and so comes under the wings of the Shekinah. The conclusion is that Hillel's patience encouraged proselytizing and even reformed those who previously had impure motives. This, it ought to be noted, is consonant with the tradition assigned to Hillel in *m. 'Abot* 1:12: "loving mankind and bringing them nigh to the Law." Thus, according to at least later traditions, Hillel was very favorable to proselytism—although again the direction is toward Hillel, not Hillel toward the Gentiles. (We do not, for instance, find Hillel pursuing Gentiles.)

In the second generation of Tannaim, Rabbi Joshua b. Hananiah wanted to abolish the limitation upon the Ammonites (Deut. 23:3) so that they could become proselytes (*m. Yad.* 4:4; *b. Ber.* 28a). He argued from Isa. 10:13 and Jer. 30:3. In *Mek. Amalek*, parashah 2, lines 177–86 (Exod. 17:14–16), Rabbi Eliezer b. Hyrcanus is reported as accepting every nation that requested citizenship—except Amalek. Eliezer infers his decision from the forgiving, loving nature of God (par. 3, lines 158–64). Few scholars accept these texts at face value; however, the aspirations present in these texts may reflect serious theological disputes at the time of their composition. Further, I suspect that they reflect social dissonance: some Jews were prone to accept proselytes while others were not.

Later rabbis also evince a positive attitude. Rabbi Eleazar, a fourth-century Tanna, saw Israel's dispersion as divinely intended for making proselytes, and this was accepted by Rabbi Johanan (*b. Pesaḥ.* 87b; cf. *T. Levi* 14:4; Wisd. of Sol. 18:4).[58] Rabbi Meir, citing Lev. 18:5 (*b. Sanh.* 59a), legitimated all as potential students of the Torah (cf. Rabbi Eleazar in *b. Sanh.* 99b). Rabbi Simeon b. Eleazar, a fifth-generation Tanna, asked for intercession for all those outside Palestine because all would become proselytes in the future (*b. Ber.* 57b), a hope that seems to find its climax in *Mek. Nezikin*, parashah 18, lines 9–48, a "hymn" on the glory of being a proselyte: "the proselyte is beloved."[59] This favorable attitude toward both proselytes and proselytizing escalated further among the Amoraim (*b. Ber.* 17b; *b. Pesah.* 91b; *b. Menah.* 44a; *b. ʿAbod. Zar.* 11a, 13b; *b. Šeb.* 39a; *b. Ned.* 32a; *t. Sanh.* 13:2), and because of this evidence it would be historically inaccurate to make a radical break in attitudes to proselytization after A.D. 70 or A.D. 135.[60] However true this may be, rabbis also record what can only be described as negative attitudes toward proselytization.

This completes a survey of the positive attitudes of Jewish literature toward proselytes. A point that has been made throughout and is worthy of repetition here is that there is a difference between aspiration and conviction, on the one hand, and social reality and practice, on the other. Thus, we have seen that Jews almost universally approved of proselytes and encouraged them to join Judaism. This, however, is not necessarily evidence for missionary activity among Gentiles for the sake of converting them to Judaism.[61]

Unfavorable Attitudes toward Proselytes and Proselytism

The evidence of unfavorable attitudes toward proselytes and proselytism is nowhere near as widespread as the positive views described above.[62] Consequently, I have chosen to look at two important pieces of evidence, the evidence from Philo and that of the rabbis.

Philo

In spite of Philo's rather utopian view of education and its potential for changing character, and even the world, he recognized that "to educate a disbeliever is difficult or rather impossible" (*Praem.* 49) and the uninitiated are therefore not to hear Philo's disquisitions on virtues (*Cher.* 42, 48; *Sacr.* 60).[63] Here we may be hearing the aspirations of Philo running aground on the rocks of practical experience among Gentiles. These rather general ideas need to be supplemented by two other passages that express an unfavorable attitude to proselytes.

First, *Mos.* 1.147.[64] The Israelites that emerged from Egypt are described by Philo (through interpretation) as a promiscuous lot, and he looked adversely on "the children of Egyptian women by Hebrew fathers into whose families they had been adopted . . ." and those converted because of miracles and punishments. Philo seems to be against "adopted converts" and those who convert as a result of miracles or God's punishments. Here Philo refers to what later become known as "lion proselytes," and these were not accepted in Jewish communities. Again, this may reflect Philo's experience with Gentiles and proselytes. In exegeting Deut. 23:1-2, Philo mentions three groups who were unworthy to enter the assemby of the Lord (*Spec.* 1.324-26): the effeminate (i.e., those with crushed organs; Deut. 23:1 [Hebrew] 23:2), the bastard (i.e., *mamzēr* [Hebrew 23:3]), and the harlot. From these he deduces classes of reprobates (*Spec.* 1.327-45): those who deny the existence of Incorporal Ideas (327-29), those who deny God (330), polytheists (331-32), those who revere the mind (334-36) and those who honor the senses (337-43). Although his method may be suspect, he reveals nonetheless an attitude toward some unworthy classes and this has some bearing on his attitude toward proselytes. He is against bastard children, impure motives, the physically mutilated, and certain philosophical tendencies that are unworthy of a pure form of wisdom.

Rabbinical Evidence

Even if it is unlikely to be historically reliable, the story of Shammai repulsing the would-be proselyte is an indicator of a negative attitude toward (at least some) proselytes (*b. Šabb.* 31a; *'Abot R. Nat.* 15:3, 24ab, pp. 91-92). This may perhaps be explained as nothing more than excessive caution. Apparently Rabbi Eliezer b. Hyrcanus (second-generation Tanna) excluded Amalekites from joining Judaism (*Mek. Amalek,* par. 2, lines 177-86).[65] Rabbi Eliezer excluded the Cutheans because he classified them as "lion proselytes," and this ban stretched forward and backward many generations (Rabbi Ishmael, Rabbi Akiba; *b. Qidd.* 75b-76a).[66] In a well-known passage from *Mek. Shirata,* parashah 3, lines 49-63, Rabbi Akiba, in a conversation with the nations, praises God (Ex 15:2). When the Gentiles petition to come to God (*Cant* 6:1), Akiba turns them away, contending that they have no part in God (*Cant* 2:16; 6:3). This cautious, if not harsh, attitude was compounded in part by those who promised to become proselytes on condition of a hand in marriage (*m. Qidd.* 3:5; cf. *b. Qidd.* 63a). Rabbi Nehemiah's classification of impure motives led him to reject proselytes who became such for advantageous motives (*b. Yeb.* 24b). External pressure led Rabbi Jose b. Halafta, a fourth-generation Tanna, to reject idol worshipers who desired to become proselytes (*b. 'Abod. Zar.* 3b).[67] The climax of this attitude is found in the dictum of Rabbi Helbo, a fourth-century, Palestinian Amora, who said: "Proselytes are as hard for

Israel as a sore" (*b. Yeb.* 47a; *b. Qidd.* 70b).[68] The Amoraim continued this viewpoint (*b. Qidd.* 62ab; *b. Yeb.* 76a, 109b; *b. Sanh.* 96b, 99b; *b. Menaḥ.* 44a; *b. Giṭ.* 56b; *b. Ned.* 13b). The statements by rabbis concerning the legal status of proselytes sheds some light on their attitude.[69] In the rabbinic literature the legal status of proselytes (Could the proselyte marry a Jew? a priest? a high priest? a *nātîn?* a Cuthean? a *mamzēr?* What happened to his or her property when he or she died—since no heritage existed after conversion?) was greatly debated, and a large portion of evidence about proselytes is found in these halakic discussions.

First, the rabbinic dictum that a proselyte is equal to a Jew in every respect is both late and most probably not a reflection of the phenomena of life—or else many of the other laws would be nonsensical (cf. *b. Yeb.* 22a, 23a, 47b, 48b).[70] Second, the very existence of separate halakot for proselytes is a revelation in itself, which demonstrates that they were not seen as Jews in every respect.[71] We turn now to a few texts.

An early attribution shows an inferiority on the part of a female proselyte: Akabiah b. Mahalaleel (*m. ʿEd.* 5:6; *b. Ber.* 19a) does not think it proper to administer *sôṭâ* waters to a female proselyte.[72] According to *b. ʿErub.* 71a, Beth Shammai made rulings on the property of a deceased proselyte. This, if reliable, would demonstrate that an absolute break was necessary for becoming a proselyte. In *b. Ber.* 28a, again, we find that Ammonite proselytes can now marry Jews, at least according to Rabbi Joshua and, finally, in *Mek. Nezikin,* parashah 1, lines 46–50 (on Exod. 21:2a), Rabbi Eliezer b. Hyrcanus contends that proselytes have an evil streak in them. Thus, however hard one wants to press the legislation of Rabbi Jose b. Halafta, the facts betray that Jews did not immediately accept converts as equals; in fact, the notion of three generations is probably closer to reality.

Conclusions

Jewish attitudes toward proselytes unfold from Jewish attitudes toward Gentiles. Just as the dominant disposition toward Gentiles was favorable, tempered as it was by a religious and ethical demand, so also the dominant view of proselytism was positive in that Jews generally accepted any who would assume the "yoke of the Torah" (the ethical consequence of conversion).

First, apart from a few minor references in Philo and the several we have cited in the rabbis, Jews were generally favorably disposed to Gentiles who were willing to convert to Judaism. There is abundant evidence to demonstrate that the Jews had only occasional (and probably justifiable) reservations about accepting proselytes. It is historically inaccurate to assert that Jews had, as a general rule, negative attitudes to proselytes.

Second, the evidence that is negative appears to be based in such factors as improper motives or inconsequential conversion, both of which led to immorality within the camp. There does not seem to be any evidence in Judaism to suggest that Jews would prohibit a Gentile from converting to Judaism if that Gentile made it clear that he or she was serious about conversion. To become a convert meant to become socialized in Judaism; to be socially acceptable within Judaism carried with it certain moral and social expectations. If Gentiles were unwilling to live up to these stipulations, it is not surprising that hesitations were made about the propriety of conversion. But these hesitations are grounded in ethical and social boundaries, not in an antipathy to Gentiles. Resistance to proselytes was not a racial issue; it was religious and ethical.[73]

Third, as negative expressions were essentially theological convictions being expressed in social terms, so positive attitudes follow suit. In other words, an important aspect of proselytization evidence pertains to Jewish privilege and responsibility (*T. Levi* 14:4; *T. Naph.* 8:3, 4, 6; *T. Benj.* 5:1-5; 10:6-10; *2 Enoch* 33:9; 48:7-8; *Sib. Or.* 3:5-10, 811-12, 194-95, 582-83, 772-79). This can only be expected: Jews were convinced that Yahweh was the God of the Universe and that he had chosen them. If Yahweh has done this, proselytizing activity will reflect the same pattern. Consequently, Jews were convinced that they had the true message and religion and that it was there for others.[74] In fact, there is even at times an expression of a consciousness of mission to the world (cf., e.g., Justin *Dial. Trypho* 121-22), although such expressions are rare and seem to have had almost no permeating influence in Jewish practice and social reality (Wisd. of Sol. 18:4; *2 Enoch* 33:9; 48:7-8).

For instance, Philo can state that "the Jewish nation is to the whole world what the priest is to the State," and Philo goes on to speak of the rites of purification, supplication, and obedience (*Spec.* 2.162-67). Further, since the One God exists, "then it was the duty of all men to cleave to Him and not introduce new gods . . ." (165). But men failed; consequently, "when they all went wrong in what was most vital, this failure of the others was corrected by the Jewish nation." In a less explicit, but nonetheless revealing, comment, Philo compares Israel to the sand of the sea (*Som.* 1.175-78). Commenting on Gen. 28:14, he says that Israel is like the sea in two respects: it is numberless and it checks the inroads of the sea, that is, sinful actions and their onslaught. Here there is a clear consciousness of mission; if this were followed out in practice, Jews would have had a visible influence through missionary activity.

Fourth, following from this third point is that proselytization is resocialization or nationalization (Tob. 13:11; Ecclus. 36:11-17; *1 Enoch* 53:1; Rest of Esther E 1-24; F 7-9; *Ep. Arist.* 187-202; *T. Benj.* 10:6-10 [hope]; Bel and Dragon 26-28; *Sib. Or.* 5:493-500 [note 501]; *2 Bar.* 42:1-8; 68:5; Philo demands Torah but it is a differently interpreted Torah; *Mos.* 1:149; 2.17-25, 36; *Spec.* 1.151-53; Josephus *Ag. Ap.* 2.209-10 *et passim*). In the words of A. F. Segal, "Joining Judaism was primarily a decision to join another *ethnos*, which was not self-evidently possible to everyone, never taken lightly, and often viewed with some suspicion."[75] If God has chosen Israel, then to convert to the religion of Israel is to convert to the nation of Israel. This form of nationalization is necessarily bigotry because it stems, as mentioned, from a conviction about truth having its locus in the revelation of God to Israel. This explains what may be called the "triumph motif" of Jewish literature (e.g., Ecclus. 36:17; *1 Enoch* 50:1-3; 90:30-33; 91:14; 4 Ezra 6:25-28); if God is on Israel's side and God will eventually triumph, then Israel will be on the winning side. It follows that those who opposed Israel will lose. This will mean for our study that the universalism and friendliness of Judaism, outlined briefly in the previous chapter, are not blanket pluralism.[76]

Fifth, a universal conviction of Judaism is that conversion is total conversion, a topic that we will address in chapter 5. That is, a seeming majority of Jews, although friendly to outsiders and tolerant enough to permit gentile participation in the cultus, did not accept partial conversion as sufficient for full inclusion in society. This conviction follows from the negative expressions toward Gentiles found in separation and condemnation of moral laxity. Thus, it is not surprising to discover that Jews demanded of their converts that they live according to the same laws and obey the same customs.[77]

Sixth, an important element of Jewish views of proselytization is that there will be a massive conversion of Gentiles at the Last Day (Tob. 13:11; Ecclus. 36:11-17; *1 Enoch* 48:4; *T. Sim.* 7:2; *T. Levi* 18:2-9; *T. Jud.* 24:6; 25:5; *T. Zeb.* 9:8; *T. Benj.* 10:5-10; *Sib. Or.* 5:493-500; 4 Ezra 6:26; *2 Bar.* 68:5; not in Philo; *b. Ber.* 57b; cf. also Philo, *Praem.* 164-72; *Mos.* 2.43-44). This is not the only view found in Jewish literature, nor is it to be construed as the dominant view, but it is nonetheless an important aspect of Jewish thought and of the evidence. This theme is related, undoubtedly, to the triumph motif and, I might suggest, to the reality of the lack of converts to Judaism in the present—or should one say, the reality of almost an entire world of non-Jews who retained a form of paganism. J. Jeremias has presented this motif of apocalyptic conversion clearly, supported with ample evidence, and I summarize his five points: (1) the epiphany of God becomes visible to the nations; (2) God beckons the world to gather before him; (3) the Gentiles set out on a pilgrimage to Zion; (4) there is world-encompassing worship at the "World-sanctuary"; (5) and there is a messianic banquet on the "World-mountain."[78]

Seventh, although there is clearly an almost universally positive attitude toward proselytes and proselytism, a positive attitude toward, and an acceptance of, proselytes is to be methodologically distinguished from aggressive missionary activity among the Gentiles. In other words, although Jews clearly admitted proselytes, and although they clearly encouraged Gentiles to convert, and although they anticipated that Day when hordes of Gentiles would convert, there is almost no evidence that Jews were involved in evangelizing Gentiles and aggressively drawing Gentiles into their religion. L. Goppelt has correctly said, "No one thought about a real evangelization of the Gentile world."[79] This point will be further underscored in the next chapter. At this point, I state again what appears to me to be the most reliable picture we can draw: Jews were *a light among the Gentiles* and were more than willing to allow others to partake of that light.

We can say confidently that Jews almost universally and always accepted Gentiles who would join their religion. But Jewish religion was a serious constitutional element of life and not a casual matter; Jews were not in the business of hawking their wares on the open market. Thus, to join Judaism meant an entire orientation of life around the Jewish religion, including its God, law, and nation. To convert to Judaism was a serious matter.

The views of B. M. Bamberger and W. G. Braude have to be seen as just as one-sided as the views of W. Bousset and E. Lerle. More accurate is the view of G. F. Moore, who said, "Speaking generally the tone of the utterances about proselytes is friendly, though not unduly enthusiastic."[80]

3

The Methods of Proselytizing

IT HAS BEEN established that Gentiles converted to Judaism and that there were proselytes, though to what extent we are no longer able to tell. It has also been argued that neither the existence of proselytes nor the widespread positive attitudes toward proselytism proves that Judaism was a missionary religion. However, this does not mean that Gentiles did not convert to Judaism. The questions that emerge from these facts are, What led Gentiles to convert? What part did Jews play in their conversion? What *methods* did Jews use in gaining converts? It is the purpose of this chapter to examine the evidence of the ancient world to discern what we can know about the Jewish methods of proselytizing.[1]

Four terms are used constantly in the literature but often without clear definitions: propaganda, proselytization, evangelism, and mission.[2] F. M. Derwacter, for instance, defines propaganda as "the deliberate attempt of the Jews to win Gentile adherents to their religion."[3] In my view, this only muddles the definitions, because scholars are not inclined to agree that both "propaganda" and "mission" mean the same thing. Furthermore, "propaganda" is usually seen as pejorative. Accordingly, in this study propaganda is *indirect* proselytizing or evangelizing, behavior that is performed through some indirect means (say, literature, speeches, etc.) but whose purpose is not spelled out. A good example of such is Josephus's *Jewish War,* which, however one reads it, seems to be an attempt to defend Judaism against charges of insurrection. Josephus's strategy, of course, is to blame the war on the Zealots and, in so doing, exonerate the "typical Jew."

If propaganda is indirect, then "proselytization" or "evangelism" is *direct,* in the sense that some Jew seeks to explain Judaism in some manner and so convert the listener to Judaism. It is obvious, then, that propaganda is a specific part or motivation of proselytization. Moreover, I take apologetics to be a form of proselytization, namely, the defense of one's beliefs. It goes without saying that propaganda, proselytization, evangelism, and apologetics can all take place within a short compass, whether it be in the form of speeches, literary works, or even possibly architecture. In general, it seems fair to distinguish between indirect and direct means of proselytization.

Further, the expression "Jewish mission" will be used for a conscious design to reach outsiders and, through conversion, to include them in the covenant of Israel. The old view that Judaism had no mission because it did not evangelize is mistaken. If Judaism did use propaganda, that would constitute a mission because mission is a broader term about one's orientation. In other words, such a view of propaganda reflects a mission consciousness. Moreover, the use of "good works" to affect non-Jews is another reflection of a mission to the world, although such is not "evangelism." Traditionally, of course, "evangelism" has been used of early Christian missionary efforts, and "propaganda" or "proselytizing" has been used of Jewish behavior. I see no reason to assign one kind of behavior to one religion and another to the other religion. In fact, it strikes me that religious apologetics has become intertwined in this use of terms (evangelism seen positively and propaganda negatively). I hope that a more consistent use of such terms can aid our discussion.

Eight Methods of Proselytizing

These are methods that Jews used or that contemporary scholars contend that Jews used to effect conversions among Gentiles. The first is actually God's "method of converting Gentiles" but because it is such a keynote of the evidence, I begin with it.

God's Intervention

Conversion to Judaism, in much of the evidence, is seen as an act of God at the end of history in which Israel plays no part; the actor is God. Thus, Gentiles will stream to Zion at the Last Day (Tob. 13:11).[4] As a result of God's display of power, Gentiles will come to know Yahweh (Ecclus. 36:1-17). A major source for this category of thought is *1 Enoch* (48:4-5; 50:1-5; 62:9-13; 90:30-33; 91:14).

A feature of this idea is the crushing defeat of Israel's foes, sometimes by the messiah, who will force submission on the part of the nations to Israel and its God (*Jub.* 26:23; 39:4; *T. Sim.* 7:2; *T. Levi* 2:11; 4:3-4; 18:1-9; *T. Jud.* 24:6; *T. Zeb.* 9:8; *T. Benj.* 10:5; 4 Ezra 6:26). This notion is found also in Philo, but only once that I have noticed (*Praem.* 95-97): a "man" will appear who will lead Israel to victory. Consequently, some will show "affection or fear or respect."[5] Such an idea is found also in the rabbis (*Sem.* 46b [7:13, p. 359]).

Associated with this "method" is the notion that God's miraculous acts—frequently just before the end of history—often yield conversions. When Judith is delivered by God, Achior converts to Judaism (Jth. 11:23; 14:6–10). *2 Baruch* 54:18 appeals to "natural revelation" as a means of enlightening the nations,[6] and much of the so-called "propaganda literature" uses the same approach (e.g., *Letter of Aristeas, Sibylline Oracles*). From Philo we know that miraculous events witnessed by Gentiles were instrumental in conversion to Judaism—although Philo does not appear to have looked favorably on those who converted for such reasons (*Mos.* 1.147). Josephus records that, after Esther's victory, many Gentiles were converted because they feared the potential danger of continued opposition to the Jews (*Ant.* 11.285–86) and Metilius promised to convert completely—to spare his life (*J.W.* 2.454: *touton gar hikteusanta kai mechri peritomēs ioudaïsein hyposchomenon diesōsan monon*).[7] A later text reads:

> Then the Holy One, blessed be he, will reveal his great arm in the world, and show it to the gentiles: it shall be as long as the world and as broad as the world, and the glory of its splendor shall be like the brilliant light of the noonday sun at the summer solstice. At once Israel shall be saved from among the gentiles and the Messiah shall appear to them and bring them up to Jerusalem with great joy. Moreover, the kingdom of Israel, gathered from the four quarters of the world, shall eat with the Messiah, and the gentiles shall eat with them, as it is written,
> > The Lord bares his holy arm
> > in the sight of all the nations,
> > and all the ends of the earth shall see
> > the salvation of our God;
> and it also says,
> > The Lord alone is his guide,
> > with him is no alien god;
> and it says,
> > The Lord will be the King of the whole world."
>
> (*3 Enoch* 48A:9–10; *OTP*)

A consistent means of conversion in Jewish thought was the acts of God that led Gentiles to convert. These acts of God were especially prominent at the end of history, effecting a massive conversion to Judaism.

Jewish Missionaries through Evangelism

Is there evidence for "Jewish missionaries" who sought converts?[8] If we can strip away modern connotations of "Christian missionaries," is there evidence that there were men or women in the Jewish world who saw their mission in life, or at least an occasional task, as penetrating the gentile world in an attempt to convert Gentiles? F. M. Derwacter has taken, in what I have read, the strongest stand in this regard: "One of early Christianity's most striking characteristics was its apostles, men sent out to preach its message and to organize the developing movement." With this he begins his chapter; at the end he states: "It is very likely, therefore, that the method of itinerant teaching and preaching was a common phenomenon of the time, and that the Jews of propagandist spirit followed it, as did the Christians and pagans."[9] Is this a reasonable and probable inference from data?

The evidence cited by Derwacter from 2 Chron. 17:7-9; 2 Macc. 1:1-2, 9, 18; 2:16; Esther 9:20, 30; Philo; Josephus; early Christians; and the Talmud is unquestionably interesting for the establishment of the so-called Jewish apostolate but shows nothing more than regulation of Jewish communities by Jewish leaders.[10] Derwacter admits that there is very little information that could be construed in this way (e.g., Dio Cassius 67.14; Josephus *Ant.* 20.17-53) but, even after this admission, he buttresses his conclusion by appealing to early Christian missionaries (Paul, Peter, etc.) and pagan itinerant philosophers. It seems to me that his "very likely" does not have sufficient evidence to support it. We must look, then, more closely at the evidence. In fact, L. H. Feldman, an authority on Jewish proselytism, has conceded that "one of the great puzzles of the proselyting movement is how to explain the existence of a mass movement [of conversions to Judaism] when we do not know the name of a single Jewish missionary."[11]

According to Ben Sira, the wise scribe is the one "who travels (*dieleusetai*) in foreign countries (*en gē allotriōn enthnōn* [i.e., *ethnōn*]), he has experienced good and human evil" (Ecclus. 39:4; NJB).[12] This is possible evidence for Jewish missionaries, but it must be observed that Ben Sira is describing here the life of a scribe who functions as a court official or ambassador; the growth being described may be in that scribe's cultural and philosophical understanding (cf. 39:1-11).[13] Further, the description of this scribe as one who declares (*ekphanei*) his wise instruction may suggest that he does so to outsiders (cf. 39:10: *ethnē*), but nothing certain can be inferred from this statement (39:8).

The *Letter of Aristeas* suggests something similar to Ben Sira at 266:

> King: "What is the purpose of speaking?" "To persuade (*to peisai*) your opponent in debate," was his [one of the king's guests] reply, "by pointing

out his errors in an orderly list. In this way you will win over your listener, not being antagonistic but using some commendation to persuade him. And persuasion succeeds through the activity of God." (*OTP*)

There are difficulties here for using this as a clear consciousness of mission to Gentiles. Is the opponent a Gentile? Probably. Is the debate over Judaism? It is impossible to tell, but one can see here an emphasis on rhetorical skill, if not psychological flattery;[14] and these skills may have been forged on the anvil of polemics with Gentiles. Again, this text does not encourage confidence in our knowledge about Jewish missionaries.

Another possible clue for Jewish missionaries is found in *T. Levi* 14:4: "For what will all the nations do if you become darkened with impiety? You will bring down a curse on our nation, because you want to destroy the light of the Law which was granted to you for the enlightenment of every man, teaching commandments which are opposed to God's just ordinances." This idea could be further supported in *T. Levi* 2:10–11; 8:4; *T. Naph.* 8:3, 4, 6.[15] What can be inferred from *T. Levi* 14:4 is that the author has a clear consciousness that Israel has a responsibility to enlighten the world with the truth of Judaism. It needs to be observed, however, that the author does not spell out how this responsibility was to be accomplished, and from the evidence of these texts there are no clues that it was to be fulfilled through proselytizing the Gentiles. Thus, I see "mission" here but neither missionary activity nor missionaries; consequently, Judaism is not presented here as a missionary religion.

Virtually the same idea is expressed in Wisd. of Sol. 18:4: ". . . for they [i.e., the Egyptians] had kept in captivity your children, by whom the incorruptible light of the Law was to be given to the world." Again, this text evinces a mission consciousness to enlighten the world, but it does not explain how that was to be worked out.

The Sibyl of *Sibylline Oracles* may have been involved in revelatory, oracular utterances that bordered on evangelistic preaching or proselytizing. *Sib. Or.* 3:5–10: ". . . compelled from within to proclaim an oracle to all? But I will utter everything again, as much as God bids me say to men. Men, who have the form which God molded in his image, why do you wander in vain, and not walk the straight path ever mindful of the immortal creator?" (see also 3:809–29). It is difficult to know what to make of these statements. Do they refer to the Sibyl's writing of oracles? There is here both a consciousness of mission and an apparent proselytizing activity, but how much of this came to life in evangelism is impossible to tell.

The Dead Sea Scrolls offer some information here. The Qumran sect claims to have discovered the truth by revelation (1QH 4:5, 17–18, 23, 27–29; 5:25; 8:16–26; 18:10–12, 19–20, 27–32; 1QS 10:24–25). Consequently, members seem to have announced this revelation (1QH 4:17; 5:22–23; 9:23–24; 18:11, 14) and declared the sin of Israel (5:22–23; 6:20; 9:9; 18:12; 1QS 10:21, 23–24a) both to sectarians (1QS 1:22; 1QH 1:23, *et passim*) and nonsectarians (1QpHab 2:7; CD 3:7).[16] The key term for public pronouncements in the scrolls is "to recount, announce" (*spr*), used thirty-one times as a verb and twenty-one times as a substantive, but, again, the revelations known to the sectarians are publicly pronounced only to sectarians (e.g., 1QS 1:21–22; 9:26; 10:23–24; 1QH 1:30, 33–35a; 3:23; 6:11; 10:14, 20–21; 11:6, 24, 28; 13:11; 18:23; CD 13:8). The decision to pronounce judgment on all those who did not follow in the way of the Teacher of Righteousness apparently led to considerable argumentation (*ríb:* see 1QS 4:18, 23; 9:16, 19; 1QH 2:14; 5:22, 30, 35; 7:23; CD 1:2, 21).[17]

This general picture of reception of revelation and pronouncement of judgment (probably after unsuccessful attempts to convert Israel) needs to be supplemented with a closer examination of 1QS 10:17–18, which reads: "To no man will I render the reward of evil, with goodness will I pursue each one. . . ."[18] Instead of wreaking wrath, this psalmist contends that he will pursue others "with goodness," and this could very well suggest deeds of charity. It may also suggest evangelism or proselytization. But, interestingly, the term "pursue" elsewhere in the Dead Sea Scrolls always indicates "pursuit with a negative end in view" (see 1QpHab 11:5; 1QM 9:5, 6; 18:2, 12; CD 1:21). In other words, it appears that the psalmist will eventually, in God's timing, overtake his enemies with goodness—that is, cause their condemnation by doing good. This is confirmed by the next sentence in 10:18: "For judgement of all the living is with God and it is He who will render to man his reward."[19] Moreover, it is strengthened by lines 20, 23–24, which further suggest proclaiming sin and judgment.

It appears then that the sect was esoteric in its use of knowledge (see 1QS 9:17; 5:11; 8:11–12; 4:6; 10:24; 11:5–6; 1QH 5:26; 9:24).[20] However, P. Wernberg-Møller ller contends that the sect was not esoteric but cautious in its passing on of revelation; he cites 1QH 2:7–8; 5:22–25; 1QS 6:13–16. But the first text (1QH 2:7–8), as a hymn of the Teacher, probably involved rejection, not for revelation of secrets but for condemning others as sinners. The second text (1QH 5:22–25) is of a similar nature in that it refers to the revelations of secrets given formerly to those who were members but who have now defected; those who are rejecting the Teacher had received knowledge prior to this persecution.[21] Finally, Wernberg-Møller cites 1QS 6:13–16 and speaks here of instruction in "all the rules of the Community." But this instruction *follows* the decision by the powers that be that the novice "is suited to the discipline" [*w'm yśyg mwsr*] (see also CD 15:10–11). Further, this piece of information pertains to initiates, and we ought not to apply this to outsiders without confirming evidence.[22] In summary, there is no solid evidence in the Dead Sea Scrolls that there was ever any time of "evangelizing or proselytizing Gentiles."

Several passages in Philo have been used to suggest missionary proclamation by Jews to Gentiles. For instance, Philo denigrates the mysteries for their esotericism "when by producing (*prothentes*) them [the truths] in the midst of the market places you might extend them to every man and thus enable all to share in security a better and happier life" (*Spec.* 1.320). Again, "let those whose actions serve the common weal use freedom of speech (*parrēsia*) and walk in daylight through the midst of the market-place, ready to converse with crowded gatherings . . ." (1.321). Through life-style and speech, he says, let the truth become known so the crowd may "feast on the fresh sweet draught of words which are wont to gladden the minds of such as are not wholly averse to learning" (1.321). Because nature does not hide its works (322), neither should men. Instead, we [the Jews] should "display in public (*protithenai*) all that is profitable and necessary for the benefit of those who are worthy to use it" (1.323). According to Philo, then, the one who grasped the truth had a moral-natural (*Spec.* 1.322–23) obligation to proclaim the truth publicly, viz., in the agora. Abraham, the good man, is almost seen as an evangelist: the divine spirit "invested his voice with persuasiveness, and his hearers with understanding" (*Virt.* 217).

We look finally at *Prob.* 74 and the expression "heralds of words and works" (*presbytai logōn kai ergōn*). In the barbarian world there were apparently some ambassadors of truth, but the emendation of F. H. Colson in his translation in the Loeb Classical Library edition seems plausible. He suggests that it would originally have been more probably *en hē presbyetai logōn erga* ("in which deeds are held in higher esteem than words"). This is almost demanded by the illustrations that follow immediately: the Magi "silently research" into things "clearer than speech"; Gymnosophists "make the whole of their lives an exhibition of virtue"; and the Essenes, by their seclusion and practice, do the same. But even if virtue outweighs words in Philo, it cannot be denied that Philo values public conversation about the glories of Judaism. If we find a specific place for proselytizing in the writings of Philo, it would be the agora, not the synagogue. The evidence from Asia Minor, especially

Sardis, suggests that the give-and-take of the agora may have been the most suitable setting for such disquisitions.

From Josephus we learn also that some Gentiles may have been converted to Judaism through preaching. Reform movements were often "instigated" by didactic and "kerygmatic" activities (*Ant.* 9.2–6; 10.43, 47–53; 18.63;[23] 20.34) and oratorical abilities were not unusual among Jews (see, e.g., *J.W.* 1.453; 4.230, 391). Such preaching often led to repentance among the Jews (*Ant.* 9.267; 10.68; 18.116–19; 20.168).[24] At times preaching is directed toward Gentiles, as when Jonah preached (*kēryssō*) and divulged (*dēloō*) his message to the Ninevites (*Ant.* 9.208–14). Jesus, "Josephus" records, won over (*epagō*) both Jews and Gentiles (18.63).[25] Finally, Ananias won over (*synanepeisen*) Izates, and Eleazar urged him (*protrepō*) to complete his conversion in circumcision (20.35–43). This text does not teach that there were such things as Jewish missionaries or that these supposed missionaries were zealous; rather, it provides evidence for traveling merchants being involved in explaining Judaism to those who were interested in it.[26] In summary, there is some evidence in both Philo and Josephus, however meager, of Jewish missionary activity, of the proselytizing and evangelizing sort, among Gentiles and done by those who tried to convert Gentiles. It remains an open question, however, to what extent this practice was typical and widespread. These problems are compounded when we ask whether these statements of Philo and Josephus are more aspiration than practice. In my opinion, the statements of Philo are particularly vulnerable to this question, but the evidence of Josephus seems to me to be more unambiguous—although some of his evidence is undoubtedly a rewriting of Jewish history.

According to a much later, Amoraic tradition, the descendants of Sennacherib, in this case Shemaiah and Abtalion (pretannaitic teachers) taught Torah in public (*b. Sanh.* 96b; *b. Giṭ* 57b; *b. Yoma* 71b).[27] In the Mishnah, we have a possible reference in *m.* ʾ*Abot* 2:14, which states that Rabbi Eleazar b. Arak (second-generation Tanna) told his disciples to "know how to make an answer to an unbeliever" (=Epicurean).[28] Some anonymous Mishnaic *halakot* contain some details in this regard. Some proselytes may have been won by persuasion (*b. Yeb.* 47b; *b. ʿAbod. Zar.* 11a; ʾ*Abot R. Nat.* 12:7, 23a, p. 76) or invitations to synagogues (*Midr. Qoh.* 8:10; *Ruth Rab.* 4:1; *Shir. R.* 1:15).[29]

In summary, there were perhaps some Jews who functioned as evangelists in Judaism. How widespread and how frequent this practice was are impossible to tell now. There is evidence to suggest that some Jews spoke publicly about their religious message and their national solidarity in defense of themselves, and it is fair to say that sometimes they were successful in gaining converts to Judaism.[30] But there is no evidence to suggest that Judaism, at any time or at any location, thought of itself in terms of a "mission" with respect to the Gentiles. Nor is there evidence that any Jews were "missionaries."

If we can agree that there was some Jewish missionary activity of an evangelistic nature, we need also to ask if in that evidence there was a neatly defined message of evangelism. If the Jews did proselytize Gentiles—and there is no evidence to prove that such took place in any organized fashion—can we speak of any sort of "kerygma" when it did occur? An affirmative answer to this question is most difficult, and the diversity of Judaism, coupled with the lack of information, works heavily against framing an adequate summary of what it would have looked like. In fact, the message would either be too reductionistic to be of value or would not reflect the historical contingencies that gave rise to various expressions of Judaism. Furthermore, in my opinion the question is slanted in the direction of cognitive affirmation, which derives largely from Christian disputes about orthodoxy rather than the facts of the ancient world of Judaism.

Because his work is general enough to avoid reductionism, I will simply summarize what P. Dalbert has concluded regarding the "essential points" of the message contained in the so-called propaganda literature and then offer a few comments.[31] Dalbert sees three aspects of expected agreement: (1) monotheism and the universal reign of God (*Sib. Or.* 3:542; 5:291; *Ep. Arist.* 16–17, 234; Wisd. of Sol. 8:4; 9:1, 9; 16:24); (2) nonphysical, spiritual revelation that manifests itself in rational ethics; and (3) the superiority of Israel.[32] I am inclined to think that Dalbert sees far too little of a place for the Torah and for the sociological importance of adhering to Israel. He pushes the evidence too much in the direction of propositional affirmation and *credo*, probably because he is asking what is too much of a later Christian question. He has not laid enough emphasis on the phenomenology of ancient religious adherence; however, his points are generally accurate and therefore useful.[33]

Literature

Distributing literature that related the truth of Judaism was, according to many scholars, a method of proselytizing in ancient Judaism. For instance, Fergus Millar states: "At any rate . . . a varied literature came into being, the direct aim of which was to convince pagans of the folly of idolatry, to win them over to belief in the one true God, and at the same time to convert them to a more serious and moral way of life by pointing towards a future reward."[34] The literature under question includes the nonextant work of Philo, *Apologia hyper Ioudaiōn*, Josephus's *Contra Apionem*, and others, including the *Letter of Aristeas*, and the authors Demetrius, Eupolemus, Aristobulus, as well as the *Sibylline Oracles*.[35] This aspect of Jewish proselytizing has been fully expounded by P. Dalbert, who attempts to explain the theology of this literature, and we refer the reader to his volume for further details. Two caveats must be mentioned.

The scholarly classification, definition, and explanation, along with the appropriate historical scenario, of Jewish-Hellenistic apologetics have not yet been delineated with sufficient rigor to be utilized determinatively in this monograph. My aim here is not directly to contest this aspect of scholarship but to deal with a broader question: Did Jews use literature to evangelize Gentiles? The question of apologetics and our question are undoubtedly related, but with apologetics we are asking questions about ideological framework and literary genre. My question pertains to evidence that speaks about methods of reaching non-Jews.[36]

Furthermore, V. Tcherikover has issued a knowledgeable challenge to this entire branch of historiography, concluding that Jews did not give their cherished writings to non-Jews for the purpose of persuasion. The implications of this work are enormous and would lay to rest a significant area of scholarship today, namely, the assumptions and explanations of certain documents as apologetics. M. Goodman, in the revision of E. Schürer, seems to agree with the challenging, and too frequently neglected, essay of Tcherikover.[37] We cannot doubt, however, that Jews responded to the calumniating discourses of non-Jews. Our problem is to discern if this debate ever left the academics and whether any literature was created that was to be given to non-Jews as counterapologetics. There is a serious question today whether a literature of this sort even existed. Until further proof is offered, I shall treat the literature as written for Jews.[38] I offer but one further comment. It strikes me that much (if not most) of this so-called literature needs to be seen as an attempt on the part of Jewish authors (who certainly arose from a particular community) to aid in Jewish self-identification. By defending its heritage (or whatever) and by responding to the charges against Judaism, this literature serves the community by reaffirming its self-identity and tradition. If this is even close to the underlying motivation for this literature, a revision of our understanding of Jewish apologetical literature is needed.

The *Letter of Aristeas* is an apology for Judaism, and the author defends the temple and the Septuagint. He writes to show that Judaism, with its law, wisdom, and God, was of the highest character as a religion and, therefore, deserved to be embraced by all. The result of his effort, as stated by V. Tcherikover, is that "Aristeas' fundamental idea is the somewhat surprising revelation that Judaism is nothing more than true Hellenism enriched by the idea of the unity of God."[39] Of a different form, but with a similar purpose, are the *Sybilline Oracles*, a collection of literature from someone who was convinced of a call from God (perhaps) to proclaim to non-Jews the message of monotheism and the superiority of the God of Israel. In the words of P. Dalbert, "The ecstatic prophetess proclaimed, under divine impulse, the will of God and predicted the fate of the nations."[40] One ought to mention also 4 Maccabees. The author states his desire to convince non-Jews of the supreme rule of inspired reason (*eusebēs logismos*) over passion and flesh, "inspired reason" no doubt being the author's form of Judaism.

Another bit of information is found at *2 Enoch* 48:6-9:

> Thus I am making it known to you, my children; and you must hand over the books to your children, and throughout all your generations, ‹and to (your) relatives› , and |among| all nations who are discerning so that they may fear God, and so that they may accept them. And they will be more enjoyable than any delightful food on earth. And they will read them and adhere to them. But those who are undiscerning and who do not understand ‹the LORD› neither fear God nor accept them, but renounce them, and regard themselves as burdened by them— |a terrible judgment is awaiting them|. Happy is the person who puts their yoke on and carries it around; for he will plow on the day of the great judgment.[41]

If we disregard, for the moment, the obviously suspicious nature of the text and the problem of dating the origin of these texts, this text does suggest that an occasional Jew propagandized Gentiles through literature. In the words of F. M. Derwacter, "It [i.e., Jewish literary propaganda] sought to make its acceptance surer in Gentile circles by obscuring its Jewish origin and by affecting names which had won a place in Gentile religious thought."[42]

Philo has great hope for the law, thinking that it will affect the entire world (*Mos.* 2.36, 41, 44; *Dec.* 81; *Spec.* 1.52). He does not tell us, however, that the literature of the Jews was given to Gentiles for the purpose of leading them into Judaism.[43] The evidence of Josephus is similar (see *Ag. Ap.* 2.279-95).

When Eleazar followed Ananias to Adiabene and found Izates reading the Torah, he exhorted Izates to do more than read it—he directed him to obey it by being circumcised (Josephus *Ant.* 20.44-46). Here we have evidence that the Torah was useful for deepening a Gentile's understanding of Judaism. It must be noted, however, that the evidence does not say that he was given the law in order to learn about Judaism. In fact, it is more likely that he was given the law by Ananias after Izates showed some interest in that law. Furthermore, we ought not to forget that what was done for kings may very well have been exceptional.

In addition to the evidence mentioned above, many scholars have argued that the Septuagint itself was a "missionary document" or that it was used at some level for the conversion of Gentiles. It is beyond the scope of this book to engage the complex questions associated with the text and transmission of the Septuagint. It is my view that the Septuagint does represent transparency at many places, showing both Hellenistic influence and a greater openness for Gentiles understanding the text. However, the translation of the Hebrew Bible in these directions can be done just as easily for Jews as Gentiles. Jews growing up, for instance, in Alexandria might more easily understand the text if it is expressed in more Hellenistic categories and in the Greek language. Furthermore, I maintain that, although the Septuagint reflects an attempt to express the biblical text in terms familiar to Gentiles, this does not prove that Gentiles were given copies of the Septuagint or that the Septuagint was designed to convert them. However, I do not want to push this point too far simply because the evidence is there to suggest that sometimes the Septuagint renderings seem to be motivated by the desire for Gentiles to understand the text, or at least to make the text more compatible with Hellenism.[44] In this sense, we may accurately contend that literature was used by Jews for proselytizing.

In addition, the Septuagint is a witness to the presence of proselytes in Judaism.[45] For instance, if the term *prosēlytos* is given the notion of "convert" in the Septuagint of Isa. 54:15 (the Hebrew text is probably using a pun that the translator missed), then one could infer that proselytes were expected (and maybe common) in Judaism.[46] But no actual missionary activity or proselytizing is transparent in the Septuagint, and the Septuagint of Isaiah was not a missionary document.[47] However, the Septuagint may be taken reasonably as first steps toward a missionary religion—but that does not mean that second and third steps were actually taken shortly thereafter.[48]

Joseph and Aseneth

The ancient story of Joseph and Aseneth is a case in point, and we pause here to look more carefully at a piece of literature, taken by many to be propaganda, that expressly deals with proselytism.[49] This legendary but compelling romance completes the biblical story about Joseph's marriage to Aseneth (Gen. 41:45) and divulges how a good Jew could marry an apparent Gentile (her father was the priest of On). The resolution is that Aseneth is a prototypical convert to Judaism.

This story, written in a simple Koine Greek and worth reading in its own right, describes an arrogant, beautiful virgin who, when requested to marry Joseph by her father, Pentephres, vehemently refused on the grounds that Joseph was an alien and a suspected adulterer (*Jos. Asen.* 3-4). However, after encountering the handsome and wise Joseph (5-6), she radically changes her mind and prays to the God of Joseph for pardon (6:1-8). After shunning a kiss from the mouth of an idolater, Joseph prays for her conversion (8:9) and Aseneth retires to her rooms in a seven-day fast of abject misery and repentance. The tale of her repentance is both illuminating and marvelous as she destroys all vestiges of her idolatry and pride (10:2–13:15). God hears her confession, sends Michael to relay the absolution, gives her the new name "City of Refuge" (because she will eventually be surrounded by Gentiles), and promises Joseph's hand in marriage (14:1–17:10). Their marriage is then narrated (18:1–21:9). Closing the first act of the tale is a poetic hymn of confession, told in the style of a repetitive, revised biography (21:10-21). The hymn, along with Aseneth's earlier prayers, express depth of sin (especially idolatry and eating food offered to idols), repudiation of idolatry, separation from family,[50] and the need for mercy. As such, the story is a monument to gentile conversion and the necessary illumination needed in coming to the God of Israel. The second act of the story, about complicity and intrigue to steal Joseph's wife, is not relevant for our topic.

The importance of this story for proselytism during Second Temple Judaism is obvious. Here we need to counter, however, a common interpretation: namely, that *Joseph and Aseneth* is an example of Jewish propaganda written for Gentiles for their conversion and, alongside this view, that the text is a testimony to widespread Jewish proselytization.[51] There are, however, serious problems with these inferences from *Joseph and Aseneth*.[52] First, the pattern of the story is the typical pattern found elsewhere in Judaism: Joseph does not seek out Aseneth (he simply happens upon the situation), nor does he "evangelize" or "proselytize" her. Rather, Aseneth seeks to convert to Judaism by approaching him— and, I might add, with very little encouragement on Joseph's part. The text of *Joseph and Aseneth* offers no evidence for "proselytizing activity."[53] Second, although Aseneth is renamed "City of Refuge" (15:7), the conversion of other Gentiles is seen as yet future—as we saw above in the case of apocalyptic vision. Conversion to Judaism is not seen as a contemporary problem or a common situation.

Third, however religious one wants to make this tale, the story remains an (erotic) romance,[54] and her motive for conversion is clearly associated with a desire to marry Joseph.[55] Finally, it is difficult to know just how much one can make out of a special man (Joseph) and a special, gloriously beautiful woman (Aseneth) as typical for conversion.

I concur with C. Burchard: "There is no hint in Joseph and Aseneth that Jewish missionaries or zealous individuals spread the good news of salvation and called for conversion."[56] "Joseph and Aseneth has often been called a missionary tract, a *Missionsschrift*, meaning that it was written to promote Jewish missions among non-Jews, or Jews, or both. This is mistaken. Judaism is not depicted as mission-minded in Joseph and Aseneth. Proselytes are welcomed, not sought, and conversion certainly is not an easy affair."[57] More pungently, S. West observes: "JA [*Joseph and Aseneth*] is as irrelevant to the problems of contemporary proselytes as *Quo Vadis* is to the oecumencial movement."[58]

In conclusion, A. Momigliano has stated, "I do not know of any Hellenistic evidence to show that a Gentile became a Jew or a sympathizer because he had the Bible."[59] His conclusion is accurate because we do not have evidence of conversion through literature. However, Josephus's thorough apologetic (and polemical) work *Contra Apionem* does justify the use of literature for propaganda at some level. We can only surmise that "Apion" read this work. I leave open the possibility that all Jewish literature of a propagandistic, apologetical, or polemical nuance might have been exclusively written by Jews for Jews in order to bolster faith and establish identity.

Later Christian evidence confirms the position here: Tertullian, speaking of Christian literature, says, "to which [literature] no one comes for guidance unless he is already a Christian" (*de Test. Animae* 1). If expressly apologetical literature is not read by outsiders—and this in the opinion of an apologist—how can we so easily assume that other literature was read by outsiders?

The Synagogue as an Institution for Proselytizing

G. F. Moore stated, "Their [the Jews] religious influence was exerted chiefly through the synagogues, which they set up for themselves, but which were open to all whom curiosity drew to their services."[60] More recently, however, A. T. Kraabel has stated: "There is no evidence from the excavations of attempts to recruit gentiles by means of these buildings. In the inscriptions the word 'proselyte' is very rare: it appears in but one per cent of the Jewish inscriptions from Italy, the largest sample available; and it does not occur in the synagogue inscriptions at all."[61] From Philo, who uses both *synagōgē* and *proseuchē* for "synagogue,"[62] the synagogue appears to have been a place for reading Scriptures, expounding passages,[63] discussing and debating interpretations,[64] catechizing, singing hymns to God, and reflecting on Israel's past (*Spec.* 2.63, 159, 244–48; *Som.* 1.118–19; 2.127; *Her.* 280–83; *Mut.* 141–43; *Abr.*

99; *Jos.* 151ff.; *L.A.* 1.59; *Det.* 22, 133; *Conf.* 190; *Prob.* 82; *Dec.* 98; *Leg.* 315; *Vita* 75–82; *Hyp.* 7:12–14). However, we must ask whether there is evidence for the view that, in the words of D. Georgi, "the continuing dialogue with paganism was then at the heart of synagogue worship, in form as well as in content."[65] In other words, was the synagogue used by the Jews to be a house for converting Gentiles? We are not asking whether or not Gentiles were converted in synagogues; we can only surmise that this did take place, but, so far as I know, there is no evidence of radical conversion there. Rather, we are asking whether Jews intended the synagogue to be an institution that had as one of its major purposes converting Gentiles.

I have found only one piece of evidence in Philo that suggests the presence of Gentiles in Alexandrian synagogues, namely, *Spec.* 2:62–63, which reads, "So each seventh day there stand wide open in every city . . . schools of good sense, temperance, courage, justice and the other virtues . . . duty to God . . . [and] duty to men. . . ." This discussion arises to show what Jews do on the Sabbath: they gain inspiration to continue their wisdom. But the question to be asked is, Does the verb "stand wide open" suggest the presence of Gentiles? There is nothing in the context to argue for gentile attendance. If the synagogue was an evangelistic platform, there is no substantial evidence for such a view in Philo. That it was used to instruct proselytes cannot be doubted, but we must be careful not to build "castles in the sky," constructed on inferences from texts that cannot hold their weight.

In light of this Philonic text, we need then to interact with the recent theory of D. Georgi, who contends, partly from Philo, that the synagogues were in fact missionary institutions. He has two points I would like to consider: First, he deduces that the great numbers of Jews in the Diaspora can be explained only by an "enormous expansion" through proselytizing. Second, he states that "the medium of Jewish propaganda was the synagogue worship and the exegis [*sic*] of the law presented there. Every pagan had free access since the synagogue service was a public event."[66] The first point, however crucial for the logic of his argument, can be dispensed with rather summarily: to accept demographics from the *Letter of Aristeas*, Philo, and Josephus and to build inferences on them are courting disaster.[67] The disparate numbers of Harnack, J. Juster, S. W. Baron, and others demonstrate that it is virtually impossible to attain the accuracy we need.[68] Consequently, to build inferences on proselytizing activity by the Jews on the basis of "growth percentages" is wildly speculative.

But, more important, we need to examine his second theory, namely, that the synagogue and its Torah exposition were the main vehicle of

converting Gentiles. Georgi adduces the following passages: Josephus
J.W. 7.45; Horace *Satires* 1.4.138-43; Juvenal *Satires* 14.96-106; Philo
Mos. 2.17-25, 26-27, 209ff.; *Spec.* 2:62ff. and *Hyp.* 7.13.

To begin with, all that can be shown from Horace's *Satires* is that, as
taken traditionally, Jews were known for "compelling" (*cogemus*) others
to become members. Though this speaks, perhaps, to the emotional
energy spilled into proselytizing, it says nothing of synagogues or of
Torah interpretation as devices in proselytizing. The recent work of J.
Nolland on this statement deserves careful consideration.[69] Because the
implications of Nolland's work are so far-reaching for understanding
this text, his work and conclusions are summarized here. The last lines
of *Satire* 1.4 are, according to Nolland, a tactical weapon for Horace's
defense of writing satires. They read, "This is one of those lesser frailties
I spoke of, and if you should make no allowance (*concedere*) for it, then
would a big band of poets come to my aid—for we are the big
majority—and we, like the Jews, will compel you to make one of our
throng." Horace threatens the use of coercion by a great band of poets
in contrast to the reason he has used prior to this point. Further,
Nolland contends that *concedere,* usually understood to mean "to pass
over or transfer," is identical in meaning in both 1.4.140 and 1.4.143. He
argues that it means "to fall in line with" or "to yield" in some way to
the acceptability of writing satire. The intention of Horace, then, is to
contend that, if he were alone in writing satire, he could be dismissed;
but, since he is surrounded by an army of poets, his readers cannot stand
against them.

Nolland contends that the comparison with the Jews concerns the
power of Jewish groups to achieve their results through concerted
effort—in an armylike fashion. A parallel to this idea he aptly finds in
Cicero, *Pro. Flacc.* 66, which speaks of political effort on the part of
Jews. Horace, in other words, is not at all speaking of the Jews' ability
to coerce conversions or of their aggressiveness in proselytizing. He is
speaking of their ability to get political or personal advantage through
public assembly. If Nolland is accurate, and I tend to agree with him,
then this text must be permanently dismissed as evidence for Jewish
missionary activity. It speaks neither of synagogue interpretation nor
of proselytizing.

Juvenal's *Satires* 14.96-106 also says nothing about a synagogue.[70]
Further, contrary to Georgi's own thesis, the text shows a slow growth
in Judaism. It is the "fearer of the Sabbath" (*metuentem sabbata*) whose
son eventually, as he matures into an adult, becomes a convert. Again,
nothing is said either of synagogues or of Torah interpretation.

What about Philo, upon whom the argument so heavily leans? In *Mos.* 2.209–16 we have a clear discussion of the Sabbath synagogue service. Those involved are those "whose names were written on his [Moses'] holy burgess-roll and who followed the laws of nature," but this is not evidence for Gentiles as far as I can see. In fact, from 216 we see that it was "the Jews" who were being discussed. There is nothing here about Torah interpretation. *De Vita Mosis* 2.17–27 shows that Gentiles have been converted to respecting the Jewish Torah and states that they hallowed the Sabbath (21–22), but it refrains from placing them in the "schools of virtue, etc." In fact, 26–27 speaks of the power of good deeds and the translation of the Torah as that which led other nations to admire Jewish laws. Here then we have Gentiles but not in synagogues and not being converted through the exposition of Torah. In *Spec.* 2.62–63 the synagogue service is described as "training in philosophy,"[71] but this says nothing about Gentiles either. From *Hyp.* 7.13 we gain information about synagogues and interpretation, but nothing about Gentiles being converted to Judaism through a propagandistic interpretation of the Torah.

By a skillful arrangement of his texts, D. Georgi, after citing the Philonic texts, concludes, "One can see from the example of the Antiochene community (adduced by Josephus, *JW* 7.45) how successful the synagogue service was."[72] In other words, if we exclude *Mos.* 2.17–27, which Georgi cites on the next page for a slightly different reason (Gentile respect for Jewish institutions), he believes he has proved that the synagogue was evangelistic in presentation. In my view, Georgi has not proved his case at all. He has said a few important things about what probably took place in a synagogue but nothing about Gentiles being converted through Torah interpretation.

We turn to Josephus, *J.W.* 7.45, in which Josephus states two things: (1) the successors of Antiochus IV gave the Jews considerable freedom and (2) during this time Jews were "constantly attracting (*prosagomenoi*) to their religious ceremonies multitudes of Greeks." What can be made of this generalized reference? It says nothing clear about leading Gentiles to synagogue services so that the Gentiles can hear an "evangelistic or propagandistic sermon" on the Torah. In fact, this verse may be nothing more than a general allusion to "the regular conversion of Gentiles to Jewish customs."

In conclusion, if we limit discussion to the evidence cited by D. Georgi, we can accurately say that the case is not proved. In other words, there is not sufficient evidence from the ancient world to demonstrate that the synagogue was used as a missionary platform—especially not through the use of Torah exposition.[73] I do not doubt that Gentiles, at least those who were on the fringe of Judaism, learned progressively more about Judaism in the synagogue and, further, that such adherents may have eventually come to convert through synagogue expositions. However, the issue is the larger one regarding the purpose of synagogue activity, and it seems to me that it was almost predominantly for the instruction of Jews. Jews evidently did not use the synagogue as an institution for converting Gentiles to Judaism.[74]

Education

Associated with the synagogue was Jewish education.[75] Is there evidence that Jews proselytized Gentiles by educating them in the knowledge of the Torah and the customs of the Jews? We ought to notice, by way of introduction, that this was almost exclusively the way Jews reared their children into Judaism: by teaching them knowledge of the Torah (Philo *Leg.* 115, 210, 230, 314; *Spec.* 2.88, 228–30, 233, 236; 4.16, 149; *Virt.* 141; *Praem.* 162; *L.A.* 1.99; *Ebr.* 80–81). Philo, for one, highly valued education (see, e.g., *Spec.* 2.21–22; *Cher.* 129). But is there evidence that *Jews* educated *Gentiles* in order to bring them into Judaism?

In *Mos.* 2.26–44 those who translated the Torah, according to Philo, had the hope "that the greater part, or even the whole, of the human race might be profited and led to a better life" (*Mos.* 2.36). One can surmise that such reading could be accompanied by a corresponding explanation, which in itself would be an education in Judaism—though the evidence is not altogether clear. Philo also tells us that Jews picked up castaways, and it is possible that the verb *anelesthai* (*anaireō*) could mean "adopt." We can reasonably assume that Jews who "adopted" such children invariably educated them in the ways of Judaism. In conclusion, from Philo I think we can fairly state that he did not see education as a normal means of proselytizing.

Very similar ideas are found in Josephus, who states, "Above all, we pride ourselves on the education of our children" (*Ag. Ap.* 1.60: *peri paidotrophian philokalountes*). But not only did Jews educate their own (*Ant.* 20:71; *Ag.Ap.* 2.204); they also had a special concern for rearing orphans in the Jewish faith. Picking up on Deuteronomic laws on the fatherless (Deut. 14:28; 26:12), the Essenes (at least), when finding orphans, nurtured them both physically and spiritually (*J.W.* 2.120).[76] This is also witnessed in rabbinical comments about educating *asufi* (foundlings) stock, who, when found, were reared in Jewish customs (*m. Qidd.* 4.1–3). We may safely conclude that Jews did use education, probably in the synagogue setting and certainly through family instruction and adoption, as a means of proselytizing. It seems to me that this method was not instrumental in numerous conversions and is to be seen as marginal for the realities of social life. Furthermore, though this may be seen as "proselytizing," it is more naturally categorized as "socialization" of the young. However, in light of the Gentile origin of the orphans and in light of their subsequent Judaism, its impact is worth noting.

Good Deeds

It is likely that the most effective and probably unconscious method Jews "used" to attract Gentiles was the compelling force of a good life. A scribe describes the power of good deeds when mixed with prayer in the *Letter of Aristeas,* saying, "My belief is that we must (also) show liberal charity to our opponents so that in this manner we may convert them to what is proper and fitting to them. You must pray God that these things be brought to pass, for he rules the minds of all" (226). In *T. Benj.* 5:1–5 we find the same notion (cf. 8:3). S. Bialoblocki stated, nearly fifty years ago, "When persons of the lower classes of people adhered to Judaism, it occurred because the manner of life and the synagogue service convincingly worked on them and enticed them to conversion; however, this occurred without the Jews being particularly concerned about it."[77]

Philo tells us that Joseph, "by setting before them his life of temperance and every virtue, like an original picture of skilled workmanship . . . converted even those who seemed to be quite incurable . . . and repented" (*Jos.* 87). Of course, this is legendary material but it may reflect the experience of Philo as seen in another text. The principle is this: "For to gaze continuously upon noble models imprints their likeness in souls which are not entirely hardened and stony" (*Praem.* 114; see also *Som.* 1.178). Good behavior, he tells us, led to the translation of the Torah: "But, in course of time, the daily, unbroken regularity of practice exercised by those who observed them [the laws] brought them to the knowledge of others, and their fame began to spread on every side" (*Mos.* 2.27).[78] The famous example of the son of the gentile "god-fearer" in Juvenal (*Satires* 14.96–106) indirectly confirms the point of the impact of behavior because the son, so infers Juvenal, is destined to become a convert to Judaism. His "conversion" takes place gradually as he becomes socialized into the life and ways of Judaism.

The rabbis also mention good deeds as a form of attracting Gentiles: "When the Israelites do the will of God His name becomes renowned in the world" (*Mek. Shirata,* parashah 3, lines 85–96 [on Exod. 15:2]).

This form of converting Gentiles is a consistent feature of the evidence and probably formed the very backbone for the majority of conversions to Judaism. The power of good life and a noble character speaks well for a religion even today; there is every reason to suspect a similar pattern in the ancient world.

Various Means

The more natural means of marriage (*m. Qidd.* 3:5; *b. Yeb.* 92b; *b. B. Meṣ* 16b)[79] and, as mentioned above, adoption that leads to education by Jews were also used to attract Gentiles.[80] Political or economical advantage is also found. Josephus, for instance, tells us that Izates' brother, Monobazus, thought it would be advantageous to convert to Judaism when he saw the admiration given to his brother (*Ant.* 20.75).[81]

Force

At certain periods in history Jewish leaders did cause a great deal of "conversions" through force and plunder. Both Judith (14:10) and Esther (8:17) provide information pertaining to forceful conversion—even if it is interpreted by various writers as God's triumph.[82] Hyrcanus, Aristobulus I, and Alexander Jannaeus each forced Gentiles to convert and be circumcised (Josephus *Ant.* 13.257–58; 318–19, 397; 15:253–54). Wryly, G. F. Moore described the effect of such as "skin-deep conversions."[83]

The Propaganda Techniques of Philo and Josephus

Having surveyed eight methods that have been called into account for evidence of Jewish missionary activity, I turn to two examples of the so-called propagandistic sort. Because two authors, Philo and Josephus, have left so much of a literary deposit for us to examine, the "propaganda technique" of both will be examined briefly. In describing the "apologetic tradition," D. Georgi provides a telling description of what such apologists were up to: "They wanted to show that the divine was expressed precisely in what was Jewish, hoping that unbiased and intelligent pagans would agree—an expectation characteristic of the Jewish missionaries on rationality."[84] In the history of the discussion of Jewish missionary activity, the propaganda literature has occupied a central place.

Philo

This Jewish author, as described briefly in chapter 1, was a man of education who believed in the encyclical.[85] Two elements of this educational pedigree were the skills of rhetoric and dialectics, which are everywhere evident in Philo's works.[86] Philo believes (and he does not even try to prove) that God is with the Jews and that he is against those who oppose them (e.g., *Flacc.* 116, 121–24, 169–75, 191; *Leg.* 138–39, 207–338; *Mos.* 1.146). In addition, the Torah, which is translated for the Gentiles, is the clearest proof of Israel's superiority (*Mos.* 2.26–44). Philo, by allegorically interpreting this Torah, is able to gain biblical *and* philosophical authority for his viewpoints.[87]

One of Philo's best examples of propaganda is his depiction of Moses.[88] In Philo's presentation, Moses combines the kingly, philosophical, legislative, priestly, and prophetic offices (*Mos.* 2.1–7, 192–287, 291; *Opf.* 8; *Hyp.* 2.5–9). He is "the greatest and most perfect of all men" (*Mos.* 1.1, 48, 59, 148). His brilliance was pushed back, like Jesus', into his childhood (*Mos.* 1.20–24), and he was "incapable of accepting any falsehood" (1.24). His murder of the Egyptian was "a righteous action" (1.44). Power did not make him arrogant; instead, he remained reasonable (1.150–54). In fact, *autos egeneto nomos empsychos te kai logikos* ("he was a reasonable and living impersonation, i.e., embodiment, of the law"; 1.162).[89] To add to Moses' prestige, Philo makes him the best legislator of all, better even than Greek legislators (2.12–25).[90] Philo elevates Moses to the point that his pre-ascension state was one of pure mind, dissolved by God from body and soul (2.288; see also Josephus *Ant.* 4.323–31). He is addressed in prayer (*Som.* 1:164–65), and, in fact, the whole earth obeys him (*Mos.* 1:155–59; *Q. Exod.* 2.40, 54).[91]

Several other comments about Philo's propaganda are worthy of observation. According to Philo, the temple is so vast and marvelous that foreigners are amazed (*Spec.* 1.73), and his use of *philanthrōpia* at 2.104 is designed to heighten foreign opinion of the Torah and Jews. Just as the Greeks borrowed legal evidence from the Jews (*Spec.* 4.61), so also Heracleitus's "discovery" was previously developed by Moses (*Her.* 214).[92]

Philo at times turns the debate into an attack on other ideas, basing his views on Jewish elective consciousness and monotheism.[93] Some of his enemies are the sophists, those whose profession was training others—for a profit.[94] The kindest statement Philo has for the sophist is that he is to the wise man what the encyclical is to virtues—nothing more than a beginning (*Sobr.* 9). Philo's basic criticism, expressed in a variety of ways, is that the sophist is concerned with pedantic words and verbal gymnastics; consequently, he never attains virtue and wisdom (*Her.* 125; *Conf.* 14, 34–35; *Mut.* 10; *Fug.* 209; *Prob.* 80; *Post.* 86; *Agr.* 12–16, 136, 143–44, 159; *Congr.* 18, 53, 67; *Migr.* 76). This method of presentation permits Philo to portray his own view in contrast. In short, it is propaganda, because Philo is saying more than what is on the surface.

Philo wrote *In Flaccum* to expose the atrocities that were purposefully permitted by Flaccus against the Jews and to demonstrate his just end.[95] Philo criticizes anyone who worships anything/anyone but the one invisible God (*Vita* 3–9).[96] He defends Moses' taking of the children of Israel from Egypt (*Hyp.* 6:2–4)[97] and the Sabbath as a day of mental, not physical, labor (*Hyp.* 7.14; see Seneca *De Superst.* [*apud* Augustine *De Civ. Dei* 6.11]). He responds to others as to why God used such insignificant creatures to punish the Egyptians (*Mos.* 1.109–12) and to the charge that the Jews robbed the Egyptians (*Mos.* 1.140–42; cf. Pompeius Trogus *apud* Justin, *Hist. Phil.* 36; *Epit.* 2.13; see also *Virt.* 141; *Conf.* 2–14, 142–43; *Migr.* 147; *Her.* 81–85, 90–93; *Fug.* 148; *Deus* 21–32; *Agr.* 128–29, 149–56; *L.A.* 3.30–31, 204–7; *Som.* 2.283–85). Moses' creation account is a critique of atheists and polytheists (*Op.* 170–72). He defends Abraham's near sacrifice of Isaac (*Abr.* 178–99) and gives a lengthy and historically important defense of circumcision (*Spec.* 1.2–11; see Petronius *Satyricum* 102.14; but cf. Strabo *Geogr.* 16.4.9; 17.2.5; Horace *Sermones* 1.5.100).[98] He defends the lack of groves in the Jewish cultus (*Spec.* 1.74–75), the Jewish laws on inheritance (*Spec.* 2.129–39), as well as Jewish restraint on Yom Kippur (2.193–94). In *De Providentia*, frag. 2, he defends, against Alexander, God's providence and activity in history. He can appeal to authorities (*Jos.* 132–33). Philo is skilled in apologetics, polemics, and propaganda. His work, in this sense, has a "proselytization" orientation. But I suspect that the absence of evidence for direct speech to Gentiles reveals that Philo's work is essentially intended to bolster Jewish self-identification.

Josephus

It has been recognized by all scholars that Josephus did not write simply to set out the facts for objective readers; rather, most today contend that Josephus wrote with an agenda, whether to glorify Israel's religion, to curry favor with Rome, to encourage Jews to respect Rome, or to exonerate himself as a reliable historian.[99]

Not infrequently Josephus uses terms that, although quite uncommon for a Jewish audience, were much more palatable to a Gentile one and so aid in presentation, for example, *to theion, aretē, tychē, heimarmenē,* and *eudaimonia*–all of which are part of his method of presenting his message.[100] In addition to these terms, there are other sundry items that reveal Josephus's hidden agendas. Not everyone would agree that the Roman-Jewish war was the "greatest . . . of all that ever broke out between cities or nations" (*J.W.* 1.1) or that no one has suffered like the Jews (*J.W.* 1.12). Jewish willingness to suffer for religion amazed Pompey (*J.W.* 1.448–51; cf. *Ant.* 14.64–68)–according to Josephus. The reader of the *Antiquities* is invited to see the wisdom of Moses and the glory of God (*Ant.* 1.15–17, 24–26), and the records of longevity for the patriarchs are not to be easily dismissed (*Ant.* 1.104–8). Even the cultus has universal symbolism (*Ant.* 3.179–87), and it had a Corinthian style (8.133). Furthermore, Moses was not struck with leprosy (*Ant.* 3.265–68)[101] and Rahab seems to have been delivered in battle (cf. Josh. 2:1 with *Ant.* 5.7, 8, 10, 13).[102] Jews, in fact, were not "inhumane by nature nor unfriendly" to foreigners (*Ant.* 8.117).[103] Even if Alexander the Great's prostration before Jerusalem seems unlikely, its import for Judaism is favorable (*Ant.* 11.329–39). In short, if one will take time, says Josephus, to examine Jewish customs, one will learn that they are superior and ancient (*Ant.* 16.44). To sum up: Josephus casts himself as a historian, but his method is not without regular brief disquisitions designed to dispose the reader favorably toward Judaism and Yahweh.

Although we cannot be sure of the identity of all of his critics, Josephus felt it necessary to demonstrate constantly the integrity of his writings, footnoting his work here and there and even offering an occasional bit of self-congratulation. For instance, both of his historical works begin by asserting the inadequacy, both in motive and result, of previous historians and the resultant need for a more accurate and truthful record.[104] Josephus contends that he can accomplish the task (*J.W.* 1.1–16; *Ant.* 1.1–17). His aims are accuracy and truth, and so he will not hide or add to the facts (*J.W.* 1.26; 6.200–13; *Ant.* 10.218; 4.196; 5.136–74, 266, 306–17; 8:190–91, 251–53; 11.299; 18.310–79). His "work is written for lovers of truth and not to gratify [his] . . . readers" (*J.W.* 1.30). In a grandiose conclusion he can boastfully state: "For I think that I have drawn up the whole story in full and accurate detail . . . no one else, either Jew or Gentile, would have been equal to the task . . . of issuing so accurate a treatise as this for the Greek world" (*Ant.* 20.259–68, quoting from §§260, 262).[105]

To bolster his arguments, Josephus regularly appeals to the scholarly practice of citing outside authorities. He appeals to Titus to show that the Jewish rebels were to blame for the war (*J.W.* 1.10) and to the eyewitnesses to attest the miracles at the end (6.299–300). Cestius confirms his statistics (6.422), and other historians record the longevity of the patriarchs (*Ant.* 1.107–8). Solomon's aid of Hiram is found in letters (8.50–56); Herodotus supports a point (8.260–62); and the lack of rain is witnessed in Menander (8.323–24; cf. 9.283–87). Even the strange death of Nebuchadnezzar is confirmed by other writers (10.219–28). Among others, he appeals to Agatharchides (12.57), Polybius (12.135–36, 358–59), Nicolaus of Damascus (13.249–52, 347; 14.68, 104), Strabo (13.284–87, 319, 347; 14.35–36, 68, 104, 110–18, 138–39; 15.9), his compatriots (20.263), and some Roman decrees (14.186–267; 16.162–73).[106]

The Jewishness of many personalities and parties is often softened when Josephus presents them.[107] For instance, Josephus presents the various groups in Judaism as "philosophical schools" (*J.W.* 2.119; 2.119–66; *Ant.* 13:171–73; 18.12–25), and he uses the notion of "fate" (*heimarmenē*) as the point of comparison (*Ant.* 13:171–73; 18:12–25).[108] He presents the heroes of Judaism in a similar manner. Thus, Abraham is intelligent, logical, persuasive, virtuous, monotheistic, and aware of astronomy (*Ant.* 1.154–57, 165–68, 256; 2:9, 43, 87, 198).[109] Note also his treatments of Moses (3.19, 328–29), David (6.160), and Solomon (8.26–34, 42–49).[110]

When it comes to the Romans, Josephus is fond of flattery. Thus, the war story begins with the underhanded comment "since the blame lay with no foreign nation" (*J.W.* 1.12). In fact, he states, the Romans were kind to the Jews (1.27–28), and this is proved by countless appeals to the Jews by Titus as well as his kindnesses (see *J.W.* 5.319, 334, 348–55, 360–61, 455–57, 519; 6.124–28, 214–19, 228, 238–43, 256, 261–66, 333–50, 409–13; 7.112–15). Although he expressly states that he does not want to extol the Romans in his account of the army, he does so anyway (see 3.70–109, esp. 108). Pompey refused to burn the temple (*Ant.* 14.72–73). The expulsion of the Jews from Rome by Tiberius had legitimate reasons (*Ant.* 18.81–84; Tacitus *Annals* 2.85; Dio Cassius 62.18.5a). Josephus, in fact, states that he knew long ago that Rome was superior; therefore, Jews should not invite trouble (*Vita* 17–19). Moreover, even if Josephus offers an occasional criticism (see *J.W.* 2.224–27, 250–51; *Ant.* 3.212, 274–75; 8.252; 18.15–161; 20.108–12, 154–57), Josephus's main impression on his readers of the Romans is a flattering one.

This attitude toward Rome fits admirably with Josephus's complementary negative attitude toward the zealots.[111] From the outset, Josephus was quick to blame the Zealots for the war (*J.W.* 1.4, 10–11, 27; esp. 2.345–456).

Is Rome an Exception?

In the history of scholarship on Jewish missionary activity, some scholars rely solely on the evidence in such writers as Valerius Maximus, Tacitus, Suetonius, Josephus, and Dio Cassius, when these writers speak of the conditions of Rome. What does this evidence say?[112] First, in spite of the rather confusing nature of the interpretation of the evidence from Valerius Maximus (early first century A.D.),[113] he does seem to provide solid evidence that some kind of missionary activity was taking place in Rome—and enough to force official action. The text is from *De Superstitionibus* and is preserved in the epitomes of Paris and Nepotianus (Stern, *GLAJJ* 147a [Nepotianus], 147b [Paris]). The evidence here is that Cn. Cornelius Scipio Hispanus (*ca.* 139 B.C.) expelled Jews from Rome "because they attempted to transmit (Paris has "infect") their sacred rites to the Romans." The Jews of this description were confusingly associated with astrologers and the "cult of Jupiter Sabazius" (perhaps a confusion for "the God of the Sabbath").[114] However confused the report might be, the evidence nonetheless speaks clearly of Jewish attempts to proselytize at some level. Whether these were political or religious attempts and whether these were exceptional or typical are not known. We do know that Jews were agitating for their beliefs, probably in Rome around the middle of the second century B.C.

About a century and a half later, in 19 B.C., Jews were expelled from Rome by the emperor Tiberius, and apparently at least one of the reasons was related to proselytes. Josephus tells us that the expulsion took place because of the financial misdeeds of some scoundrels who had managed to obtain some money from Fulvia, a woman of high rank who was also a proselyte (Josephus *Ant.* 18.81–84). Tacitus tells us about a resolution of the Senate to the effect that Egyptian and Jewish worship, two growing superstitions, be checked by sending four thousand of the infected men to the island of Sardinia. The remaining believers of these superstitions were to leave Italy (*Annals* 2.85). Later Dio Cassius explicitly states that Tiberius expelled Jews from Rome for "converting many of the natives to their ways" (Dio Cassius 62.18.5a). We know that later Nero's wife was described as a "worshiper of God" (*theosebēs*) (Josephus *Ant.* 20.195).

What can we make of this evidence? Admittedly, this evidence is solid and the data point plausibly to missionary activity of some proportion in Rome, at least at the middle of the second century B.C., if not around 19 B.C. But very little can be made of Nero's wife. In light of the evidence discussed in this chapter, I would like to hazard the suggestion that the evidence from Rome is perhaps only an exceptional and sporadic situation.[115] Thus, what we see in Rome, at only two known periods in history (and perhaps only one), is perhaps nothing more than a sporadic attempt by Jews to convert Romans to Judaism. This evidence is exceptional, and, furthermore, it comes by way of antagonists, who may very well be exaggerating the behavior of Jews to exonerate the actions of Rome. Furthermore, the inscriptional and epigraphical evidence shows a few meager traces of proselytes: 7 inscriptions of the 534 inscriptions available are proselytes.[116] If proselytization were taking place regularly and as intensively as some scholars have argued, it would be more than likely that a greater number of proselytes would appear in the archaeological data.

On the other hand, there is evidence for a rather consistent presence of "God-fearers," or Jewish sympathizers, in Rome from the earliest times (Suetonius *Tiberius* 32.2; *Domitian* 12.2; Epictetus *Dissertationes* 2.19–21; Dio Cassius 67.14.1-3; see also Martial *Epigrammata* 4.4, lines 7–12 [Stern, *GLAJJ* 1:523–24]; Plutarch *De Superstitione* 3.166a [Stern, *GLAJJ* 1:549]).

Conclusions

What, then, were the methods used by Jews to proselytize Gentiles? No method is found pervasively throughout Jewish literature; neither is there a consistent consciousness of mission to the Gentiles. This makes it more than likely that Judaism was not a missionary religion.

First, although there is significant evidence that Jews expected an act of God that would lead to mass conversions of Gentiles to Yahweh, this hope is largely localized in apocalyptic and prophetic literature. For this reason, it would be wrong to suppose, as J. Jeremias apparently has,[117] that this notion is the dominating concept in Judaism pertaining to Gentile conversion and the method of that conversion. Significantly, this notion is not found in the majority of Jewish literature, especially in literature that describes the "phenomena of Jewish life." In fact, the shape of this idea, future conversion, probably indicates for that author and his community that Gentiles were not converting to Judaism. It certainly witnesses to the absence of Jewish missionary activity.

Second, there is evidence that miracles were instrumental in leading to conversions, but such miracles appear not to have been frequent and the numbers of conversions do not appear to have been numerous. This "method," if one may call it that, is not significant for Judaism, although it probably played a much greater role in earliest Christianity.

Third, is there evidence for Jewish missionaries to the Gentiles? It must be admitted that the evidence is scanty and scattered throughout Jewish history. Further, scholars have relied heavily on inferences from general statements, such as those we have cited from *Letter of Aristeas*, *Testaments of the Twelve Patriarchs*, and *Wisdom of Solomon*. Such inferences too often are not capable of demonstration from the evidence that we do possess. There is, however, some evidence that would suggest that some missionary activity did take place. I think of *Sib. Or.* 3.5-10, 809-29, which, however, probably pertains more to the revelation of oracles than to direct evangelism of the Gentile world. Perhaps some statements by Philo are the best evidence we have for the actual practice of public preaching. He criticizes the mysteries for esotericism, contending that they ought to come public with their ideas, and he comes close to suggesting that there were Jewish teachers and preachers who, as it were, "stood on their soap box" in the agora (*Spec.* 1.320-33). Philo comes close to this, but he does not state it explicitly. Josephus records Jonah, Jesus, and the Ananias–Eleazar encounter with Izates as those who were involved with forms of evangelistic preaching. Jonah, of course, is a singular chapter of Jewish history, and the text about Jesus is undoubtedly suspect; this leaves the Izates story, and the problem here is that this was certainly not "public announcement." In addition, the evidence from the rabbis is both scarce and difficult to assess regarding reliability.

In sum, I think it is safe to say that Judaism did have its occasional evangelists, but these appear to have been few and far between (Rome?). In other words, there appears to be some evidence for Jewish missionary activity through proselytizing Gentiles, but that evidence is too scarce and scattered to be considered a commonplace in Judaism. We must remember that the significant data can be reduced to about a handful—and it strikes me as hasty to base far-reaching conclusions on such an amount of evidence.

Fourth, though it is regularly contended that Jews consciously and consistently addressed the Gentile world through literature, there is almost no positive evidence that such took place. I am aware of an entire branch of scholarship that speaks of an "apologetic tradition," including such scholars as G. Klein, M. Friedländer, P. Dalbert, and D. Georgi, but I am also aware that this approach is valid only as long as such a literature is assumed to have been apologetic and evangelistic (though these scholars often operate with unclear definitions of the terms). The point I want to make is that the positive evidence that Jews used literature to convince non-Jews is minimal at best and there is the further problem that some learned scholars are thoroughly convinced that Jews would not, in fact, have given their literature to non-Jews for fear of reprisal or destruction of that literature. After all, publication was slow and expensive.[118] However, it is accurate to say that propagandistic forms are present in Jewish literature. To say that entire bodies of literature are propaganda in form and were given to Gentiles is to go beyond the evidence that has survived.

What does the evidence suggest? First, I admit that there is a great deal of literature that has an apologetical tendency, seen in such books as *Letter of Aristeas,* 4 Maccabees, Philo, and Josephus. But the question to be asked is, Who read these books? Jews or Gentiles? There is, to my knowledge, not one shred of evidence for a non-Jew reading a Jewish book who was not a sympathizer already. In other words, perhaps we ought to consider Jewish apologetic literature to have been written for Jews to bolster their confidence in the Jewish faith in response to attacks on Judaism. Second, there is some evidence that Jews aspired to have their writings read by non-Jews (2 *Enoch* 48:6–9; Philo *Mos.* 2.36, 44; *Dec.* 81; *Spec.* 1.52; Josephus *Contra Apionem*). But again, the evidence is not widespread and, in fact, often no more than an aspiration. I conclude then that literature was neither a common nor a significant method of Jewish missionary activity. I confess that it is possible that the cause of accusations against Jews was the latter's aggressive missionary activity; the issue is one of proving that this is the cause.

Fifth, was the synagogue used as a platform for evangelizing the gentile world? I have criticized already D. Georgi's theory, but a few more comments are in order. I think it is certain that Jews permitted sympathizing Gentiles to attend the synagogues. Further, it seems just as likely that such Gentiles, being already open to the religion of the Jews, heard apologetical defenses for Judaism and polemical diatribes against paganism in these services. Thus, I do not doubt that Gentiles both heard the message of Judaism and were possibly converted to Judaism through the synagogue service, but I do doubt that there is sufficient evidence to suggest that the synagogue was, in effect, a proselytizing platform through the exegesis of Torah. Instead, the synagogue was almost surely a place for Jews to be instructed about the Torah and Judaism.

Sixth, the same conclusion applies to education. Although Jews highly valued education, and although Jews undoubtedly educated their children and foster children in the traditions of their fathers, there is no evidence that Jews had "adult evening schools" to which they invited Gentiles and during which they sought to convert Gentiles to Judaism.

Seventh, in my view the surest piece of evidence for a method for converting Gentiles is to be found in the good deeds and life-style of the Jews in their integrated life-style with Gentiles. But again, the evidence is not pervasive; it is found in *Ep. Arist.* 226; *T. Benj.* 5.1–5; 8:3; Philo *Jos.* 87; *Praem.* 114; *Som.* 1.178; *Mos.* 2:27 and in the rabbis. We do know that Jews attracted Gentiles to synagogues and that the practices of the Jews generated a great deal of discussion and criticism by Gentiles;[119] this can only mean that the behavior of the Jews was noticeable to Gentiles. I would like to suggest that the good deeds of Jews are what attracted Gentiles to the synagogues, but I recognize that this can be no more than a suggestion.

Finally, other "methods" are found—marriage, political and economic advantage, and force—but these are not worthy of consideration in a study on missionary activity.

I conclude, then, that some Jews saw an act of God at the end of history as a "method" of conversion, that there was some missionary activity through evangelistic preaching, perhaps some through literature and the synagogue, and that the good deeds of Jews were probably influential on Gentiles. I further conclude that the evidence does not permit us to infer that there was any such thing as an "organized mission to the Gentiles" or that missionary activity was a consistent or important feature of Jewish piety. J. J. Collins has it right:

> It has been said that the crucial question which confronted first-century Judaism was that posed by the Gentile world. This is probably true in the sense that the very survival of Judaism depended on working out a *modus vivendi* with the Gentile world. It is not true, however, that first-century Judaism was greatly preoccupied with the salvation of the Gentiles. That was ultimately a matter for the eschatological age.[120]

In short, it can be said that Judaism was not a missionary religion.

Even if Judaism is not to be accurately described as a missionary religion, it is a fact that many Gentiles converted to Judaism. One of the most interesting features of conversion to Judaism is the nature of the requirements for conversion. To this we now turn.

4

The Requirements
for Proselytes

IT IS EVIDENT THAT Gentiles converted to Judaism for a variety of reasons and through an assortment of methods, even if it is also clear that Judaism was not truly a missionary religion. A further question needs to be asked at this point, one that has generated a great deal of discussion: What was required of a Gentile to be considered a proselyte?[1] Put differently, if Judaism saw itself as clean, what were the ritual steps needed to make the unclean clean? What were the steps needed to make a full transition from one sociological group (paganism — in all its variety) to another (Judaism — in all its variety)? In the terms of D. A. Snow and R. Machalek, were "demonstration events" a necessary accompaniment of conversion for insiders to accept the outsiders?[2] An answer to this question will shed some light on our larger question about the nature and extent of Jewish missionary activity. In answering this question, however, an important aspect of Judaism needs to be kept in mind, namely, the diversity of Judaism. The evidence discussed below will not permit neat categories, as if "Judaism" had a set of requirements for "pagans." The "officials" of "Judaism" never met to discuss the matter of requirements, come to a decision, and send out the decision through official "apostles." In fact, the evidence suggests that different Jews had different requirements at different periods in history, and it further seems that individual Jews may have shown an amazing diversity themselves. It may be the fact, as I intend to show, that general principles/requirements may have been consistent (say, obeying the Torah), but even within that general principle there was flexibility.

In the history of scholarship, the consensus has been that during the Second Temple period circumcision, baptism, and sacrifice were required before a Gentile's conversion was complete. The standard reference work, E. Schürer's *History of the Jewish People*, states: "All three are regarded as traditional already in the Mishnah; indeed, they are so much taken for granted in rabbinic Judaism that even in the absence of definite proof they can be considered as prevailing in the Second Temple period."[3] The task of this chapter is to examine this conclusion to see if it can be sustained for the first century. Admittedly, the evidence[4] is not secure enough to enable us to deal carefully with questions of diversity (did different "sects" have different requirements?) and geography (did the Diaspora have different requirements from the homeland?). Differing social conditions made their presence felt here as well. Rather than trying to trace out the possible shades of difference, a task I take to be virtually impossible because of the nature of the evidence, our task is a more moderate one: Is there evidence for requirements as such as a general rule?[5]

A final word of caution is necessary here: the evidence of the ancient world pertaining to requirements is seriously beset by the androcentrism latent in the texts and interests of ancient writers.[6] Josephus tells us, and probably accurately, that more women were "converts" than men (*J.W.* 2.559–61). However, the evidence of the ancient world deals with the requirements for men and not women.[7] This observation naturally skews the discussion, both then and now. So far as I know, there is no serious discussion about the requirements for women. Accordingly, I will keep this in mind throughout this chapter; I mention it here because I do not want this chapter to be seen as furthering what Ross Kraemer called "gender myopia."

Circumcision

The rite of circumcising men for participation in the covenant is believed by Jews to have been commanded by God, and its practice throughout the history of Judaism is anchored in Scripture (Gen. 17:9–14).[8] We know that Jews practiced the circumcision (*milah*) of men as a self-identity marker[9] and that as early as *ca.* 160 B.C. we find a convert being circumcised at conversion (Jth. 14:10) to demonstrate a complete break from an idolatrous and immoral past in order to join Judaism—with its nation, God, land, and Torah.[10] The text reads, "When Achior saw all that the God of Israel had done, he believed in God completely (*episteusen tō theō sphodra*). So he was circumcised (*perietemeto tēn sarka tēs akrobystias autou*) and was admitted to the community of Israel, as are his descendants to the present day."[11] We do not know from this text that the rite was demanded from him by others for conversion to be "authentic" or whether he decided on his own to do this as a demonstration of his zeal. What we do know is that in the middle of the second century B.C. we have clear evidence—and there is no reason to doubt this report—that converts were circumcised. What is surprising is that there is no further unambiguous evidence of circumcision for converts until the writings of Josephus.

Philo, for instance, speaks of a "twofold" circumcision, an inner and an outer circumcision (*Som.* 2.25; *Spec.* 1.304–6; *Q. Exod.* 2.2).[12] He also divulges six reasons for the significance of circumcision (*Spec.* 1.2–11; *Q. Exod.* 3.48).[13] However symbolic the rite may be, for Philo it must be performed physically (*Migr.* 92).[14] Although we find no traces of converts being circumcised in Philo—and there are plenty of references to proselytes where such could have been mentioned—it seems reasonable to me to conclude that in Philo's Alexandria circumcision was probably required for those men who truly converted to Judaism—even if *Migr.* 92 seems to indicate that some did not think it necessary. There may well have been a diversity in Alexandria. However, circumcision is Torah, and to become a Jew meant to live according to Torah. Therefore, it seems likely that circumcision was required for men. One reason why Philo was somewhat "open" on the matter may have been the presence of female converts to Judaism.

Some Gentile men were circumcised, according to Josephus, out of fear (*J.W.* 2.454; *Ant.* 11.285; cf. Esther 8:17), but this ought not to be taken as evidence for requirements except that it was seen (by some) as a sign of full conversion. Others were forced (*Ant.* 13.257–58, 318–19, 397; 15.253–54).[15] Further, circumcision was required at times for marriage (*Ant.* 16.225; 20.139, 145–46). What these three examples show is that circumcision, Judaism, and national identity were intertwined. Such a connection could be utilized for proselytizing since, if being a male Jew meant being circumcised, then becoming a Jew would probably involve being circumcised. This is perhaps supported by *Ant.* 3:318, where refusal to permit some from beyond the Euphrates to participate in the cultus may very well be related to circumcision—though it is far from obvious. Josephus's success at dissuading some Jews from demanding circumcision of two nobles from Trachonitis who were residing in Palestine shows both open and closed attitudes on the part of various Jews. The closed view certainly would follow up conversion with circumcision (*Vita* 112-13). The Izates narrative is of a similar cloth; here we find apparently two attitudes toward conversion: Ananias seemed to permit conversion without circumcision (and to perceive Izates as a "convert" or at least as one who had done all that was necessary), but Eleazar did not (*Ant.* 20.35–49).[16] Josephus describes as converts those males who undergo circumcision, and it seems likely from this that Josephus saw the rite as a requirement.

The evidence from Pauline correspondence is interesting in this regard: whereas Paul, in seeking to distance himself from Judaism and a Judaizing tendency in earliest Christianity, argues that circumcision is unnecessary for conversion to Christianity (e.g., Gal. 5:2, 6, 12; 6:15;

Phil. 3:2), the obvious need on his part to counter the Judaizers in this regard suggests that this group of Jews (the Judaizing wing of Palestinian Christianity) saw it as necessary (see also Acts 15:1-2; Gal. 5:12; 6:12-13). Further, Paul's former calling of "preaching circumcision" suggests the same (5:11).[17]

The earliest attributions of which I am aware in the rabbinic literature are to disputes between Beth Hillel and Beth Shammai. Beth Shammai permitted a "Passover eve proselyte" to submit to the *ṭĕbîlâ* bath and then simply eat of the meal, but Beth Hillel required circumcision. Therefore, the convert could not partake because of the need to be purified for seven days (see *m. ʿEd.* 5:2; *m. Pesaḥ.* 8:8; *b. Pesaḥ.* 92a; *t. Pisha* 7.14).[18] However, in the *Gemara* to *m. Šabb.* 19:3 (*b. Šabb.* 135a),[19] Beth Shammai required a heathen who had been circumcised as a heathen (for heathen practices) to shed "a few drops of blood"; Beth Hillel did not require this.[20] These two accounts about circumcision seem to conflict, and therefore very little should be based on them.[21] In the Jamnian fathers we find an attribution to Rabbi Eliezer b. Jacob I by an Amora, arguing from the practice of the forefathers that only circumcision was necessary for full conversion (*b. Yeb.* 46a). Thus, the evidence prior to the mid-second century A.D. is meager but, since Beth Shammai may have expected circumcision later, we can conclude that circumcision was probably required — at the least as an act of obedience to the law. Furthermore, it is very possible that these disputes arose not from the issue of whether circumcision was required but from the issue of at which point a Gentile became a convert. In other words, the issue may have been one of social and religious status not legal requirement.

Later rabbis are much clearer on this matter: circumcision was required. Thus, Rabbi Akiba wanted circumcision (*b. Yeb.* 71a), although Ketiah b. Shalom, perhaps a contemporary of Akiba, did not allow himself to be circumcised until just before his death (*b. ʿAbod. Zar.* 10b). Rabbi Jose b. Halafta required both circumcision and baptism (*m. ʿEd.* 5:2; *b. Yeb.* 46b). Debate continued concerning those who had been circumcised before conversion to Judaism (Rabbi Judah b. Illai; *b. Yeb.* 46b). A *Baraita* of Rabbi Meir attests the need for circumcision (*b. ʿAbod. Zar.* 26b). The consummation of this debate is found in Rabbi Judah the Patriarch, who demanded circumcision, baptism, and sacrifice — at least he did according to later traditions (*b. Ker.* 8b-9a; *m. Ker.* 2:1).

The rabbinic tradition shows that circumcision would have been seen at least as an act of the obedient convert. Further, I do not doubt that by and large it was seen as a requirement and that it was practiced.[22] However, in light of the debates over the matter, it is probable that circumcision as a requirement had not yet become established custom or tradition prior to the first century A.D.

In conclusion, it seems quite probable to me that circumcision was seen as an act whereby the male convert demonstrated his zeal for the law and his willingness to join Judaism without reservation. I hesitate to conclude that circumcision was a requirement throughout Second Temple Judaism, because the evidence is not completely unambiguous and there may well have been some diversity on the matter. Circumcision was probably required for male converts most of the time and in most local expressions of Judaism. It was *the* ritual that separated the Jew from the Gentile (at least in Jewish perception), and therefore it would have been *the act* that permitted the would-be convert to cross the boundary and enter the community.

Baptism

The important issue here is not whether there were lustrations and water purifications in the Jewish community; that there were is clear.[23] Rather, the issue is whether there is evidence for Jews of the Second Temple period practicing an initiatory, unrepeated rite for entrance into the community.[24] The distinction being made is fine, and the evidence is not always clear. However, unless one recognizes the distinction between a simple religious lustration (e.g., washing hands to effect ceremonial cleanness or even a ceremonial bath) and an initiatory, unrepeated baptism (e.g., Christian baptism), then one cannot speak of "entrance" rites. The importance of baptism for this topic is obvious: baptism is not restricted by gender; this rite may serve as a direct path to evidence both for requirements and the extent of Jewish missionary activity.

Perhaps the earliest allusion to what can perhaps be taken to be baptism is found in *Sib. Or.* 4:162–65, which reads, "Ah, wretched mortals, change these things, and do not lead the great God to all sorts of anger, but abandon daggers and groanings, murders and outrages, and wash your whole bodies in perennial rivers."[25] E. Lerle, and others, contend that this text of *Sibylline Oracles* 4 refers to a ritual act of baptism as a necessary initiation rite for Judaism.[26] However, problems here require a certain amount of caution. First, the passage is heavily metaphorical in nature. Are we also to assume that "daggers and groanings, murders and outrages" are literal? Second, the date of this passage is difficult to determine; many argue for a date around A.D. 80.[27] If the metaphorical nature of the passage has any weight in our decision, and I suspect that it ought to have, then this text is at best suspect evidence for determining the origins of "proselyte" baptism. We would be wise to move to other evidence.[28]

Philo speaks of water lustrations as he does of circumcision: "the most profitable form of 'cleansing' (*katharsin*) is just this, that a man should know himself and the nature of the elements of which he is composed, ashes and water" (*Spec.* 1.264; cf. *Cher.* 95–96) and that "it is absurd that a man should be forbidden to enter the temples save after bathing and cleansing (*lousamenos phaidrynētai*) his body, and yet should attempt to pray and sacrifice with a heart still soiled and spotted" (*Deus* 8; cf. *Som.* 1:210, 214, 220). It is quite unlikely that Philo speaks here of a known initiation rite; his evidence is ambiguous.

The evidence in Josephus is inconclusive in that baptism appears to be an abnormal event for his readers, requiring explanation (*Ant.* 18:116–19), and there are no records of baptism of converts. His silence in this regard as pertains to Izates, who could have been let off the hook had baptism been an ersatz for circumcision, may be quite significant. Little then can be inferred from Josephus or, for that matter, from any prerabbinic data.[29] Furthermore, although it is an argument from silence, the *absence* of the rite of baptism in texts describing the conversion of Gentiles, especially women (e.g., *Joseph and Aseneth*), may well be the most determinative piece of evidence at hand. We now turn to the rabbis.

The first piece of evidence to be considered from rabbinic data is *t. Pesaḥ.* 7.13, a record of an incident that is possibly dated *ca.* A.D. 67. Here soldiers are baptized and permitted to eat of the paschal lamb on Passover eve. It is possible that this lustration is evidence for proselyte baptism being a mandatory, initiation rite, especially because the context is illustrating the nature of a proselyte.[30] But the term *ṭûbĕlîn* can simply indicate a (here, pre-paschal) lustration for the sake of ritual purification and thus have nothing to do whatsoever with proselyte baptism—though a radical distinction between purification rites and initiation rites ought not to be too rigidly drawn. This interpretation would indicate that a Gentile can convert to full participation (if bathed) on Passover eve.[31] What we can conclude from this passage confidently is that someone can convert on Passover eve, that water lustrations were required prior to Passover, and that possibly a proselyte had to be baptized before acceptance.

A proselyte is required to undergo ritual water purification in the dispute of Beth Shammai and Beth Hillel (*m. 'Ed.* 5:2; *m. Pesaḥ.* 8:8; *b. Pesaḥ.* 92a).[32] Beth Shammai requires that the "Passover eve proselyte" take the *ṭĕbîlâ* bath and then eat of the meal (*t. Pesaḥ.* 7.13). Hillel, because he sees the one who is circumcised as one who has touched a grave (cf. Num. 19:18–19), requires a later water purification.[33] If this action reflects the origin of baptism for proselytes, it began as a "purification-from-uncleanness" ritual, or as a purity rite for paschal meals.[34] It is also possible that the act was self-performed; in fact, both H. Danby and J. Neusner translate *ṭûbl* "he may immerse himself" (*m. 'Ed.* 5:2).[35] However, this passage is unclear as to whether the act is an initiation baptism as a rite for inclusion or a simple purification.[36]

The second generation of Tannaim (*b. Yeb.* 46a) disputed *the* essential requirement for proselytes: Is it circumcision, as with the fore*fathers* (Rabbi Eliezer b. Jacob I), or baptism, as with the fore*mothers* (Rabbi Joshua b. Hananiah)?[37] The *Baraita* and the debate form both speak against the pericope as stemming from the first century. The later ruling in the rabbis is for both, and the pericope is constructed to bring such a conclusion. In the third generation, Rabbi Akiba, according to Rabbi Shemaiah, expected both circumcision and baptism (*b. Yeb.* 71a). In the fourth and fifth generations, the rite was becoming clearer in halakic discussion: Rabbi Judah b. Illai (according to Amoraim) required baptism even if the pagan had been circumcised for sinful reasons (*b. Yeb.* 46b).[38] But Rabbi Jose b. Halafta (fourth generation) wanted both circumcision and baptism (*b. Yeb.* 46b). According to the minor tractate *Ṣemaḥot* (46b; 7.13, p. 359), Rabbi Simeon b. Eleazar permitted a captive woman to marry legally into Israel after immersion. Again, the climax of this debate is found in Rabbi Judah the Patriarch: "As your forefathers entered into the Covenant only by circumcision, immersion and the sprinkling of the blood, so shall they enter the Covenant only by circumcision, immersion and the sprinkling of the blood" (*b. Ker.* 9a, p. 66).[39]

To sum up, rabbinic sources are clear only in the later strata, probably near the end of the third century A.D. Prior to this, baptism as an initiation rite may have been practiced—indeed, probably was—but its status as an institutional requirement cannot be proved. In fact, F. Millar's caution is admirably sensitive: "All that is known is that it is post-biblical and pre-Mishnaic."[40] However, in light of the sociological nature of a Jewish community and in light of needed rituals for women, it is more than likely (in my opinion) that baptism became a requirement for most of Judaism during the Second Temple period.

When did proselyte baptism begin? Some scholars have argued that it is pre-Christian and pre-70 (e.g., J. Jeremias, G. R. Beasley-Murray, A. Oepke, A. Bertholet, G. Alon, H. H. Rowley, J. H. B. Lübkert, T. F. Torrance, L. H. Schiffman, K. Pusey, and many others); others have contended for a date after A.D. 65–70 (G. Polster, D. Michaelis, S. Zeitlin, T. M. Taylor, R. J. Z. Werblowsky); still others have admitted ignorance (L. Finkelstein, B. J. Bamberger). I will look at the deductive and inductive arguments before offering a suggestion.

Deductively, scholars have argued that since women joined Judaism as converts and since all religions have entrance rites, there must have been a Jewish rite and that rite would probably have been baptism.[41] Others have contended that since Gentiles were unclean, a rite of purification would have been in order for the convert.[42] Third, some have contended that it is unlikely that John the Baptist introduced something new into Judaism; therefore, he probably borrowed the rite from Judaism. Finally, the typical argument is that it is unlikely that Judaism would have borrowed a distinctive rite from Christianity and adopted it as its own initiation rite.[43]

Inductively, many scholars point to *t. Pesaḥ.* 7.13, to *m. Pesaḥ.* 8:8 and *m. ʿEd.* 5:2, to *b. Yeb.* 46a, to *Sib. Or.* 4:165, to 1 Cor. 10:1–2, or to Epictetus *Diss.* 2.9.19–21, which reads, "But when he adopts the attitude of mind of the man who has been baptized and has made his choice, then he both is a Jew in fact and is also called one." I have already dealt with the problems of dating these texts (and Epictetus is not first century). The problem here is that these texts do not antedate the early Christians.

So when can we date proselyte baptism? Taken together, the evidence and arguments adduced above can be used for a strong case for a first-century dating of Jewish proselyte baptism. But an argument is only as strong as its individual "links" and, it must be admitted in this case, there is not one unambiguous piece of evidence for a pre-Christian dating. I would like to suggest, then, that the rites in Judaism and Christianity owe their origin to a common Jewish milieu in which water lustrations became increasingly important for converts and that Judaism's rite of baptism may very well have received a decisive impetus from John the Baptist, Jesus, and the earliest Christians. The origins of Jewish proselyte baptism, then, may have been in the entrance requirements of Jewish Christianity.

Sacrifice

One cannot separate Second Temple Judaism from its worship center. It is not surprising that halakot regarding sacrifice were devised to bring the convert into proper association with the temple. Just as Philo was more concerned with the inner meaning than the outer form of circumcision, so it is with his attitude to sacrifice: "What is precious in the sight of God is not the number of victims immolated but the true purity of a rational spirit in him who makes the sacrifice" (*Spec.* 1.277). But, when it comes to the practice of sacrifice,[44] Philo appears to be more lenient than he is with circumcision: "But, if he is pure of heart and just, this sacrifice stands firm . . . , even if no victim at all is brought to the altar" (*Mos.* 2.107–8). One could appeal to *Migr.* 92 as well as the countless worshipers at the temple (*Spec.* 1.68-70), but one still comes up short of a statement *requiring* sacrifice in Philo. A Diaspora setting could well account for Philo's view of sacrifice.

Josephus says nothing about converts being required to sacrifice, and he could have in the case of Izates. It is, however, possible that Helene of Adiabene went to the temple to sacrifice in order to fulfill her requirements for conversion (*Ant.* 20.49)–but the evidence is far from making this clear.

The rabbis, not surprisingly, are almost silent in this regard, and the paucity of evidence here is probably to be explained as much by the absence of the temple as the absence of the problem. Certainly before A.D. 70 Jews offered sacrifices annually in Jerusalem, but did Jews demand an initial sacrifice as a requirement for full incorporation into Judaism? G. F. Moore has said, "The offering of a sacrifice is, thus, not one of the conditions of becoming a proselyte, but only a condition precedent to the exercise of one of the rights which belong to him as a proselyte, namely, the participation in a sacrificial meal."[45] In other words, sacrifice would have been seen as part of the life of the obedient Jew but not as a rite of entry.

In an Amoraic source, from an attribution to a fifth-generation Tanna (Rabbi Simeon b. Eleazar), who, in turn, makes an attribution to Rabbi Johanan b. Zakkai (first generation)–the tradition is beginning to sound suspect!–the latter sage annulled halakah that required a proselyte to lay aside a quarter (denar/shekel) because it was a source of temptation (*b. Ker.* 8a; *b. Roš Haš.* 31b). This ruling reflected the following process: proselytes must offer initiatory sacrifices; the temple was destroyed; rabbis ruled the need to lay aside money to buy sacrifices in the event that the temple was rebuilt; it became a temptation to the proselyte; Rabbi Johanan annulled the halakah. It is all but impossible to demonstrate that this halakah had Second Temple moorings; rather, we probably ought to suppose that the ruling and its history are all intertwined in later situations. However, I suspect that halakah demanding sacrifices probably did not originate after A.D. 70.[46]

Another tradition to this effect pertains to Rabbi Eliezer b. Jacob II (*m. Ker.* 2:1), a fourth-generation Tanna: a proselyte's atonement is incomplete until he has made a sacrifice. Again, this tradition climaxes in the ruling of Rabbi Judah the Patriarch, who requires circumcision, baptism, and a sacrifice (*b. Ker.* 8b–9a; on *m. Ker* 2:1).

What can we conclude? The temple was a focal point of most of Judaism during this period, and thus we must think that some converts did at times participate in temple sacrifice for the first time. This may have been construed by some as a requirement. Further, there is evidence that some Jews did see sacrifice as a requirement. But, as is so often the case, we simply do not have the evidence to conclude confidently that Jews generally saw sacrifice as a requirement. I can conclude only that sacrifice was probably required by at least some Jewish leaders.

Others

Jewish literature, in general, places high value on repentance and obedience (*1 Enoch* 50:2, 4; *Sib. Or.* 3:624–31, 762–65; 4:24–34, 162–78; CD 2:5; 8:16; 10:17; 15:7; 19:29; 1QH 2:9; 6:6; 1QS 5:1–11; 6:15; 14:24; Josephus *Ant.* 13.257–58, 318, 397; 16.225; *Joseph and Aseneth*).[47] These moral virtues were undoubtedly expected of converts, and some form of "pledge" (or a pre-understanding) of obedience to the Torah was undeniably an integral aspect of conversion to Judaism.

From Philo we learn that the "purpose is as important as the completed act" (*Det.* 97) and that purity of soul is what makes one acceptable to God (*Spec.* 1.277; *Cher.* 95–96); however, the letter cannot be easily dismissed (*Migr.* 92–93).[48] For Philo the requirements for a convert were monotheism and moral transformation, a conversion to the law that very probably led to circumcision and social integration. Note that, for him, a proselyte is accepted "because he has turned his kinsfold . . . into mortal enemies, by coming as a pilgrim to truth and the honouring of One who alone is worthy of honour, and by leaving the mythical fables and multiplicity of sovereigns . . . to a better home" (*Spec.* 4.178; *Q. Exod.* 2:2).[49]

I find it intriguing (and perhaps revealing) that the tradition that speaks of Hillel's accepting for conversion the pupil rejected by Shammai bears no trace of the necessity of circumcision, baptism, or sacrifice (*b. Šabb.* 31a; *'Abot R. Nat.* 15:3, 24a–b, pp. 91–92).[50]

Later rabbinic evidence speaks of the public nature of conversion. Rabbi Judah b. Illai (fourth-generation Tanna) contended that a confession had to be made before a Beth Din (*b. Yeb.* 47a) and, according to Rabbi Simeon b. Gamaliel (fourth-generation Tanna), any daughters and sons had to accompany the confessor before three *ḥăbērîm* (*b. Ber.* 30b).[51] Rabbi Jose b. Judah (fifth-generation Tanna) taught that the initiate had to accept all the Torah, even the minutiae of the experts (*b. Ber.* 30b).[52] A much later Amoraic instruction is interesting as well. In *b. Yeb.* 47a–48b a proselyte is interrogated, instructed, circumcised, baptized, and thereby becomes a "new-born child."[53]

Conclusions

My basic conclusion is that we know very little substantial about what was required for converts to Judaism during the first century. (1) It is probable that many Jews thought circumcision was necessary for true conversion to Judaism for the male – at the least as an act of obedience to the law. (2) It is possible that baptism was required for converts, but it is not possible to date this before John the Baptist, Jesus, and the development of earliest Christianity. (3) It is likely that sacrifices were performed by some converts and that therefore some may have seen this as part of initiation, but it is difficult to determine the date when such a notion became halakic ruling. (4) It is certain that converts were expected to join Judaism, worship the one God, repent from sin and idolatry, and obey the law (some specifics of which may have been, for the male, circumcision, and for others perhaps sacrifice).[54]

Finally, it seems to me that the *absence* of firm data regarding initiation is an argument, albeit from silence, that Judaism was not a missionary religion. Had Judaism been a missionary religion in any centralized sense, greater attention would have been given to entrance requirements. Further, had Judaism been aggressively involved in converting Gentiles, there would have been greater attention to entrance requirements. But I admit that this argument is from silence and ought not to be given priority.

In conclusion, I suggest that we turn to the idealized account of Aseneth's conversion to Judaism. This account is informative here, especially if the text is to be dated in the first century.[55] Aseneth's conversion, particularly emphatic on her internal perceptions, is rehearsed in detail in *Jos. Asen.* 10–18, and the text, I suggest, rehearses some Jewish aspirations for true conversion to Judaism.[56]

First, Aseneth radically departs from her previous religion and idolatry, demonstrating this by destroying her idols and religious food (10:10–13; 11:4–5, 7–9; 12:5; 13:11). Second, Aseneth's repentance is deep, prolonged (cf. 10:1–8, 14–17), and evidences itself in the threefold ascetic confession of sin (11:1–13:15).[57] Third, Aseneth learns to trust in the God of Joseph, the God who pardons and shows mercy. Aseneth thereby learns to address this God as father (12:14–15). Fourth, the effect of her confession is a humble resignation to God's will (13:15).

Subsequent to this elaborate confession, God's angel informs her of her acceptance, symbolized in a change of clothes and a meal (15:3-6; cf. 15:13–17:4).[58]

If this text is actually from the first century and reflects conditions at that time, our previous conclusions are confirmed: (1) For whatever reasons, there are no ritual requirements for Aseneth, not even baptism.[59] (2) The emphasis of the text is repentance from sin and the abolition of idolatry (cf. 19:4-7). (3) From this time on Aseneth serves Joseph (13:15), who may symbolize Israel (e.g., 22:1-10).[60] This new family and religion thus evoke a reconstructed biography on her part (21:10-21). I suggest, then, that baptism was not an established tradition for requirements for proselytes. The real requirement here is repentance from sin and communion with Israel. In other words, perhaps the most determinative factor for converts to Judaism was sociological (transfer to Israel) rather than rituals and theology. Aseneth has passed from death to life, she was a new creation (27:10): the symbol for this was becoming a part of Israel.

5

Levels of Adherence
to Judaism

LATER RABBINIC TEXTS show clearly that certain proselytes received (quasi-)official categorization according to the level of the commitment that had been made or according to the degree to which they had penetrated Judaism.[1] Is there evidence that distinctions regarding levels of adherence were made in the first century? Is it accurate to argue, perhaps, that Jesus prohibited the evangelism of the Gentiles (Matt. 10:5-6) because he knew the primary motives of the Gentile "converts" as seen in Galilee or because he was so familiar with the superficial conversions of Gentiles? Was this a motivating factor behind some of the reticence of early Jewish Christianity's reluctance to evangelize Gentiles (e.g., Acts 10–11)?

I have mentioned several times the social nature of conversion to Judaism: that is, to convert was essentially (for most converts) to switch nations and sociological groups. In the case of slaves it may have been more complete integration into the household; nonetheless, a major shift was involved. It seems that there were various levels of participation in the gentile society by Jews (see chap. 1), and so it naturally follows that there were various levels of gentile participation in Jewish society (and therefore religion), depending, of course, on such things as the strength of the Jewish community or the desire for the favor of the potential associates. The various levels, as one proceeds more and more to the core of Judaism where one becomes a full convert, would involve definite boundary markers, for example, knowledge of the Torah, Sabbath practices, circumcision, etc. I wish to point to the social nature of the various levels of attachment to Judaism and to suggest, from the outset, that various levels of adherence are *a priori* likely.

This observation about society may be illuminated (and confirmed) by some recent studies in sociology. Rosabeth Kanter distinguishes three levels of "commitment," not from the perspective of the individuals but from the point of view of how the "committed one" serves the community: (1) *affective* commitment involves a commitment to the members of the organization, (2) *instrumental* commitment involves a commitment to the organization itself and its rules, and (3) *moral* commitment involves commitment to the organization's ideas as explained by the leaders of that group. These various aspects of commitment to a social group (in our case, to Judaism) generate various aspects of retaining members, group cohesion, and social control.[2] The implication of this sociological model for our study is that it shows outsiders (and insiders) making commitments at different levels for different reasons, and these commitments were most likely perceived by the insiders according to the various contributions they might make. Whereas social exclusion might lead to affective commitment and commercial needs to instrumental commitment, guilt or moral aspirations might lead to moral commitment. Even if it is clear that modern historians do not have sufficient evidence (in the vast majority of cases) to discern the "converts'" motives or the community's needs that were met by the "converts," it is still useful to appropriate these categories in our search for levels of adherence to Judaism.[3]

To complicate this discussion, we also are now fully aware that different groups would have had different perceptions of the various levels of adherence. Thus, whereas it is probably accurate to say that the Essenes had no "adherents" (as distinguished from "converts"), it is also accurate that the Pharisees had more "adherents" (and fewer "converts") because they were more tolerant toward outsiders but just as tight on "crossing the boundary" into Pharisaism.[4] In other words, "the boundary that separates Jews and Judaism from pagans and paganism is distinct but broad."[5]

With respect to "levels of adherence," scholars have focused particularly on the "God-fearers," a title known mostly from the Acts of the Apostles. Although this title deserves consideration in this chapter, we postpone this discussion until the next chapter, which focuses on New Testament data. At that point I will discuss also the Greco-Roman evidence. We treat here the evidence from Philo, Josephus, and the rabbis, and we focus on material pertaining to noncasual relations (e.g., political treaties).

General

In the bulk of the literature of the Second Temple period one does not find any terminological distinctions reflecting levels of adherence as seen in the later rabbinic evidence. For example, the author of *1 Enoch* 50:3 speaks of honorless converts at the end of history even though the same will be saved. Further, although there is evidence for both Jews (Ecclus. 1:8, 11–20; 10:24; Jth. 8:8; *T. Gad* 3:2; 5:4; *T. Jos.* 11:1; *T. Benj.*

3:4; Sus. 2, 62; *Pss. Sol.* 3:16; 4:24, 26; 5:21; 6:8; 12:4; 17:44; 18:8, 9-10, 13; 4 Macc. 15:8; *Joseph and Aseneth; 2 Enoch* 34:1; 42:6 [J]; 43:3; *Sib. Or.* 3:573; *2 Bar.* 54:4) and Gentiles (Ecclus. 10:22; *T. Naph.* 1:10; *Pss. Sol.* 2:37; 17:38; *2 Enoch* 48:7-8; *Sib. Or.* frag. 1:3) being described as those who "fear" God, there is insufficient evidence to conclude that the term "fearing" was a technical designation in this literature for those who "partially converted."[6] In fact, from the evidence just cited, one notices that the same books often describe both Jews and Gentiles with similar expressions. Various levels of adherence do not seem to be fixed by terms in these authors, although there are undoubtedly various attitudes to Gentiles and particularly positive ones for those who honor and fear God (see chap. 1).

Philo

Philo speaks acceptingly of a general reverence by Gentiles for Judaism (*Leg.* 211; *Mos.* 2:17-25; *Spec.* 2.70).[7] He speaks of levels of perception in the migration of life.[8] Thus, in an ascending order, there are atheists, agnostics, the superstitious, natural revelation theists, those who see God (Israel) and Moses (*Praem.* 40-44; cf. *L.A.* 3.97-99; *Spec.* 1.33-35). One sees God and comprehends (*katalambanein*), but only the one who infers from natural order understands (*lambanein;* cf. *L.A.* 3.100-103). There are the uninitiated, the initiated, and the hierophants (*Cher.* 42) as well as the imperfect and the perfect (*Sacr.* 43-45; cf. *Post.* 130-31) and the earth-born, the heaven-born, and the God-born (*Gig.* 60-64). He views some people as "cosmopolitans," whether Gentile or Jew (*Spec.* 2.44-48). These classifications by Philo are not unimportant for the matters pertaining to "kinds" of proselytes, though the categories he uses are drawn from epistemology and wisdom speculation rather than from the legal halakah which we find in later rabbinic literature. In other words, it is quite difficult to know from these categories how Philo views such people (say, the "heaven-born") in the categories of proselytes.[9] But it is very clear that he does see various levels of perception and, therefore, various levels of adherence to Judaism (conceived of as the truth). This permits only the general observation of the presence of various levels of adherence in Philonic thinking. It may be simply a classification grid that Philo uses of all people, including Jews, and not a distinction between Gentiles and Jews.

Further information about Philo can be provided from his expositions of Old Testament texts (e.g., Lev. 19:33, 34; Deuteronomy 23). Here Philo distinguishes clearly the "convert" (*epēlytēs*) from the "metic" (*metoikoi; Virt.* 102-8) in that, whereas the convert receives equal status, equal love, and becomes a national, the metics, because they pay only some honor, are simply received hospitably. In addition, Philo speaks of Egyptian converts who are not to be fully accepted until the third generation (108). From this text, then, we can conclude that Philo did perceive some distinction in levels of adherence—from the "nonproselyte" metic to the Egyptian convert to the full proselyte. How such distinctions worked themselves out in Alexandrian Judaism would be interesting to know, but because we lack data, nothing firm can be argued.

However, I want to suggest that there is one revealing, and to my knowledge almost completely neglected, text which does clearly teach that Philo made some distinctions with respect to "kinds of proselytes" that are known otherwise only from later rabbinic evidence, namely, *Mos.* 1.147, where Philo interprets Exod. 12:38.[10] Two separate items in this text call for interpretation: (1) Why did Philo interpret Exod. 12:38 as he did? (2) What is the significance of this interpretation for the history and antiquity of proselyte *halakot*?[11]

To answer the first question we need before us the textual history of Exod. 12:38. The Masoretic Text reads: *wĕgam-'ēreb rab 'ālâ 'ittām* ("and many other people went up with them"). The Septuagint, with no significant variants (for our purposes), reads *kai epimiktos polys synanebē autois* ("and a numerous mixed company went up with them"). In later Jewish writings there are some significant variations and interpretations of the Hebrew. *Targum Neofiti* Exod. 12:38 reads *w'p gywryn sgyn slqw 'mhwn* ("and many strangers[12] also went up with them"). Both *Targum Pseudo-Jonathan* and *Targum Onqelos* read essentially the same on the points under discussion: *w'wp nwkr'yn sgy'yn slyqw 'mhwn* ("and also many foreigners went up with them").

Later rabbinic elucidations on the "mixed multitude" (*'ēreb rab*) were many, and mention can be made here of only some of these, our concern being with the Philonic view. The group was seen pejoratively by all texts: they were not protected by the cloud; they were much larger in number than the Israelites; they did not join the Israelites until after the exodus and still wanted share in the booty; they induced Israel to worship the golden calf; they were permitted to accompany Israel only after a lengthy persuasion of God by Moses; they clamored after the pots of Egypt; they murmured against Moses and Aaron, etc.[13]

We can now turn to Philo and his construal of Exod. 12:38 in *Mos.* 1.147. Philo renders the "numerous mixed company" (*epimiktos polys*) in the following manner (translation below): *migadōn de kai sygklydōn kai therapeias ochlos synexēlthen hōsanei nothon meta gnēsiou plēthous.* He further delineates this group into three separate divisions: *houtoi d'ēsan* (1)*hoi ek gynaikōn gennēthentes Aigyptiōn tois Hebraiois kai tō patrōō genei prosnemēthentes*, (2) *kai hosoi to theophiles agamenoi tōn andrōn epēlytai egenonto*, (3)*kai ei dē tines tō megethei kai plēthei tōn epallēlōn kolaseōn metebalonto sōphronisthentes*.

> They were accompanied by a promiscuous, nondescript and menial crowd, a bastard host, so to speak, associated with the true-born. These were (1) the children of Egyptian women by Hebrew fathers into whose families they had been adopted, (2) also those who, reverencing the divine favour shown to the people, had come over to them [*epēlytai egenonto*], (3) and such as were converted and brought to a wiser mind [*metebalonto sōphronisthentes*] by the magnitude and the number of the successive punishments.

It is obvious, and striking, to observe how much evolution has taken place since the simple "mixed multitude" ('*ēreb rab*); it has developed from a simple ill-defined or nondefined collection of people into a clearly demarcated threefold (*hoi, hosoi, tines*) division of Gentile "proselytes." Interestingly, like the later rabbinic explanations, Philo's attitude toward this group is decidedly negative. An important question comes to the surface at this point: Why does Philo describe this group as *converts* to Judaism (*epēlytai egenonto, metebalonto sōphronisthentes*)? How did he arrive at such a meaning? It seems certain that he could not have arrived at this definition of "mixed multitudes" ('*ēreb rab*) by means either of his typical allegorical exegesis or etymology. How then did he come to this?

Philo more probably is reflecting a contemporary midrashic interpretation of "mixed multitudes" ('*ēreb rab*) found in his community (or his awareness of that community) and that this community interpretation is the middle factor between "mixed multitudes" ('*ēreb rab*) and his threefold breakdown. What was this middle factor?

I suggest that the middle factor is the targumic tradition, which construed this group as proselytes. The process seems to be able to be detected in the following stages: (1) The Hebrew text ('*ēreb rab*) was translated by a targumist as *gywryn*, meaning either "stranger or foreigner." Thus, *Tg. Neofiti* on Exod. 12:38. (2) This construal was then interpreted, perhaps even at the outset of the targumic renderings, as referring more specifically to "proselyte," a definition of *gywryn* that has been well documented by M. Jastrow.[14] However, I am not suggesting that Philo had read *Neofiti* targums, nor that Aramaic targums were given in Alexandria. But Philo's interpretation of Exod. 12:38 is both too far from the original Hebrew and too close to targumic and rabbinic understandings to be accidental. One could posit either that these renderings circulated in Alexandria or that Philo had come into contact with such an interpretation either through travel to Palestine or by means of contacts with those from Palestine. It is not possible for us to determine with any probative force the provenance of Philo's rendering, but it does seem probable that he was in contact with such a targumic understanding. With the constant tie of Alexandria and Palestine, on the one hand, and the regularity of midrashic activity in the synagogues, on the other, it would not at all be an exaggeration to think that Philo received his interpretation by way of targums.[15]

This seems to answer the question, Why did Philo interpret Exod. 12:38 as he did? We turn to the second question, What is the significance of Philo's (or, better yet, the targumist's) translation and interpretation? Here we recall Philo's threefold breakdown, which reflects a negative attitude toward such people. He shows converts (groups 2 and 3) who altered their allegiance for two different reasons. The second group converts to "Judaism" because of God's favors upon the people: "those who became converts because of the divine favor upon the people." The third group is converted as a result of fear of God's punishments: "some were converted to a better mind by the greatness and number of successive punishments."

Several factors need now to be put together. First, Philo's attitude is negative. Second, these converts changed as a result of miracles or the fear of experiencing God's punishing hand. Third, rabbis later had the same attitude toward those who converted for motives that were other than religious. Thus, I suggest that we have here, in Philo, groups analogous to the gēr ḥălōmôt (the dream proselyte), the gēr of Mordecai and Esther (the advantage proselyte), and the gēr 'ărāyôt (the lion or fear proselyte).

To answer the question of the significance of Mos. 1.147 for the history of proselyte halakah, I suggest that Philo uncovers for us notions about proselytes that have not been documented prior to the second century A.D. We are familiar with similar distinctions made by rabbis, but it has been impossible to demonstrate that such distinctions were present in the first century A.D. Whatever one calls it (proto-rabbinic or not), from this text in Philo I think we can now say that (some) Jews at the beginning of the first century had already begun to take negative stances toward those who converted for dishonorable reasons and to classify them as such. However, these groups probably had not yet received "official epithets," such as gēr ḥălōmôt.

Furthermore, this view of Philo's rendering receives slight confirmation from another passage in Philo, Virt. 102–8. In this passage Philo makes a clear distinction between the "incomer" (*epēlytēs*) and the "settlers" (*metoikoi*). The former are to be loved, not just as friends and kinsfolk but both in body and soul (*keleuei dē tois apo tou ethnous agapan tous epēlytas, mē monon hōs philous kai syngeneis alla hōs heautous, kata te sōma kai psychēn*). The latter are to be given hospitality (105), because Egyptians had "originally" (*tēn archēn*) treated the Israelites with kindness in a similar situation. Thus, Philo speaks here of a distinction that later came to be known as the *gēr ṣedeq* and the *gēr tôšāb* (*b. 'Abod. Zar.* 64b; *b. Git.* 57b). If the "metics" converted (*ei tines ethelēseian autōn metallaxasthai pros tēn Ioudaiōn politeian*), they were not to be fully accepted until the third generation (108). This concern with the third generation was also developed in proselyte halakot (e.g., *b. Sota* 9a). It seems reasonable, then, to infer that proselyte halakot on such matters as levels, motives, and even how long it was to take for a Gentile to be fully admitted were known to Philo, and these texts in Philo enable us to anchor such ideas firmly to the beginning of the first century A.D.

Thus, from Philo I think we can safely conclude that "kinds" of proselytes were already known and that those who converted because of miracles or out of fear were distinguished as "unworthy" of the name. They were those of "instrumental commitment"; Philo wanted "moral commitment" and "affective commitment" (though I suspect that Philo also knew of the advantage of some "instrumental commitments"). From Philo we can speak confidently, then, of various levels of adherence.

Josephus

Josephus in several places alludes to Gentile participation in the cultus (e.g., *J.W.* 4.262, 324; 5.15, 17–18; 5.363, 563; *Ant.* 3.217; *Ag. Ap.* 2.123; 2.280–86, 293; 11.84–87);[16] in one text he comes close to describing actual levels of adherence in Jewish life (*J.W.* 7.45: in Antioch many Greeks were attracted to Judaism, "and they had in some measure incorporated themselves" (*tropō tini moiran*). One could infer from Metilius's conversion that there were some who did not go "even so far as circumcision" (*J.W.* 2.454); they were not fully committed "morally." There remained in Syria, after Syria had purged itself of Jews, some "Judaizers" (*J.W.* 2.463).[17] There were some who converted out of fear (*Ant.* 11.285ff.), who ought not to be seen as proselytes, and Poppaea was a "worshiper of God" (*theosebēs*), but nothing is stated here with clarity (*Ant.* 20.195; *Vita* 13–16).[18] Some were attracted to Judaism but were not permitted to participate in sacrifices (*Ant.* 3.318–19). One could infer from the Izates story that some converts were seen on higher levels than others if they went through circumcision (*Ant.* 20.38–42).[19] Finally, an interesting statement is made in *Ant.* 14.110: "for all the Jews of the habitable world, and those who worshipped God" (*pantōn tōn kata tēn oikoumenēn Ioudaiōn kai sebomenōn ton theon*). Josephus here is speaking of the wealth of the temple, and he attributes this to the fact that Jews and "God-fearers" had contributed to it for so long a time. The question here is whether Josephus is referring to two separate groups, that is, Jewish people and (Gentile) God-fearers. The following clause, "even those [or, including those] from Asia and Europe" seems to me simply to let the reader know the scope of the contributors rather than to comment on the God-fearers. Furthermore, there is here the difficulty of a single article being used for both "Jews" and "worshipers," which may very well suggest one group, not Jews and Gentile God-fearers, but God-fearing Jews (i.e., honorable, pious Jews), who demonstrate their loyalty to Judaism by contribution to the temple treasuries. In other words, it is possible that the text does indicate levels of attachment with official terms (Jews and "God-fearers" – whatever the term means), but it is far from clear if that is what Josephus has in mind.[20]

In conclusion, although the evidence in Josephus is ambiguous and he does not use the technical terms that were later to be used, we can conclude that Josephus reveals some stratification of attachment.[21] Thus, Josephus speaks of "partial converts" (*J.W.* 2.463; 7.45; *Ant.* 20.195; *Vita* 13–16) and "full converts" (*Ant.* 20:40–42), the latter marked by circumcision. One could conclude that the former were called "God-fearers" (see *Ant.* 14.110; 20.195; *Vita* 13–16) – but such a conclusion must be cautious. We reserve a conclusion to the appropriateness of this term until the next chapter.

Rabbinic Statements

Throughout rabbinic literature some very interesting distinctions are made regarding the "kinds" of proselytes, notably, the "God-fearer," the "true proselyte," the "lion proselyte," and the "*gēr tôšāb.*"[22]

Gēr ṣedeq ("True Proselyte")

Shemoneh Esreh, bar. 13, contains this expression, but, in spite of the many attempts to date this piece of liturgy, scholars have been unable to come to anything approaching a consensus.[23] I have not been able to trace any attributions of this expression to any first-century Tannaim, but it does appear in the fourth-generation Tannaim, notably, Rabbi Meir (*b. Pesah.* 21b) and Rabbi Joshua b. Karha (*b. Git.* 57b). One could possibly insert *Mek. Bahodesh,* parashah 7, lines 97–99 (on Exod. 20:10) into the upper layer of the Tannaim. Thus, even if one may speak generally of distinguishing "true" from "false" proselytes, as we have seen in the evidence from Philo and Josephus, there is no evidence that the "true" proselyte would have been technically called *gēr ṣedeq* in the first century A.D., however appropriate the term would have been.

Gēr tôšāb

There are two tannaitic references to the "resident alien."[24] In an attribution to Rabbi Meir, who lived in the middle of the second century, there is an answer to the question, Who is the *gēr tôšāb?* He replies: "Any Gentile who takes upon himself in the presence of three *ḥăbērîm* not to worship idols" (*b. 'Abod. Zar.* 64b). The sages responded: "Any man who takes upon himself the seven precepts accepted by the sons of Noah" [= pre- and non-Abrahamic people] (see also *b. Sanh.* 56b). It is also said of Rabbi Joshua b. Harha (fourth generation) that he called Naaman *gēr tôšāb,* but Nebuzaradan a *gēr ṣedeq* (*b. Giṭ.* 57b). Thus, we are again confronted with the conclusion that very little can be said regarding first-century practice. In fact, the words of B. J. Bamberger are quite insightful: "the law regarding the *ger toshab* describes the way in which the Rabbis *would have liked* to regulate the conduct of pagans dwelling in Palestine, *if they had had the power to do so.*"[25]

God-fearer

What is noticeable here is the *absence* of this expression as a designation for Gentiles in the tannaitic period, even though some references appear in later haggadic material.[26] B. J. Bamberger explains this politically: namely, it would have been much more difficult to be associated loosely with Judaism after the destruction of the Temple.[27] His explanation lacks force, however.

Gēr 'ărāyôt ("Lion/fear Proselytes")

This category ultimately stems from the terms of 2 Kings 17:25 and describes the Gentile who converts out of fear. The term does not appear until Rabbi Akiba and Rabbi Ishmael (third-generation Tannaim; ca. A.D.120–140) (*b. Qidd.* 75a–b), and it does continue into the next generation (*b. Yeb.* 24b; *b. B. Qam.* 38b; *b. Nid.* 56b); it cannot be dated to the first century.

Gēr ḥălōmôt ("Dream Proselyte")

The same conclusion can be drawn for this expression: it is later (*b. Yeb.* 24b; *b. Menaḥ.* 44a).

Various other expressions are used in rabbinic sources. These include the proselytes of Mordecai and Esther (advantage proselytes; see *b. Yeb.* 24b), money proselytes (*b. B. Meṣ.* 72a), marriage proselytes (*m. Yeb.* 2:8; *b. Yeb.* 24b).[28] *B. 'Abod. Zar.* 3b (Amoraic) speaks of the "self-made proselyte" or "dragged-in proselyte."[29] Both Philo and Josephus give evidence of the proselyte of Mordecai and Esther, though without such official designation.

Conclusions

It is safe to conclude, both from social probabilities and the evidence cited above, that within Judaism of the Second Temple period there were various levels of attachment to Judaism by Gentiles. The different levels of adherence to Judaism were simply different choices made by Gentiles. There is no evidence for a "schema of categories"; furthermore, there was no mechanism to enforce such a schema before Jamnia or later.

Before moving into a more refined discussion of "God-fearers" in the next chapter, I propose a fourfold breakdown of this adherence. This breakdown, however, needs to be seen as aspects of commitment; there were undoubtedly some Gentiles who fit into more than one category (e.g., the gentile male who married a Jew but also was a sabbatarian, a non-idolater, who refused circumcision but donated large sums of money or influenced society toward Judaism).

(1) General and peripheral participation: Some Gentiles were held in respect, either for their perception of truth, for their political rank, or for their social standing. They were allowed to participate in a general way in Judaism; they could attend synagogues or offer sacrifices in the temple or were simply held in high regard by the Jewish community at large. Most of these "feared" the God of Israel, either through a confession of monotheism or through the legalization of monotheism in an official public act. Others honored the Sabbath, fasted, or refused to eat pork. Various forms of penetration could be mentioned, but one interesting form, perhaps at the lowest level of participation, is the "cursing and blessing" of Ampikles, who, though pagan, clearly utilized

the formulas of Deuteronomy 28.[30] Shaye Cohen observes seven forms of respecting the God and religion of the Jews, and Ross Kraemer has detailed some of the ways gentile women, some of whom were converts, participated in Judaism.[31] The levels of commitment involved in this general participation could be derived from social, commercial, and moral reasons, and undoubtedly various Jews would have seen these motives from different angles. The evidence is sufficient to show that Gentiles participated in Judaism in various ways. The wall between Judaism and paganism may have been high, but it was a wall made from steps and there were Gentiles at each level.

(2) Official recognition: Some Gentiles received an "official hand of fellowship," either through patronage or acts of obedience to the Torah. I include here the "God-fearers" (see chap. 6), those who funded projects, such as building synagogues (see, e.g., Luke 7:1–10), and those who converted partially but were of sufficient social status to make their contribution to Judaism helpful (Izates of Adiabene). The number of Gentiles in this category is impossible to estimate; suggestions range from an insignificant minority to a massive following.

(3) Social integration: It is a known fact that intermarriage took place in Judaism (see chap. 1 for evidence).[32] Intermarriage most certainly generated some awkward social situations for some Jews (see, e.g., Acts 16:1-3; Gal. 2:3), but, when the gentile spouse did not convert, it also created social integration of Gentiles with Jews and blurred the boundary lines. This kind of social integration places a non-Jew in direct contact with Judaism without conversion. We think of the son of the "God-fearer" in Juvenal (*Satires* 14.96–106): although the father was only minimally connected with Judaism, his social integration led to the conversion of his son. Furthermore, Philo speaks of Egyptian converts who were not permitted full participation in Judaism until the third generation and who therefore were held in abeyance. It must be remembered that "social integration" in Judaism is more than "social contact," because the Jewish society is, in effect, the locus of God's blessing. To use Christian terms, the Jewish society is a sacrament of God's covenantal grace. Nonetheless, there is sufficient evidence to see as a common pattern that there were Gentiles who were socially integrated with Jews but were neither "converts" proper nor typical pagans.

(4) Conversion: When a Gentile decided to join Judaism totally, he or she converted to Yahweh, to his law and to his people, Israel. For males, this was demonstrated most probably through the supreme act of obedience to the law, namely, circumcision. Women, no doubt, would have been assessed differently but with just as much concern. This conversion could have taken place from alternation to radical

conversion and transformation. Even here, however, if later rabbinic evidence is to be taken as a reflection of social conditions, and not just theological speculation, converts may have never been seen as fully Jewish. If this is so, we would have in effect, five classes, adding those who are Jewish by birth.

In conclusion, I argue that for much of Judaism there would have been at least five "levels of adherence" to Judaism: (1) There were Gentiles who simply preferred to do some things that Jews did; these were not converts but a fringe element of Judaism. (2) There were some Gentiles who were officially recognized, most of whom probably had what R. Kanter has called "instrumental commitment." (3) For whatever reasons, most probably marriage, some Gentiles were socially integrated into Judaism but remained Gentiles. I suspect that this level of commitment is more typical of males than females because of circumcision. As I will show in the next chapter, it is unwise to restrict the term "God-fearer" to this group, although that term would be nonetheless accurate for them. It could also be used for those in the first two levels. (4) Some Gentiles were converted to Judaism. Conversion is seen here as acceptance of Judaism, socialization into the Jewish community, and an inevitable restructuring of one's universe of discourse, one's biography. (5) The fifth level of adherence is not really "adherence" at all: it is the Jew by birth, for whom Judaism is a natural home.

6

Jewish Missionary Activity
in the New Testament

BECAUSE EARLIEST JEWISH Christianity saw itself in some sense
as "eschatological Israel," or as a remnant movement within Israel, it
perceived itself vis-à-vis Israel. Accordingly, we need to look at the data
we find in earliest Christianity separately. This separation requires
some explanation. In so separating the earliest Christian evidence from
the Jewish evidence I do not mean to suggest that these early Christians
were not Jewish. Rather, whether at times the dramatic split was
formed quickly or at other times slowly, Christianity did eventually
separate itself from its parent religion, Judaism, and saw itself as the
completion of that religion, practically forming another religion. But
because the evidence of earliest Christianity is so frequently related to
Judaism in a polemical and apologetical fashion, I have chosen to
examine this evidence separately. But this separation should not create
distortions. It is remarkable how little new information is gleaned from
the New Testament, and yet it is also notable how that information
significantly meshes with the evidence from non-Christian sources.
Rather, the evidence from Judaism influences how we are to understand
the New Testament data.

This chapter will be limited to Jewish missionary activity in its non-
Christian components; thus, Paul and Peter are excluded as Jewish missionaries even if they saw themselves as "true Jews." I am concerned
primarily with the data and hints found in early Christian literature
that pertain to the nature and extent of (non-Christian) Jewish missionary activity. I will move from the earliest Christian traditions (e.g.,
Mark, Q, and early traditions) to the latest traditions (e.g., Lukan
theology), without seriously engaging in discussions about the various
shades of reliability of a given datum for reconstructing the message and
praxis of the historical Jesus.

Long ago S. Bialoblocki made a statement that has not been given
much attention in studies of Jewish missionary activity: "It is unjustified
to assign to the Pharisees a particularly active mission of propaganda."[1]

It is the purpose of this chapter to investigate earliest Christian evidence to see what light it sheds on Jewish missionary activity, with a view to testing this conclusion of Bialoblocki.

Earliest Christian Traditions

Is there evidence of Jewish missionary activity in the earliest gospel traditions (Q, pre-Markan traditions)?[2] In a Q tradition, Matt. 15:14// Luke 6:39 (L9; S11, Q6:39; cf. Matt. 23:16), there is a possible piece of evidence of Jewish missionary activity. The logion is found in Luke's Sermon on the Plain, and it appears that Luke has placed it here without significant contextual concerns, perhaps to develop the idea of "teaching" found also in Luke 6:40 or around the theme of judging.[3] Matthew, however, places the same logion in the context of the debate with the Pharisees over true defilement. At any rate, this *Sprichwort*[4] is applied by Matthew to Jewish leaders who are attempting to guide those who do not understand, and a similar meaning is found also in Luke.[5] Thus, it is safe to conclude that the logion reflects Jewish leadership (which Jesus describes as blind) in its capacity of leading others from blindness into sight.

The problem for us is that the contexts provide no clues that the "blind," who are perceived by Jewish leadership as needing guidance, are Gentiles. A parallel in Rom. 2:19–20 could suggest that the "blind" were Gentiles, but it is difficult to make a convincing case.[6] It can be said that similar expressions are used for a Jewish consciousness of possessing the light of truth, as has already been seen in such texts as Wisd. of Sol. 18:4; 2 Enoch 33:9; 48:7–8. But it is most difficult to conclude that this was the original meaning of this logion; the evidence is inconclusive.

Another piece of evidence suggestive in this regard is the Q logion found at Matt. 23:13//Luke 11:52 (L36:36–39; S34, Q11:52). Here Jesus castigates Jewish "lawyers" (*tois nomikois*) for preventing others from entering into knowledge (Matthew has "the kingdom"), to which they alone had access.[7] Again, this logion may point to missionary activities. Several comments are in order. First, I tend to agree with the majority of Q scholarship, which contends that the mention of Pharisees in Matt. 23:13 is to be attributed to Matthean redaction.[8] Second, more important for our study, it is very difficult to determine if the leaders are preventing *Gentiles* from entering the kingdom.[9] As with the previous saying, the language, particularly in Luke, could be explained in the context of the Jewish consciousness of tradents of the truth, but there is no clear evidence to tip the balance in favor of Gentiles. Again, the evidence is inconclusive.

In these two early Jesus traditions we find no unambiguous evidence of Jewish missionary activity on the part of Jews. It is possible that both evince a consciousness of responsibility for passing on knowledge to others, but it is not possible to tell if those to whom the knowledge is imparted are Gentiles.

Pauline Corpus

In studying the literature on Jewish missionary activity I have been amazed at how infrequently scholars turn to Paul for information about Jewish missionary activity. Paul's own testimony of his past shows that he had an intense zeal for the causes of Pharisaism – but, as far as I can see, no zeal for missions. Paul apparently was acting largely as a theological guardian of the Torah and its interpretation. However, Paul was acting with authority when he persecuted the churches of Jesus (Gal. 1:13–14, 23; Phil. 3:4–6). Before his conversion Paul was not a Jewish missionary to Gentiles, so far as we can tell.[10]

When we turn to traces of information about Jewish missions in Paul's letters, we find some interesting details. In Galatians Paul seems to be opposing "Torah missionaries" who are involved in a *Gegenmission*. These missionaries can be identified plausibly as Jewish missionaries who are of the Pharisaic persuasion.[11] My concern here is not with identifying the opponents; rather, we need to specify their missionary practices and aims. What is interesting is that we have Jewish Christians who are "out and about" on a sort of missionary movement but whose sole concern seems to be with Christians and the "completion" (Gal. 3:3) of their conversion through the total submission to the Torah.[12] In other words, these are Judaizing Christians who, through the influence of their previous Judaism,[13] were attempting to turn those whom they saw as "partial converts" (perhaps as "God-fearers") into "full converts" (proselytes). Put differently, their concern was with Gentiles but not with Gentiles *qua* Gentiles; rather, their concern was with Gentiles who had already shown an interest in "completed Judaism." They form a striking similarity to Eleazar of the Izates story, with Paul functioning as Ananias. If Paul was accused of knocking down some boundary markers, they were concerned with reconstructing the same.

This seems to be how Gal. 5:11 ought to be understood. When Paul asks, "If I am still (*eti*) preaching circumcision, why then (*eti*) am I being persecuted?" he probably means that he previously did "preach" circumcision in some sense, although he no longer does and consequently he is being persecuted (6:12).[14] Which is to say, there was a time in Paul's life when his zeal (i.e., "he preached" is metaphorical) was directed, as these Judaizers' is now, toward compelling (cf. Gal. 2:3) "God-fearers" to complete their conversion by undergoing circumcision, or more sociologically, by joining the Jewish community.[15] To sum up: Galatians shows that there were Judaizers, some of whom had become Christians, who spent their energies for the total conversion of Gentiles, Gentiles who had previously become associated either with Judaism or Judaism more recently in its newer, Christian form.

Two passages need to be noted from Romans. Romans 2:17-24 is an attack on some form of Judaism as seen through the eyes of a former Pharisaic Jew.[16] In this section is a diatribe against Judaizers, 2:19-20: "and if you are sure that you are a guide to the blind, a light to those who are in darkness, a corrector of the foolish, a teacher of children, having in the law the embodiment of knowledge and truth" (RSV).[17] Several terms must be examined to see if they reflect Jewish missionary activity. The term "guide" (*hodēgos*) can be used in missionary contexts (Acts 8:31; cf. also Matt. 15:14 par.; 23:16, 24).[18] Further, in Jewish literature the term and the ideas are connected with Jews leading Gentiles into the light (e.g., Wisd. of Sol. 18:4; *1 Enoch* 105:1; *Sib. Or.* 3:194-95; Josephus *Ag. Ap.* 2.293). Furthermore, the terms "blind," "light," and "darkness" are used similarly (cf. Isa. 42:6-7; *T. Levi* 14:4; Philo *Vita* 13; *Virt.* 179; *Heres* 76-77; note also Matt. 4:16; 5:14; Luke 2:32; John 1:4, 5, 9; 3:19, 20-21; 8:12; 9:5; 11:9, 10; 12:35-36, 46; Acts 13:47; 26:18, 23; 2 Cor 6:14; Eph. 1:18; 5:8; 1 Pet. 2:8; Rev. 21:24).[19] None of the other terms can be taken so clearly in a missionary sense.[20]

Thus, the conclusion we are driven to by the evidence of this passage is that the Jews with whom Paul is disagreeing[21] saw themselves as the bearers of truth and that these same Jews saw themselves as conscious of a superiority and mission to the Gentile world. This idea is found regularly in Jewish literature, as I have shown in previous chapters, but it does not follow that a consciousness of possessing the truth necessarily leads to active Jewish missionary activity among the Gentiles. It may reflect nothing other than an attitude of national privilege or a willingness to permit Gentiles to convert to a nationalistic concept of religious faith.[22] Thus, from Rom. 2:19-20 we learn that (probably Pharisaic) Jews saw themselves as guardians and dispensers of the truth found in the Torah. One might suggest that they applied such a consciousness to missionary activity, but that could only be inferred; it is not explicit.

A second passage is Rom. 16:17-18.[23] If these opponents are Jewish Judaizers, then the clues must be found in "difficulties," "which you have been taught," and "appetites" (*skandala, hēn hymeis emathete, koilia*). It is possible that the "difficulties" could refer to the issue of circumcision (cf. 1 Cor. 8:13; 2 Cor. 11:29) and that "appetites" may refer to the types of issues that emerge again in Phil. 3:19, a text that refers to typically Jewish (and Pharisaic) concerns. If so, then we find marginal evidence of Jewish missions. But all of this is rather farfetched, and it is best that we agree with Cranfield's healthy skepticism about the identity of these opponents.[24]

To discuss all the opponents of Paul and their potential for Jewish missionary activity would be to embark on an endless discussion, which would not achieve probabilities. The evidence presented here—and these texts are probably the clearest—suggests three conclusions with respect to Pauline letters: (1) Some Jews, who were probably Pharisees, had a clear sense of religious superiority over Gentiles, because they had been entrusted with the truth. (2) The evidence in Paul permits one to conclude only that the energies of these Jews were directed at those who had become attached to Judaism, or to this "new Judaism." (3) We find no evidence that Jews were evangelizing Gentiles in competition with Paul's missionary efforts. In other words, the "missionaries" with whom Paul had to contend were "Torah missionaries" (Jewish-Christian advocates of Torah piety), and they were probably from the Pharisee party. If so, they would not be true parallels to Paul himself (who evangelized Gentiles) or to many early Christian missionaries. They were similar to Eleazar, who sought deeper conversion for Izates.

Matthew and His Tradition

When we turn to Matthew we are directly confronted with the text that has formed the basis for the conclusion that Judaism, and Pharisaism in particular, was a missionary religion, namely, Matt. 23:15: "Woe to you, scribes and Pharisees, hypocrites! For you traverse sea and land to make a single proselyte, and when he becomes a proselyte, you make him twice as much a child of hell as yourselves."[25]

The logion is peculiar to Matthew and contains a number of possible redactional traits: "Woe to you" may be redactional;[26] "scribes and Pharisees, hypocrites" is probably redactional;[27] "son of hell" is a Semitism and may be Matthean.[28] Thus, though there is some evidence for redaction, there is insufficient evidence to attribute all of this logion to Matthean redaction. What is noteworthy, however, is that nothing that pertains to missionary activity in this logion can be demonstrated to derive from Matthew's diction. Thus, I would conclude that the missionary element of this logion is traditional and, in light of the

Semitisms noted by J. Jeremias, that the saying ought to be given serious consideration as being an authentic word of Jesus uttered against Jewish leaders (perhaps even against Pharisees).[29]

The logion states that the Pharisees will go to "great lengths"[30] to make one[31] proselyte. S. Bialoblocki continued the translation with what he judged to be implicit: "in the pursuit of new conversions."[32] Is his explication accurate? I suggest not for the following reasons.

First, the term "proselyte" (*prosēlytos*) and the verb "to make" (*poiēsai*), upon which everything here hinges,[33] almost surely mean "a circumcised Gentile," that is, a "total convert."[34] Second, it cannot be demonstrated from the evidence from the ancient world that there was such a thing as an "aggressive" (which is usually argued from "sea and land") mission to the Gentiles among the Jews. This makes the interpretation of S. Bialoblocki, and virtually every commentator after him,[35] most unlikely. Third, the evidence we have marshaled so far, both Jewish and early Christian, would suggest much more of a guardian type of activity. I suggest that it is of the sort that we see in Eleazar's urging of Izates to go all the way (Josephus *Ant.* 20.40–42),[36] that is, activity in which Jewish leaders would be urging Gentile "God-fearers" to become "proselytes" by undergoing circumcision. In other words, what we see here is the kind of thing Paul faced in Galatia: (Pharisaic Christian) Jews who were seeking to turn "partial converts" into "total converts." Matthew's redactional addition of Pharisees harmonizes closely with what was being done by Pharisees at his (and Jesus') time. Fourth, such a view is supported by the *cause* of the woe, the intended focus of the logion: "and when he becomes a proselyte, you make him twice as much a child of hell as yourselves."[37] That is, Matthew's Jesus castigates these leaders for turning their converts into zealotic fanatics of the way of life being taught by the leaders. In the context of Matthew, this "zeal" can only be construed as "zeal for Torah minutiae."[38] This cause, I am suggesting, provides a clue to what is going on in the first half of the logion: Torah proselytization. The criticism reveals the problem; it is not missionary activity that Jesus is against. He is against their understanding of the law and their imposition of that understanding on others (here, Gentile "God-fearers").

To sum up: This logion confirms what we have seen already: Jews were essentially uninvolved in such a thing as "evangelism." Rather, (Pharisaic) Jews were undoubtedly open to Gentile conversion but, more important, they were especially concerned that the "God-fearers" "go the whole way," that is, that they convert to Judaism through circumcision and so assume the yoke of the Torah. K. Axenfeld stated it accurately:

Rarely would they come into contact with true heathens; we are not permitted to think [here] according to the manner of Paul who preached publicly in Athens. Rather, they and those in the Diaspora communities would predominantly have approached half-judaized heathens individually and privately in order to bring them to full submission to the Law, in particular to accept circumcision.[39]

Lukan Writings

The best source in the New Testament for Jewish missionary activity is the Acts of the Apostles. Surprisingly, though the author of Acts was surely the author of Luke, there are no significant traces of Jewish missionary activity in Lukan redaction of his gospel traditions. Our study, consequently, will concentrate on Acts. I will look at various groups (proselytes, non-Jewish participants in Judaism, and "God-fearers") and then at the kinds of missionary activity glimpsed in Acts.

Groups

Proselytes

Three references to "proselytes" are found in Acts. On the day of Pentecost, people from various places throughout the Roman Empire[40] heard the disciples speaking in their own dialect/language. Some of these were from Rome, "both Jews and *proselytes*" (2:11).[41] One of the seven[42] who was appointed "to serve tables" was Nicolaus, a proselyte from Antioch (6:5). Following Paul's address at Pisidian Antioch, both Jews and "devout proselytes" (*sebomenoi prosēlytoi*) inquired further about Paul's message (13:43).[43]

Several observations can be made from Luke's usages. First, the "proselyte" is a Gentile (2:5–12; 6:5; 13:16, 26, 43)[44] who seems to participate in Judaism in different ways, including such practices as celebrating Pentecost (2:5–12), attending synagogue (6:5, 9; 13:43) or caring for the widows (6:1). More narrowly defined, it is possible that the distance traveled and the adjectival "devout" indicate that some "proselytes" were marked by religious zeal (2:9–11; 13:43).

What can we say from Acts about the meaning of "proselyte"? The common assumption of scholars is that the term designates a "Gentile who converts through circumcision in contrast to the God-fearer." However firmly entrenched this view is, it is simply not demonstrable from the evidence in Acts. That it indicates "convert" is unquestionable; that some converts were circumcised is clear. But that the term "proselyte" in Acts means "a circumcised Gentile in contrast to the God-fearer" is not possible to demonstrate, though it may very well be a reasonable inference from other evidence (see chap. 2). What we can say for Acts is that a proselyte is a Gentile convert to Judaism, but we cannot specify the degree of adherence for that Gentile. It may be the case that "proselyte" is a general term in Acts, from anyone who is loosely associated with Judaism (and the synagogue) to the one who makes a full conversion. We cannot forget that 13:43 is unusual in this regard; if "devout" is adjectival, then Luke may very well see at least two classes of proselytes.

For our findings for Jewish missionary activity I think it is safe to say that Acts indicates that there were proselytes to Judaism throughout the Roman Empire. How they became proselytes is not specified; that they did so is fully clear. Very little can be inferred from this fact about the nature or extent of Jewish missionary activity, however.

Non-Jewish Participants in Judaism

We are concerned here with the permission granted to Gentiles to participate in Judaism at a general level, something on the order of John 12:20, without adducing evidence from our next section on the God-fearers.

Acts 8:26–40 records the encounter of Philip with the Ethiopian eunuch.[45] In his introduction to the event, Luke describes the eunuch and then asserts that a eunuch "had come to Jerusalem to worship" (*elēlythei proskynēsōn eis Ierousalēm;* 8:27)[46] and also that "he was reading the prophet Isaiah" (8:28).[47] The eunuch, a non-Jew,[48] had probably participated in a festival and was now reading an actual text of Isaiah. What this incident shows is openness to participation in Judaism and probably some kind of proselytization in Ethiopia; beyond these two points nothing firm can be inferred.

Throughout Acts we see the presence of Gentiles in Jewish synagogue services (13:44, 48; 14:1; 17:12; 18:4). This evidence particularly has led some scholars to conclude that Gentiles were regularly welcomed in synagogue services, but we must recognize that these "Gentiles" in Acts may very well have been the "God-fearers" and so were not simply disinterested observers. One can certainly conclude from Luke's evidence here that Jews were open to gentile participation in the synagogue, and I think that the number of participants was large (cf. 17:12). But the evidence will not permit us to infer that the synagogue was a missionary platform for Judaism. It may have been, and it may not have been.

God-fearers

The issue of God-fearers has been hotly disputed of late,[49] and several conclusions seem to have emerged. First, it is now clear that there was such a group of Gentiles attached to Judaism at some level that may fruitfully be labeled "sympathizers."[50] Second, as Kraabel and Feldman (among many others) have shown, the terms *phoboumenoi ton theon*, etc. were not technical terms for a special class of Gentiles; the terms were used univocally throughout the Roman Empire. It is now clear that the terms so used by ancient writers could be used both for Jews and Gentiles (e.g., *Jos. Asen.* 4:7; 23:9-13; 27:1; 28:7; 29:3; Josephus *Ant.* 20:41).[51] Thus, the issue needs to be focused on how individual authors use the various terms and what groups are seen to be associated with Judaism and in what respects these Gentiles did associate with Judaism. Traditionally, of course, each God-fearer has been seen as a partial convert and has also been depicted as having had religious motivations for associating with Judaism. This is no longer the case. In light of these remarks, we move now to the evidence.

The general point governing this debate was stated long ago by K. Lake: "The point at issue is to what extent *phoboumenoi ton theon* is a technical description of the non-Jewish fringe attending the Synagogue, or is merely an honourable epithet applicable to Jew, Gentile, or Proselyte, as the context may decide."[52] But what is perhaps just as significant is this: Because the terms "God-fearer/devout one" (*phoboumenos, sebomenos*) are used both for Jews (e.g., Josephus *Ant.* 1.96) and Gentiles (Acts 13:16, 26, 43), what importance is to be given to the use of this term for a Gentile?[53] What connotations can be deduced from the contexts when the term is used to describe a Gentile?

Peter encounters a certain Cornelius (Acts 10:1–11:18) who is a gentile Roman military officer (10:1-2, 4, 7, 14, 17, 22, 28, 34-35; 11:3, 7-8, 18).[54] Cornelius is described as "pious" (*eusebēs;* 10:2), "upright" (*dikaios;* 10:22), one who gave alms to Israel (10:2, 4, 31),[55] and one who was respected (10:22). He is also described as "a fearer of God" (*phoboumenos ton theon;* 10:2, 22). However, since he was an outsider, Peter wanted nothing to do with him (cf. 10:28, 34-36, 38, 45; 11:2-3, 17-18),[56] even though Cornelius seems to occupy a fairly well-defined (positive) relationship to Israel. For defining "God-fearer" we can say from this text that it refers to a Gentile who participates (at some "introductory" level) in Judaism. However, A. T. Kraabel has properly warned New Testament scholarship that Cornelius is not necessarily the "archetype" God-fearer, and we need to examine other evidence to understand the term and category accurately.[57]

At Pisidian Antioch, Paul addressed the Jews and a group described as "God-fearers" and "devout ones" (*phoboumenoi . . . sebomenoi ton theon;* 13:16, 26, 43, 50). When the Jews opposed Paul (13:45), he turned exclusively to the Gentiles. From this passage we deduce, first, that here "God-fearer" is used for a Gentile. This is seen in the parallel structure of 13:16, 26, and 43, virtually equating the *phoboumenoi* with the *prosēlytōn.*

13:16:	*andres Israēlitai*	*kai hoi phoboumenoi ton theon*
	men, Israelites	and the God-fearers
13:26:	*andres adelphoi*	*kai hoi . . . phoboumenoi ton theon*
	men, brothers	and the God-fearers
13:43:	*polloi tōn Ioudaiōn*	*kai tōn sebomenōn prosēlytōn*
	Many of the Jews	and the devout proselytes.

Further, this conforms to the Lukan pattern of Paul in Acts: after entering the synagogue and preaching to the Jews, Paul is rejected by some Jews and accepted by both Jews and Greeks (13:5, 32, 38, 45, 49–51; 14:1, 2, 4–5; 17:2–9, 11–13, 17; 18:4–6, 19, 26; 19:8–9).[58] In addition, it is unlikely that the high-standing women of 13:50 are Jews (cf. 16:14). Thus, in contrast to M. Wilcox, I think a strong case can be made here for these *phoboumenoi* being Gentiles.[59]

Second, this passage allows us to make a firm distinction between "God-fearers" and "Gentiles" (cf. 13:43 and 46), because Paul is turning from "Jews" and "God-fearers," some of whom responded positively to Paul's message and would therefore stay with him, to Gentiles.[60] Third, although not all the evidence has been considered, it appears that Luke uses the terms *phoboumenoi* and *sebomenoi,* on the one hand, and *prosēlytoi,* on the other, almost synonymously (cf. 13:16, 26, 43, 50). Even if *tōn sebomenōn prosēlytōn* is peculiar, one has to admit that the two terms are so closely connected that Luke seems unconcerned with any distinction.[61] Here, then, we learn that the "God-fearer" is a Gentile who has apparently sympathized with Judaism—to some degree. Put differently, it appears that Luke, at least, classes the "God-fearer" as a quasi-official sympathizer.

According to Luke, in both Thessalonica and Athens, Paul preached to Jews and "God-fearers" (17:4, 17). Acts 17:4 speaks directly of non-Jewish origin (*tōn sebomenōn Hellēnōn*),[62] whereas 17:17 is slightly ambiguous (*tois sebomenois*), though the article is probably anaphoric. This evidence clearly suggests that "God-fearers" are Gentiles who participate in synagogue services (17:2–4, 17).

The final piece of evidence in Acts is found in 18:7 where Titius Justus, whose home was annexed to the synagogue, is described as "a worshiper of God" (*sebomenos ton theon*). Paul's statement of 18:6 lends support to the gentile origin of Titius, and the name probably (although not necessarily) does the same. The same result emerges: "God-fearer" was used by Luke for a Gentile who participates in Judaism.

What can we say, then, about the "God-fearer" in Acts, whether historically accurate or not? First, we ought to note that the "God-fearer" is viewed positively because he (or she) is marked by Jewish piety, whether described with the term *phoboumenoi* or *sebomenoi*. Second, the terms can refer to Gentiles and, when the term designates a Gentile, it marks him or her off from the rest of the gentile world. Third, the "God-fearer" is a Gentile who participates in Judaism, in such aspects as almsgiving and synagogue services. Fourth, the presence of "God-fearers" in Judaism may indicate some form of missionary activity on the part of Jews but what kind and to what extent are impossible to tell. Fifth, Luke seems to indicate that the "God-fearer" is to be classed within the broader class of "proselytes." In other words, for Luke a "God-fearer" is a sympathizer or a kind of proselyte. I suggest that for Luke there were two kinds of proselytes: full converts and "God-fearers." Finally, there is no information on how these Gentiles were attracted to Judaism. In fact, "God-fearer" evidence in general ought not to be used as evidence for Jewish missionary activity. Evidence for God-fearers, or sympathizers, even if abundant, can be explained in various ways. But circumstantial evidence does not encourage us to explain their existence (or number) as the result of missionary activity.

Our conclusion on the rather "fixed" definition of "God-fearer" as a pious Gentile who is also a fringe member of Jewish society, even if the term occasionally is used for a Jew, is implicit in many ancient texts but has been partly confirmed by a recent inscription found on stele that dates to *ca.* A.D. 210 in Aphrodisias.[63] In a list of subscribers to a Jewish institution,[64] there are three who are proselytes (*a.* ll. 13, 17, 22) and two who are "God-fearers" (*theoseb[ēs]*; ll. 19–20). On face *b.*, there is a list of fifty-four Jews and then, after a break, a list of fifty "God-fearers" (*kai hosoi theosebis;* ll. 34ff.), whose names are either Greek or Greco-Roman, which clearly suggests a gentile origin. Here, then, is clear evidence that in Aphrodisias, in the second-third century A.D., there were clear social distinctions between Jews, proselytes, and "God-fearers," and the last group is associated in some official way with Judaism. Although neither is this evidence from the first century, nor is there evidence as unambiguous as this anywhere else,[65] nor is the *degree* of their participation clear,[66] the clarity of this inscription for separating Jews, Gentiles, and God-fearers lends considerable weight to the Lukan presentation and suggests that the "God-fearers" were a socially distinct group in their relationship to Judaism. In my view, this inscription takes several strides toward settling the debate about the "God-fearer": the "God-fearer" is a Gentile who participates in Judaism without having become a convert;[67] however, this evidence says nothing about Jewish missionary activity.[68]

This interpretation of the evidence is further strengthened by some other Greco-Roman evidence about those who sympathize, in various ways, with Judaism. The most important text in this regard is Juvenal *Satires* 14.96–106. Juvenal remarks that some children have fathers who "revere the Sabbath" (*metuentem sabbata*)[69] and that these children end up worshiping "nothing but the clouds, and the divinity of the heavens" (14.96–97). Scornfully, Juvenal comments that these also adopt the Jewish customs pertaining to eating pork (14.98–99). Eventually, he argues, they are circumcised (*praeputia ponunt*)(14.99) and learn to practice the Jewish law (14.100–103). For his part, Juvenal puts the blame for this "progressive conversion" on the shoulders of the father "who gave up every seventh day to idleness" (14.105–6). Two points may be made: (1) Here is sufficient evidence that there were Gentiles who became attached to Judaism, who did not convert the whole way but were given a particular social status (*metuentem sabbata;* 14:96). (2) What is often not observed from this context is the secretiveness of the convert. Lines 103–4 assert that this gentile convert, having learned to obey the Jewish law, refuses "to point out the way to any not worshipping the same rites, and conducting none but the circumcised to the desired fountain." In the very text that scholars use to point to the widespread nature of Jewish missionary activity, there is pointed evidence in the opposite direction. The initiative is seen here on the part of the Gentile, not on the part of some Jewish proselytizer. At any rate, this text sheds some light on the "God-fearer" question and is most likely to be seen as evidence for a gentile unofficial, but nonetheless, association with Judaism.[70]

We can say confidently, then, that during Second Temple Judaism there was a distinguishable group (however sharply we may distinguish them) in different Jewish communities for Gentiles who had taken one or more steps toward Judaism and were therefore different from the "ordinary pagan." To say that they were officially called "God-fearers" appears to be the case for only a small portion of the evidence, but the category exists whether the term is technical or not. However, the evidence does not permit us to say anything about Jewish missionary activity.

Missionary Activity

Synagogue Activity

We can safely infer from Acts, the practice of Paul, and the evidence found in Jewish literature that the synagogue often functioned as a place for public address and for the public propagation of a variety of ideas within Judaism.[71] Paul, then, seemed to have been exploiting a normal practice in making the synagogue a platform for expounding messianic Judaism. Consequently, it was probably the content of what he proclaimed rather than his practice that generated such stiff opposition. It does appear that Gentiles attended the synagogue services, and the odd Jewish visitor seems to have been afforded an opportunity to give a "word of consolation"—if that visitor felt constrained to do so (Acts 13:15).[72]

From Paul's practice we can infer that early Christians took advantage of what may have been a custom: the invitation of a Jewish visitor to address the congregation. We know also that Paul piqued the interest of, and successfully evangelized, at least God-fearing Gentiles through his messages. However, there is insufficient evidence in Acts to infer that what Paul did as an evangelist was common among Jews or that Jews regularly evangelized unevangelized Gentiles through synagogues. It can be safely inferred, as so many have done, that early Christianity depended in large measure on the synagogue for its remarkable growth.[73] But the inference that what Christians did is what Jews were doing—namely, evangelize Gentiles—is not possible to document.

Public Missionary Activity

If one accepts the record of Acts pertaining to Paul's Areopagus address (17:22–34), one can infer that Paul (and perhaps other Christians and Jews) engaged in public debate over theological tenets. Jewish ability in debate and persuasion was probably not uncommon (see, e.g., Josephus *Ant.* 13.406). Apollos publicly debated Jews in Achaia (18:28), but Acts does not record sufficient information for us to know that Jews regularly engaged in public debate or that orators were involved in sophisticated verbal apologetic for the purpose of evangelism. The evidence is simply too scanty for us to make historical inferences about the nature of Jewish missionary activity.

Summary of Results for Acts

It is safe to conclude, first of all, that Gentiles were converting to Judaism and that such conversion took place throughout the Roman Empire. The presence of "proselytes/God-fearers" indicates quite clearly that conversions were taking place. Second, Jews regularly permitted Gentiles to participate in their religious ceremonies and institutions — such as synagogue services and almsgiving. Third, if we make any conclusion regarding the missionary activity of Jews I suggest that it appears to be along the lines of instructing inquirers rather than evangelizing Gentiles. At the least, there is no direct evidence from Acts that Jews were involved in proselytizing Gentiles.

Conclusions

In summarizing the data from the New Testament pertaining to Jewish missionary activity I observe that we are dealing with authors who, in varying degrees, perceived Judaism as either a former religion or the enemy of the truth. Although Paul loved his fellow Jews (Rom. 9:1-5), he did not spare any words regarding their final destiny if they chose not to heed his message regarding Jesus as the Messiah. Having stated this, however, I find that the New Testament does not intentionally skew the evidence against the Jews with regard to missionary activity. In fact, we find a remarkable similarity between the evidence of the New Testament, incidental though it is, and the portrait we have drawn from the Jewish sources.

First, at least some Jews had a clear consciousness of a mission to the world. Although this idea is found here and there in Judaism and occasionally in the New Testament, it is not a common, consistent theme of the literature and ought not to be regarded as a fixed element of Jewish consciousness. Second, Jews did attract Gentiles to Judaism and Gentiles did convert to Judaism. The New Testament does not betray how Jews attracted Gentiles, but we can safely infer that it was through the kinds of activity found in Jewish literature: a general openness to others, good deeds, instructions about Judaism in the synagogue, and perhaps literature and marriage. Third, in conformity to our previous conclusions, I find no trace of a widespread practice of missionary activity among Gentiles by Jews in Acts.

Conclusions

OUR TASK HAS BEEN to describe the nature and extent of Jewish missionary activity during the Second Temple period. Admittedly, a major impulse for this study is the desire to understand the origins of the aggressive missionary behavior of earliest Christianity even though such an attempt is not to be made here. Having described the former movement, we now wish to draw two of the more important threads together.

It has been shown that Jews were not isolationist in their attitudes and relations with Gentiles. In fact, just the opposite was the case: Jews were integrally related to the non-Jewish society in which they were living. Owing largely to the prophets, many Jewish thinkers began to perceive the world as a unity and consequently developed a sense of universalistic religious outlook. If God was the creator of the world and if he had revealed his truth to Israel, then it was the truth also for the whole world, even if Israel was the custodian and tradent of that revelation. Furthermore, even if many Jewish authors expressed themselves in nationalistic, and even condemnatory, terms regarding other nations and paganism in general, those expressions of thought are more accurately described as religious convictions in social dress. We cannot dismiss the fact that Judaism never condoned immorality and polytheism, but its resistance is grounded in its faith. In fact, the evidence almost universally speaks of a general friendliness of Jews to non-Jews and a willingness to be flexible, if that adaptation did not force them to deny their God, their law, and their nation. This adaptability of the Jews is perhaps most visibly seen in permitting Gentiles to participate in their religious activities and to attend their religious gatherings. Finally, Jews joined themselves to gentile society through citizenry, education, and even intermarriage. Such a penetration of gentile society, which became proverbial for both Philo and Josephus, did have its dangers. Some Jews carried integration to the point of apostasy, but that merely illustrates the fact of Jewish enculturation.

This permeation of gentile society raises the crucial issue of how it was that Jews related to that society with respect to conversion. It is the conclusion of this work that Judaism never developed a clear mission

116

to the Gentiles that had as its goal the conversion of the world. Further, although there may have been a few "evangelists" scattered throughout Jewish history, and although Jewish missionary activity may have existed at times in Rome, there is no evidence that could lead to the conclusion that Judaism was a "missionary religion" in the sense of aggressive attempts to convert Gentiles or in the sense of self-identity. However, this does not mean that Judaism was characterized by a general isolation or an esotericism, except in marginal cases. The evidence clearly points to a serious openness by Judaism to Gentiles to participate in Judaism at the level desired by individual Gentiles. There is evidence that Gentiles converted to Judaism through a variety of means, especially through the good deeds of Jews, and there remained the hope of God's decisive apocalyptic intervention at the end of history. Although there is some evidence for conversion through literature and missionaries, the predominant means of conversion appear to have been the life of individual Jewish citizens. The behavior of Jonah, then, appears to have been typical. In other words, it is my contention, contrary to a great deal of Christian and Jewish scholarship today, that Judaism was not truly a "missionary religion" except in the most general of definitions of missionary. Rather, the evidence adduced above leads to the conclusion that Judaism was a light among the nations—a "light" because Judaism was fully assured that truth was on its side; "among the nations" because Jews were thoroughly woven into the fabric of the Roman world.

Abbreviations

AB	Anchor Bible
AGAJU = AGJU	Arbeiten zur Geschichte des antiken Judentums und des Urchristentums
AJSRev	*Association of Jewish Studies Review*
AJTh = AJT	*American Journal of Theology*
ALGHJ	Arbeiten zur Literatur und Geschichte des hellenistischen Judentums
ALUOS	*Annual of Leeds University Oriental Society*
AnBib	Analecta biblica
AnnRev of Soc	*Annual Review of Sociology*
ANRW	*Aufstieg und Niedergang der römischen Welt*
APOT	R. H. Charles, ed. *The Apocrypha and Pseudepigrapha of the Old Testament* 2 vols. Oxford: Clarendon, 1913.
ARW	*Archiv für Religionswissenschaft*
ASTI	*Annual of the Swedish Theological Institute*
ATANT	Abhandlungen zur Theologie des Alten und Neuen Testaments
BA	*Biblical Archaeologist*
BAR	*Biblical Archaeologist Review*
BASORS	Bulletin of the American Schools of Oriental Research, Supplement
BEvT	Beiträge zur evangelischen Theologie
BFCT	Beiträge zur Förderung christlicher Theologie
BHT	Beiträge zur historischen Theologie
BJRLUM	*Bulletin of the John Rylands University Library of Manchester*
BJS	Brown Judaic Studies
BSNTS	*Bulletin of the Society of New Testament Studies*
BTB	*Biblical Theology Bulletin*
BTH	Bibliothèque de Théologie Historique
BZ	*Biblische Zeitschrift*
CAH	*Cambridge Ancient History*
CBQ	*Catholic Biblical Quarterly*
CIJ	*Corupus inscriptionum judaicarum*
ConBNTS	Coniectanea Biblica, New Testament Series

ConsJud	Conservative Judaism
CPJ	V. Tcherikover, A. Fuks, eds. *Corpus Papyrorum Judaicarum.* 3 vols. Cambridge, Mass.: Harvard University Press, 1957–64.
CPSSV	Cambridge Philological Society, Supplementary Volume
CUASCA	Catholic University of America Studies in Christian Antiquity
DB	*Dictionnaire de la Bible*
DBSup	*Dictionnaire de la Bible, Supplément*
EJMI	R. A. Kraft, G. W. E. Nickelsburg, eds. *Early Judaism and Its Modern Interpreters.* Philadelphia: Fortress, 1986.
EncPhil	*Encyclopedia of Philosophy*
EvT	*Evangelische Theologie*
ExpTim	*Expository Times*
FFNT	Foundations and Facets: New Testament
FRLANT	Forschungen zur Religion und Literatur des Alten und Neuen Testaments
FzB	Forschungen zur Bibel
GRBS	*Greek, Roman, and Byzantine Studies*
HAR	*Hebrew Annual Review*
HNT	Handbuch zum Neuen Testament
HNTC	Harper's New Testament Commentaries
HSS	Harvard Semitic Studies
HTKNT	Herders Theologischer Kommentar zum Neuen Testament
HTR	*Harvard Theological Review*
HUCA	*Hebrew Union College Annual*
HUCAS	Hebrew Union College Annual, Supplement
ICC	International Critical Commentary
IDB	G. A. Buttrick, ed. *Interpreter's Dictionary of the Bible.* Nashville: Abingdon, 1962.
IEJ	*Israel Exploration Journal*
JAC	*Jahrbuch für Antike und Christentum*
JBL	*Journal of Biblical Literature*
JES	*Journal of Ecumenical Studies*
JHUSE	Johns Hopkins University Studies in Education
JJS	*Journal of Jewish Studies*
JPT	*Jahrbücher für Protestantische Theologie*

JQR	*Jewish Quarterly Review*
JR	*Journal of Religion*
JRS	*Journal of Roman Studies*
JSJ	*Journal for the Study of Judaism in the Persian, Hellenistic and Roman Period*
JSNT	*Journal for the Study of the New Testament*
JSP	*Journal for the Study of the Pseudepigrapha*
JSSR	*Journal for the Scientific Study of Religion*
JTS	*Journal of Theological Studies*
LCL	Loeb Classical Library
LEC	Library of Early Christianity
MBT	Münster Beiträge zur Theologie
MGWJ	*Monatschrift für Geschichte und Wissenschaft des Judentums*
MHUC	Monographs of the Hebrew Union College
MNTC	Moffatt New Testament Commentary
MUS	*Münchener Universitäts-Schriften*
Mus.Helv.	*Museum Helveticum*
NedTTs	*Nederlands theologisch tijdschrift*
NewDocs	G. H. R. Horsely, ed. *New Documents Illustrating Early Christianity.* 3+vols. North Ryde, N. S. W.: Macquarie University Press, 1981-(=editing of MS finds of 1976-).
NIDNTT	C. Brown, ed. *New International Dictionary of New Testament Theology.* 3 vols. Grand Rapids: Zondervan, 1975-1978.
NISBE	G. W. Bromiley, ed. *International Standard Bible Encyclopedia,* new edition. 4 vols. Grand Rapids: Eerdmans, 1979-1988.
NJB	New Jerusalem Bible
NovT	*Novum Testamentum*
NTL	New Testament Library
NTS	*New Testament Studies*
OBT	Overtures to Biblical Theology
OCD	*Oxford Classical Dictionary*
OLZ	*Orientalische Literaturzeitung*
OTP	J. H. Charlesworth, ed. *Old Testament Pseudepigrapha.* 2 vols. Garden City, N.Y.: Doubleday, 1983-1985.
PEQ	*Palestine Exploration Quarterly*
PTMS	Pittsburgh Theological Monograph Series
QD	Quaestiones disputatae

RAC	*Reallexikon für Antike und Christentum*
RB	*Revue biblique*
REJ	*Revue des études juives*
RelSRev	*Religious Studies Review*
RelStuTheol	*Religious Studies and Theology*
RevQ	*Revue de Qumran*
RHPhR	*Revue d'histoire et de philosophie religieuses*
RSV	Revised Standard Version
SB	H. Strack, P. Billerbeck, eds. *Kommentar zum Neuen Testament aus Talmud und Midrasch.* 6 vols. München: C. H. Beck'sche, 1922–1961.
SBLDS	Society of Biblical Literature Dissertation Series
SBLSCS	Society of Biblical Literature Septuagint and Cognate Studies
SBLMS	Society of Biblical Literature Monograph Series
SBT	Studies in Biblical Theology
SecCen	*Second Century*
SHR	Studies in the History of Religions
SJLA	Studies in Judaism in Late Antiquity
SNTSMS	Society for New Testament Studies Monograph Series
SPB	Studia postbiblica
SSS	Semitic Study Series
ST	*Studia theologica*
StPhilonica	*Studia Philonica*
SUNT	Studien zur Umwelt des Neuen Testaments
SVTP	Studia in Veteris Testamenti pseudepigrapha
TAPA	*Transactions of the American Philological Association*
TBl	*Theologische Blätter*
TDNT	G. Kittel, G. Friedrich, eds. *Theological Dictionary of the New Testament.* 10 vols. Grand Rapids: Eerdmans, 1964–1976.
TDOT	G. J. Botterweck, H. Ringgren, eds. *Theological Dictionary of the Old Testament.* 5 vols. Grand Rapids: Eerdmans, 1974–.
TF	*Theologische Forschung*
THK	Theologischer Handkommentar zum Neuen Testament
TLZ	*Theologische Literaturzeitung*
TQ	*Theologische Quartalschrift*
TSK	*Theologische Studien und Kritiken*
TWNT	G. Kittel, G. Friedrich, eds. *Theologische Wörterbuch zum Neuen Testament.* 9 vols. Stuttgart: W. Kohlhammer, 1933–1973.
TZ	*Theologische Zeitschrift*

UNDCSJCA	University of Notre Dame Center for the Study of Judaism and Christianity in Antiquity
VC	*Vigiliae christianae*
WBC	Word Biblical Commentary
WUNT	Wissenschaftliche Untersuchungen zum Neuen Testament
ZAW	*Zeitschrift für die alttestamentliche Wissenschaft*
ZMR	*Zeitschrift für Missionskunde und Religionswissenschaft*
ZNW	*Zeitschrift für die neutestamentliche Wissenschaft*
ZRGG	*Zeitschrift für Religions- und Geistesgeschichte*
ZST	*Zeitschrift für systematische Theologie*
ZTK	*Zeitschrift für Theologie und Kirche*

Qumran Documents

CD	Cairo (Genizah text of the) Damascus Document
1QH	Thanksgiving Hymns (1Q=cave one)
1QM	War Scroll
1QpHab	Pesher on Habakkuk
1QS	Manual of Discipline
1QSa	Appendix one to Manual of Discipline
4QFlor	Florilegium (4Q=cave four)
11QTemple	Temple Scroll (11Q=cave eleven)

Notes

Complete bibliographical data for each entry may be found in the bibliography.

Introduction

1. Schürer, *History* 3.1: 150; this statement is written by the reviser, Fergus Millar, and expresses his view of the late 1980s.

2. Georgi, *Opponents*, 84.

3. Kuhn, "*prosēlytos*," *TWNT* 6:731, 1.5; see also Kuhn and Stegemann, "Proselyten," col. 1259. This seems to be the view also of Simon, "Débuts."

4. Georgi, *Opponents*, 175 n. 1.

5. G. F. Moore, *Judaism* 1:323-24. Moore qualifies this statement by distinguishing the manner of Jewish missions from that of earliest Christianity.

6. J. Jeremias, *Jesus' Promise*, 11, 12, 17; see also Oepke, "Internationalismus."

7. J. Jeremias, *Jesus' Promise*, 55-73; cf. Sanders, *Jesus*, 213.

8. For a useful survey of the literature, see Vande Kappelle, "Evidence," 4-20; see also the various comments of this cross section of scholars: Collins, *Between*; Schoeps, *Paul*, 220, 228; Rosenbloom, *Conversion*, 37-39; Lerle, *Proselytenwerbung*, 9-23, 63; Bousset, *Religion*, 80.

9. Kraabel, "Roman Diaspora," 451.

10. In private conversation I have learned that Dr. A.-J. Levine of Swarthmore College is presently working on a book on Jewish missionary activity (forthcoming from Edwin Mellen Press). I anticipate that our conclusions will converge at several points. See also Kraabel, "Roman Diaspora," 451-52.

11. On "missionary religion," unfortunately rarely defined by scholarship, see Hahn, *Mission*, esp. 18-25 (German 12-18), which is too Christian; and Vande Kappelle, "Evidence," 20-25, emphasizing "centrifugal" and "centripetal" categories. Classic treatments, e.g., those of Moore, Nock, and Schürer, did not define these terms.

12. On "conversion," see Nock, *Conversion*, 7; S. J. D. Cohen, "Conversion"; idem, "Respect," 410-12; idem, "Crossing the Boundary," 26, 31; Segal, "Costs"; Gaventa, *Darkness*, esp. 1-16; from the angle of sociology, see esp. Rambo, "Current Research"; Snow and Machalek, "Sociology"; idem, "Convert"; Staples and Mauss, "Conversion."

13. Nock, *Conversion*, 13.

14. Ibid., 14-16; the quotation is from p. 16. On this latter point, Nock has found agreement in S. J. D. Cohen ("Conversion," 32), but R. MacMullen has correctly pointed out that conversion does not take place in the cults because

conversion is not the appropriate response ("Conversion," 75). A. F. Segal sees Nock's view here as too "stereotypic," too Pauline, and too "first generation" ("Costs," 336–37).

15. S. J. D. Cohen, "Respect," 410. Cohen has authored some careful studies of conversion; see further "Conversion" and, most recently, "Crossing the Boundary."

16. Snow and Machalek, "Sociology"; "Convert."

17. Snow and Machalek, "Sociology," 170.

18. Staples and Mauss, "Conversion," 146.

19. Gaventa, *Darkness;* Segal, "Costs."

20. Gaventa, *Darkness*, 3.

21. Ibid., 12.

22. I do not mean to suggest that conversion requires theological sophistication; however, true conversion involves at least some form of mental shift (say, from nonmonotheism to monotheism).

23. On the variety of conversion perspectives, see esp. Segal, "Costs."

24. Compare, for instance, the various dates assigned to the pseudepigraphical documents published in J. H. Charlesworth, ed., *OTP.*

25. One of the most active areas of research today concerns the diversity of Judaism. See G. F. Moore, "Normative Judaism"; Neusner, "'Judaism' after Moore"; McEleney, "Orthodoxy"; idem, "Replies"; Aune, "Orthodoxy"; Grabbe, "Orthodoxy"; Baumbach, "Volk Gottes"; Blenkinsopp, "Interpretation"; Dexinger, "Sektenproblematik"; Smith, "Palestinian Judaism"; Schiffman, "Jewish Sectarianism"; Porton, "Diversity"; Collins, *Between;* see also the numerous studies of A. T. Kraabel listed in the bibliography. This discussion has been extended fruitfully into New Testament research by J. D. G. Dunn, *Unity;* cf. earlier Moule, *Birth,* 201–34.

26. To avoid encumbrance of expression, I use "Judaism" for the religion as a whole. I am aware of the "particularism of reality," namely, that Judaism expressed itself in (or is encompassed by) a multiplication of various forms. Judaism may, however, stand for a "diverse number of groups with a reasonably harmonious picture"; see Kraabel, "Social Systems."

27. I believe that the Tannaim are the products of the development of first-century Pharisaism; see Neusner, *Rabbinic Traditions* 3:5–100; idem, *Politics,* 7–11; Schürer, *History* 2:391–403, 467 n. 21. I am of the suspicion that first-century Pharisaism, as criticized by Jesus, was dominated by Shammaites and that, after the Great War, Hillelites gained the ascendancy. This means that the rabbinic writings reflect only indirectly the kind of Judaism Jesus faced. When one reads the debates between the schools of Hillel and Shammai, one finds in the Shammaite view a clearer picture of what Jesus was combatting.

28. On the attributions, see Neusner, *Rabbinic Traditions* 3:3, 89–100, 180–238 (esp. 180–85). He sees Ushan attributions as extremely reliable; post-70 Jamnia authorities are to be taken seriously, but pre-70 attributions are less reliable. The following statement relieves some skeptical pressure: "The legal materials attributed by later rabbis to the Pharisees are *thematically* congruent

to the . . . Gospels, and I take them to be accurate in *substance,* if not in *detail,* as representations of the *main* issues of Pharisaic law" (*Idea of Purity,* 65). In my view, this contrasts with his heavier skepticism in *Rabbinic Traditions* and *Politics.*

29. For concise summaries of these masters, see Schürer, *History* 2:356–80; G. F. Moore, "Normative Judaism," 365–73; 1–38.

Chapter 1

1. On tendentiousness in recent studies of Judaism, see Sanders, *Paul and Palestinian Judaism,* 1–24, 33–75; Neusner, "Moore to Urbach" (who also turns on Sanders).

2. On Judaism and the Gentiles, including Hellenism, see Hengel, *Judaism and Hellenism;* Schürer, *History* 2:29–80, 81–84, 309–13; 3.1: 1–176; Tcherikover, *Hellenistic Civilization;* Gilbert, "Hellenization"; Momigliano, *Alien Wisdom;* Goodenough, *Jewish Symbols;* Smith, "Image of God"; Freyne, *Galilee;* Collins, *Between;* S. J. D. Cohen, *Maccabees to Mishnah,* 27–59; Porton, *GOYIM.* An important but neglected voice in this discussion is that of D. Flusser ("Paganism"). The traditional view that Jews gradually withdrew from social intercourse with Gentiles is, gladly, no longer seriously entertained; see for the traditional view Axenfeld, "Propaganda," 59–69; SB does not help either (1:926–31); see also Derwacter, *Preparing,* 138–52. A most insightful scholar in this regard is Kraabel; among his many works, see especially "Paganism." From a more sociologically sensitive angle, see Rajak, "Jews and Christians."

A preliminary glimpse of the impact of our revised understanding of Judaism on the study of early Christianity may be seen in Meyers and White, "Jews and Christians"; van der Horst, "Aphrodisias."

On the effects of self-consciousness, historical circumstances, and individual vision, see Rosenbloom, *Conversion.* Compare, for example, the Qumran community's self-conscious conviction to be the elect, true people of God with other Israelites and also with the gentile world. This consciousness apparently was a factor leading to separation from, and condemnation of, the world (1QSa 1:1–3). Various elements of this discussion can be found in Steiner, "Warum?"; Priest, "Mebaqqer"; Schubert, *Community,* 28–29; Baumbach, "Volk Gottes," 39–40; Neusner, "Time of Crisis," 317–19; Urbach, "Self-Isolation," 273–74; Sanders, *Paul and Palestinian Judaism,* 244–50; Wernberg-Møller, "YAHAD," 71.

3. Hengel, *Hellenism* and *Jews, Greeks and Barbarians.* It ought, however, to be remembered that Hengel's work does not attempt to examine the evidence of the first century A.D. Therefore, his study should not be cited for evidence of Hellenization at the time of Jesus. The resistance movements, which he details, may have played a larger role in the first century than they did in 150 B.C. However, I do not want to suggest that first-century Judaism somehow was immune to Hellenism, because this would certainly be false. New Testament scholarship does need a study that demonstrates the influence of

Hellenism on Jewish culture, religion, and life in Palestine for the first century A.D. See the important reminder of Flusser, "Paganism."

4. See Collins, *Between*, 8-10.

5. Heinemann, *Die griechische Weltanschauung*, 3 *et passim*.

6. Schmidt, "Israel's Stellung."

7. See, e.g., Bertholet, *Stellung*, 91-122; G. F. Moore, *Judaism* 1:219-34; Hempel, "Wurzeln"; Schürer, *History* 3.1: 159-60; Rosenbloom, *Conversion*, 28-31; Vande Kappelle, "Evidence," 26-52.

8. See here the recent study of Senior and Stuhlmueller (*Foundations*, 83-138).

9. In *Spec.* 1.172, *physis* is the actor; see here Koester, "ΝΟΜΟΣ."

10. This is significant redaction of Gen. 43:29, based perhaps on "be gracious." For Josephus's monotheism, see Montgomery, "Religion," 284-87; Schlatter, *Wie Sprach Josephus*, 68; Georgi, *Opponents*, 120-22.

11. For the secondary nature of this account, see S. Kanter, *Rabban Gamaliel*, 213-15; Graetz, "Proselyten," 23.

12. On Sardis, see esp. Hanfmann and Mierse, *Sardis*; the charts and pictures of Hanfmann will be assumed in what follows. See also Kraabel, "Diaspora Synagogue," 483-88; idem, "Impact"; idem, "Paganism"; Trebilco, "Studies," 28-50, 188-204, 205-34. Some of the inscriptions can be seen in Lifshitz, *Donateurs*, 24-30 (nos. 17-27). The evidence from Aphrodisias is perhaps quite similar in implication for integration; see, e.g., Reynolds and Tannenbaum, *Jews*; van der Horst, "Aphrodisias."

The "place" (*topos*) of the decrees cited by Josephus (*Ant.* 14.235, 259-61) refers most likely to the community center that precedes the ruins now pieced together; see Kraabel, "Paganism," 16-18.

13. It ought not to be assumed, without strong evidence, that this kind of evidence for integration is equivalent to apostasy or "caving in" under the pressure of non-Jewish forces. Jews lived among Gentiles and expressed themselves in a variety of ways, most of which were not religious. See Kraabel, "Diaspora Synagogue," 502.

14. See Applebaum, "Legal Status," 448-49.

15. Kraabel, "Diaspora Synagogue," 487-88.

16. See esp. Kraabel, "Paganism," 19-25. The most notable feature is the "Eagle Table"; see Hanfmann, *Sardis*, figs. 256, 257.

17. Trebilco suggests that the building was designed to attract non-Gentiles. He infers this from the architecture and inscriptions that bear the name "God-fearer" ("Studies," 45-46). That the synagogue was "attractive" is not doubted; that the intention of its architects was to attract is unproved (and probably unprovable).

18. See Lifshitz, *Donateurs*, no. 19; see also the discussion in Trebilco, "Studies," 37-38.

19. See Trebilco, "Studies," 38; for further discussion of similar kinds of evidence, see 38-47; Kraabel, "Paganism," 22-23.

20. Trebilco, "Studies," 39-41; see also the evidence from Aphrodisias.

21. Again, see Trebilco, "Studies," 110–35, for a survey of the evidence and scholarship.

22. Rabello, "L'observance"; Schürer, *History* 2:309–13; Delling, "Heidnische Religionen," 267; Bickermann, "Altars"; Hoenig, "Oil," 71-72. See now S. J. D. Cohen, "Respect for Judaism"; idem, "Crossing the Boundary"; Porton, *GOYIM,* 259–68. See also the various inscriptions in Liftshitz, *Donateurs.*

23. In Josephus, see further *J.W.* 4.324; 5.17–18; *Ant.* 8.116–17 (adding to 1 Kings 8:41–43); 11.84–87; 17.237. Tertullian notes that Gentiles observed some Jewish customs while they also retained the worship of pagan gods (*Ad. Nat.* 1.13.3–4). See also Tacitus *Histories* 5.5: "The most degraded out of other races, scorning their national beliefs, brought to them [the Jews] their contributions and presents." See also S. J. D. Cohen, "Respect," 412–15.

24. See Stern, *GLAJJ* 1:361–63; see also Hecataeus in Diodorus *Bibl. Hist.* 40.3.6; Ocellus Lucanus *De Univ. Nat.* 45–46; Josephus *Ag. Ap.* 2.282; Tibullus, *Carmina* 1.3.18; Horace *Sermones* 1.9.68–72 ("sum paulo infirmior, unus multorum" is significant in that it implies scruples in this matter); Ovid *Rem. Am.* 219–20; Seneca *De Superst.* in Augustine *Civ. Dei* 6.11; Seneca *Ep. Mor.* 95.47; Persius *Saturae* 5.180–84; Plutarch *De Sup.* 3; Josephus *Ant.* 3.214–15; 16.43–44; *m. Šabb.* 2:6–7.

25. See Goldenberg, "Jewish Sabbath."

26. See S. J. D. Cohen, "Crossing the Boundary."

27. The literature on citizenship is extensive; see Stern, *GLAJJ* 1:399–403; Schürer, *History* 3.1: 107–37; Smallwood, *Jews,* 120–43, 220–55; Tcherikover, "Decline"; Bell, *Jews,* 10–21; Applebaum, "Legal Status"; Jones, "Claudius"; Feldman, "Orthodoxy"; Wolfson, "Jewish Citizenship," 165–68; Trebilco, "Studies," 9–27.

On *politeuma,* see Ruppel, "*Politeuma*"; Fischer, "Beziehungen."

28. On this treaty, see Wirgin ("Judah Maccabee's Embassy"), who comments on the economic side of the arrangement; Giovannini and Müller, "Beziehungen"; Timpe, "Vertrag"; Smith, "Rome and the Maccabean Conversions." This treaty did not withstand the test of time; see Ginsburg, "Fiscus Judaicus."

29. See Ginsburg, "Sparta and Judaea"; B. Cardauns, "Juden und Spartaner." These scholars debate the reliability of Josephus's report about Sparta, though both agree that there was some relationship.

30. See Wirgin, "Simon Maccabaeus' Embassy."

31. See Horsely, "Name Change as an Indication of Religious Conversion in Antiquity," *Numen* 34 (1987) 1–17, esp. 2–3; see also his *NewDocs* (1976) 92–93 (no. 55).

32. Schürer, *History* 2:415–63; Drazin, *Education*; Barclay, *Educational Ideals*; Ferguson, *Backgrounds,* 83–87. On the scholars, see Hengel, *Judaism* 1:65–102; Schürer, *History* 2:48–52; Bickermann, "Historical Foundations," 110–12; Culpepper, *NISBE* 2:21–27.

33. See esp. Mendelson, *Secular Education*; Schürer, *History* 2:415–63; Drazin, *Education,* 11–27; Drummond, *Philo* 1:260–63; Goodenough, *By Light,* 91–94; see also Laporte, "Wisdom Literature."

34. He sent Alexander and Aristobulus to Rome to have a "princely education" (*presbytatous basilikōs* [*J.W.* 1.435; *Ant.* 16.6]). See also Wacholder, "Greek Authors." On Herod's relationship with Roman power, see Bammel, "Rechtsstellung"; Schürer, *History* 1:287–329; see also Josephus *Ant.* 16.445, 623.

35. In the latter reference we discover that Archelaus was educated in Rome at the feet of a Jew.

36. De Vaux, *Ancient Israel*, 31; S. J. D. Cohen, "Matrilineal Principle"; Kittel ("Konnubium"), who concludes that the first century A.D. was a time of "Vermischungsprozess." In spite of its sponsorship under Hitler, the article needs to be read. For the rabbinic evidence, see SB 4:378–83.

37. See Kittel, "Konnubium," 40–41, 48, and the Septuagint at Esther 4:17u. On Josephus's presentation of Esther, see Feldman, "Hellenizations." On Herod, see Cook, et al., *CAH* 10: *The Augustan Empire*, 316–39; Schürer, *History* 1:287–329.

38. Gressmann, "Jüdische Mission," 173; Lerle, *Proselytenwerbung*, 43–51; SB 4.1: 31, 33–34.

39. See Dalbert, *Theologie*, 70–92; D. Winston, *The Wisdom of Solomon: A New Translation with Introduction and Commentary*, Anchor Bible 43 (Garden City, N.Y.: Doubleday, 1979), 271–74; Reese, *Hellenistic Influence*, 25–30, 154–62; Goodrick, *The Book of Wisdom* (London: Rivingtons, 1913), 404–11.

40. See also Pseudo-Phocylides 11.11, 18, 27, 39, 45, 128; see also van der Horst, *Sentences*, 81–83, 139–40.

41. See Trebilco ("Studies," 135–53), who counters the theory of F. Cumont, who saw in this title evidence for syncretism. See also Kraabel, "Hypsistos."

42. Tcherikover, "Decline," 22.

43. Ferguson, *Backgrounds*, 381; see also Schürer, *History* 3.2: 813–14, 871–80.

43. I have seen no separate study on this in Philo. See Vlastos, "*Anamnesis*"; Bartels, "Remember," *NIDNTT* 3:230–34; G. Ryle, "Plato," *EncPhil* 6:314–33, esp. 325–26.

45. See esp. H. A. Harris, *Greek Athletics*, 51–56; see also Schürer, *History* 2:44–48; 3.2: 819 n. 27; Tcherikover, *CPJ* 1:39 n. 99.

46. H. A. Harris, *Greek Athletics*, 13; interestingly, Harris wrote this book after a previous comprehensive account of Greek athletics in which treatment he neglected Jewish authors because of what he supposed was a wholesale antipathy to athletics. Observe that Harris infers that physical education was an essential feature of Jewish education; see *Spec.* 2.229–30 (*Greek Athletics*, 91–95). Although Harris notes the positive emphases in Philo, he does not appear to have observed the more negative comments found in *Abr.* 48; *Agr.* 116; *Praem.* 52.

47. Harris, *Greek Athletics*, 51.

48. See esp. Douglas, *Purity and Danger*.

49. See Feldman, "Orthodoxy," 227–28; Wolfson, *Philo* 2:73–78.

50. Jewish abstemiousness about pork was a constant jibe against Jews; see Erotianus *Voc. Hip. Collc. Frg.* F33 (Stern, *GLAJJ* 1: n. 196); Plutarch *Quest. Conv.* 4:4.4–5.3.

51. For comments on *Ag. Ap.* 1.176-83, see Stern, *GLAJJ* 1:47-52; Jaeger, "Greeks," 130-31; E. N. Adler, "Aristotle and the Jewish Sage according to Clearchus of Soli," *HTR* 31 (1938): 205-35; Lewy, "Aristotle."

52. On resistance, see Bertholet, *Stellung*, viii, 79-90, 105-9, 123-52, 208-349; Schürer, *History* 2: 81-84; Kuhn, "*prosēlytos*," *TWNT* 6:727-45; Lerle, *Proselyten-werbung*, 9-13; Grünebaum, "Fremden." For Philo, see Wolfson, *Philo* 1:27-55. For Josephus, see Thackeray, *Josephus*, 75-99. On the rabbis, see SB 1:353-414; Urbach, *Sages* 1:525-54; Jeremias, *Jerusalem*, 275-376; Bamberger, *Proselytism*, 33-36; Braude, *Jewish Proselytizing*, 49-73; Büchler, "Levitical Impurity"; Alon, "Uncleanness"; idem, "Bounds"; S. J. D. Cohen, *Maccabees to Mishnah*, 27-59.

53. Anti-Semitism is a dangerous disease, as history has proved; as a Christian, I deplore the actions of professing Christians that have led to, and actually performed, acts of violence against Jews. The recent work of R. P. Ericksen (*Theologians*) ought to be read by all theologians. Anti-Semitism has a long history; see, e.g., Stern, *GLAJJ*; Schürer, *History* 3.2: 150-53; Sevenster, *Roots*, esp. 89-144; Conzelmann, *Heiden*, 43-120; Wilken, "Judaism"; Gager, *Origins*; idem, "Judaism," in Kraft and Nickelsburg, eds., *EJMI*, 99-116. These latter four scholars trace the origins to varying elements, such as strangeness, aloofness, self-autonomy, monotheism, and social factors. See also Schürer, *History* 3.1: 595-609. On the other hand, it ought also to be observed that statements against another religion (e.g., Judaism) are not necessarily racial prejudice (e.g., anti-Semitism). I will try to show that Judaism was not guilty of racial comments; rather, the condemnations are religiously, not racially, motivated. Research in this area continues to grow; see now Feldman, "Pro-Jewish."

54. Dalbert blames hostilities on nationalism and Torah allegiance, as well as historical factors (*Theologie*, 17-18; see also pp. 137-43).

55. See Schürer, *History* 3.1: 614. Too frequently scholars simply assert that the aspersions cast on the Jews by the ancient historians were the reaction to successful attempts to convert non-Jews. But the problem here is that this is simply an unproven assumption that works well as an explanation – but explanations are to be distinguished from proofs.

56. See Axenfeld, "Propaganda," 37-38; Bertholet, *Stellung*, 251; Sanders, *Paul and Palestinian Judaism*, 374-75.

57. See Smallwood, *Legatio*, 152-55, on the origin of this incorrect etymology.

58. On the rabbis and Gentiles, the evidence for which we will not cite, several comments need to be made: (1) It is virtually certain that there was strong disagreement among rabbis (see Sanders, *Paul and Palestinian Judaism*, 208-11). (2) The dating is not clear, but it is almost certain that these attitudes stretch back into the first century A.D. – at least (see Alon, "Uncleanness"; SB 4.1: 374-78; *contra* Büchler, "Levitical Impurity"). (3) Taken from their contexts, many of the statements by rabbis can be exploited into misanthropy, but it is very clear that rabbis had a concept of God's universal creation. (4) However, it is unfair to conclude that rabbis were wholly favorable to Gentiles; *contra* Bamberger, *Proselytism*, 36; esp. Braude, *Jewish Proselytizing*, *passim*; Büchler,

"Levitical Impurity," 24–31. Porton makes the important point (see *GOYIM*, 173–258, 269–83) that rabbinic text is not necessarily (or even probably) a reflection of the real world. I believe many rabbinic texts that speak of separation from Gentiles are not reflections of real world situations. In fact, if they are, then many of the rulings would not be needed.

59. Buchanan, "Role of Purity"; Goldstein, "Jewish Acceptance"; Urbach, "Self-Isolation."

60. It is possible that attitudes became more harsh at Qumran; see Baumgarten, "Exclusion of Netinim"; idem, "Exclusions"; Blidstein, "4QFlorilegium"; Sutcliffe, "Hatred"; Urbach, "Self-Isolation."

61. A sensitive essay on this is Johnson, "Anti-Jewish Slander."

62. For a general survey of Philo's negative attitudes, see Wolfson, *Philo* 1:27–55. Tcherikover points out that Philo's polemic against the Egyptians is rooted in the soil of the Jewish plea for superior status to native Egyptians; see "Decline," 7–12; see also Wolfson, *Philo* 1:27–32. Philo's nationalistic denunciations are not reserved only for the Egyptians; he also censors the Germans (*Leg.* 10), Ascalonites (*Leg.* 205), Persians (*Spec.* 3:13–14, 17–19), Greeks (*Spec.* 3:15–16, 22; *Jos.* 30; *Cher.* 63), Sybarites (*Spec.* 3:43–45; 4:102), Spartans (*Spec.* 4:102), Arabians (*Virt.* 34–50), Ammonites, and Moabites (*L.A.* 3:81; *Post.* 177), the Cynics (Plant 151) as well as the Chaldeans (*Ebr.* 94; *Migr.* 178–79). Wisely, he avoided denigrating remarks about the Romans!

63. Is *Som.* 2:78–79 really Joseph? See Popeius Trogus, in Justin, *Hist. Phil.* 36; *Epit.* 2:7; Harrington, "Joseph," 127–31; Goodenough, "Philo's Exposition," 109–25; idem, *Politics,* 21–63.

64. See Bickermann, "Warning Inscriptions," 389–94; Porton, *GOYIM,* 259–68.

65. Cf. Lev. 22:25, but esp. 1 Kings 8:41–43. The latter is a most difficult passage and flatly contradicts statements in Josephus and the historians; see, e.g., Schürer, *History* 2:309. I have not seen a treatment of this deserving passage.

66. Mentioned or described in Josephus (*J.W.* 5.193–94; *Ant.* 15.417; 12.145–46; *J.W.* 6.124–28; Philo *Leg.* 212; *m. Mid.* 1:1–3; 2:1–3). See esp. Fry, "Warning Inscriptions"; Bickermann, "Warning Inscriptions"; idem, "Altars"; Baumgarten, "Exclusions." Fry suggests that the letters were painted in red to make them more obvious ("Warning Inscriptions," 23–24). On the possibility of death, see Fry, "Warning Inscriptions," 42–44, 111–210.

67. See Schürer, *History* 2:83–84; Schlatter, *Theologie,* 130; Baumgarten, "Exclusions"; Hoenig, "Oil," 63–65.

68. Büchler contests this view, but he fails to offer a reasonable explanation of this mishnah ("Levitical Impurity," 16–21). More to the point is Alon, "Uncleanness," 148. There is an attribution to Johanan b. Zakkai in *y. Šabb.* 16:8 regarding Galileans, but this probably refers to disobedient Jews. See Malinowski, "Torah Tendencies," 30; Chernick, "Some Talmudic," 402.

69. In general, see Schürer, *History* 2:81–84; see esp. Bilde, "Emperor Gaius"; Brandon, *Jesus,* 83–88; Smallwood, "Gaius' Attempt"; Porton, *GOYIM,* 241–58.

70. See S. J. D. Cohen, "Prohibition of Intermarriage."

71. See esp. Hengel, *Judaism* 1:175–218, 255–309; Schürer, *History* 1:137–63; 1:1–84; Bickermann, *Gott.*

72. Bickermann, *Gott,* 137 (translation mine). See further Davies, "Hasidim." Büchler argued that some legislation was made at this time that declared gentile women permanently unclean ("Levitical Impurity," 15).

73. See Philo *Leg.* 299–305; Maier, "Golden Roman Shields"; R. Meyer, "Figurendarstellung," esp. 1–13; Schürer, *History* 2:58–59, 81–83; Gutmann, "Second Commandment"; Delling, "Heidnische Religionen," 265–67; Swain, "Gamaliel's Speech"; Kraeling, "Roman Standards"; Roth, "Ordinance against Images"; Atkinson, "Historical Setting," esp. 246–62; Jervell, "Imagines," 197–204.

74. Hengel, *Judaism* 1:112; Axenfeld makes much of the juxtaposition of "Fremdenhasse" and "Propagandatrieb" in Judith ("Propaganda," 25); Bertholet, *Stellung,* 234–36.

75. See Schüpphaus, *Psalmen,* 97–99, 108–12.

76. See the important inferences of Porton (*GOYIM,* 110–11).

77. See Kraabel, "Roman," 452–53.

78. See Reynolds and Tannenbaum, *Jews,* 25–77, 116–23.

79. Porton, *GOYIM,* 2.

80. See Sanders, *Paul and Palestinian Judaism.*

Chapter 2

1. Bertholet, *Stellung,* 191; his emphasis; my translation.

2. Braude, *Jewish Proselytizing,* 7–8.

3. Bamberger, *Proselytism,* 3.

4. See, e.g., Flowers, "Matthew xxiii.15," 67–69; Munck, *Paul and the Salvation,* 264–71.

5. On proselytism in Judaism, the following works are standard: Bertholet, *Stellung;* Bamberger, *Proselytism;* Braude, *Jewish Proselytizing;* Kuhn, "*prosēlytos,*" *TWNT* 6:727–45; Kuhn and Stegemann, "Proselyten"; Kellermann, "*ger,*" *TDOT* 2:439–49; J. Jeremias, *Jerusalem,* 246–67; Lerle, *Proselytenwerbung;* G. F. Moore, *Judaism* 1:323–53; Schürer, *History* 3.1: 150–76; Derwacter, *Preparing;* De Ridder, *Dispersion;* Sanders, "Covenant," 25–38; Wolfson, *Philo* 2:352–74; Rosenbloom, *Conversion,* 40–60; S. J. D. Cohen, "Conversion"; idem, "Crossing the Boundary." Apart from Bertholet and Kuhn, there is very little study that is either critical or comprehensive.

On the various terms, A. Bertholet's demonstration that *ger* developed from a "foreigner as a physical-national immigrant" to a "foreigner as a religious convert with protection" has gone down as a secure result (*Stellung*). One of the remaining problems, however, is when this development took place and whether it was consistent throughout Judaism. In the Qumran literature one is not always sure when *ger* means "foreigner, immigrant" and when it means "proselyte," and, whereas Matt. 23:15 is quite clearly "convert, proselyte," Acts 13:43 is perhaps simply "resident alien." On terms, see also G. F. Moore, *Judaism*

1:326–31; Lerle, *Proselytenwerbung,* 24–27; Kuhn, *"proselytos"*; Meek, "Translation"; Rosenbloom, *Conversion,* 16–27; Allen, "Septuagint"; Derwacter, *Preparing,* 20–23; Pope, "Proselyte," *IDB* 3:921–31; Schreiner, "Proselyte," *NISBE* 3:1005–11; Schürer, *History* 3.1: 170–71 n. 78; Simon, "Débuts," 510–12; Overman, "God-Fearers," 18–20; Lake, "Proselytes"; Kuhn and Stegemann, "Proselyten," cols. 1249–54 (and the collection of ancient definitions in col. 1254).

6. See the observations of Axenfeld ("Propaganda," 51); see also Bertholet, *Stellung,* 297–301; H. Graetz, "Proselyten"; Dr. Hasenclever, "Christliche Proselyten der höheren Stände im ersten Jahrhundert," *JPT* 8 (1882): 34–78; Bamberger, *Proselytism,* 174–266; Feldman, "Jewish Proselytism," MS pp. 2–7 (forthcoming). One probably detects a similar phenomenon in James 2:1–13 as well.

7. See C. A. Moore, *Daniel, Esther and Jeremiah: The Additions. A New Translation and Commentary,* AB 44 (Garden City, NY: Doubleday, 1977), 236–37.

8. On *Mos.* 1.7, see Mack, *"Imitatio,"* 31–32 nn. 60–63; Knox, "Abraham," 56–59.

9. See Schiffman, who provides a sketch of a reasonable tradition-critical history of *Ant.* 20.17–96 ("Conversion," 295–98). He contends that Josephus is reliable here (p. 306). See also Teixidor, "Kingdom." Neusner (*Babylonia* 1:61–67; "Conversion") clarifies the political expediencies of such a conversion; see also Graetz, "Zeit"; Schürer, *History* 3.1: 163–64; Feldman, "Jewish Proselytism," MS p. 5. Snow and Machalek, confirming the view of Neusner, have drawn attention to the sociological factors at work in the constitution of a convert's (the narrator's) report about that conversion ("Sociology"). These features, which reveal much about what Josephus (and perhaps some of Judaism) thinks about these converts, are certainly at work in this tradition ("Sociology," 175–78). In light of their work, one needs to be cautious about equating this report with what took place in reality.

10. See also *CIJ* 21, 72, 202, 222, 462, 523; Kuhn, *"proselytos,"* *TWNT* 6:733 n. 61. On Poppaea Sabina, see Smallwood, "Alleged"; Williams, "Tendencies."

11. See esp. Michel, "Studien zu Josephus"; Stern, "Zealots," 145–47.

12. On the inscriptions and names, see Kuhn, *"proselytos,"* *TWNT* 6:733–34; Kraemer, "Hellenistic Jewish Women," 192–200. Furthermore, it is possible, perhaps even likely, that in some cases the term "Ioudaios/Ioudaia" may mean "convert" (e.g., *CIJ* 21 for the mother [*metros Eioudea Is[d]raēlitēs*] and possibly *CIJ* 68, 202); see the insightful study of Kraemer ("Term 'Jew'").

13. See Bamberger, *Proselytism,* 174–226; Graetz, "Proselyten," 23–33; Braude, *Jewish Proselytizing,* 26–38.

14. Cf. *t. Hag.* 2.8. See Neusner, *Rabbinic Traditions* 1:11–23, 81; 3:184–85, 228.

15. For more general treatments of the Gentile and rabbis, see Montefiore and Loewe, *Anthology,* 556–65; Sanders, *Paul and Palestinian Judaism,* 206–12; W. D. Davies, *Paul,* 58–85; Y. Cohen, "Attitude to the Gentile"; De Ridder, *Dispersion,* 110–20.

16. See esp. Stern, "Jewish Diaspora"; Safrai, "Relations"; also Hegermann, "Das hellenistische Judentum"; Axenfeld, "Propaganda," 29–36; Dalbert, *Theologie,* 12–21; Georgi, *Opponents,* 83–84 and nn.; Harnack, *Mission* 1:1–11.

17. Josephus *Ant.* 4.203–4; 14.115–18; 15.14. The evidence in *CPJ* shows that Jews were numerous in Alexandria. No. 4 evidences "Hellenization" (the letter begins "to the gods" (*tois theois*); no. 6 shows a Jew powerful enough to resist taxation; no. 10 relates Jewish Sabbath scruples in 250 B.C.; nos. 19–28 reveal Jews living as mercenaries. See also *Ep. Arist.* 12–16, 19, 37, where one hundred thousand Jews are counted in Alexandria. But cf. Jellicoe, "Occasion"; Murray, "Aristeas"; also Dalbert, *Theologie,* 15. 3 Macc. 4:15–21 has a legend to the same effect; see also *Pss. Sol.* 9:2; 11:1–9; 17:20; *As. Mos.* 4:9; *Sib. Or.* 3:271–72; Philo *Flacc.* 43, 45–46.

18. See, e.g., Tcherikover, "Prolegomena," in *CPJ* 1:1–111; G. Kittel, "Das kleinasiatische Judentum"; Kraeling, "Jewish Community"; Schürer, *History* 3.1: 1–176.

19. Harnack, *Mission* 1:11–12; J. Jeremias, *Jesus' Promise,* 12–14. Others who have followed Harnack here are Schoeps, *Paul,* 221–22; G. F. Moore, *Judaism* 1: 348–49; Bonsirven, *Judaïsme Palestiniens* 1:24–25; Schürer, *History* 3.1: 171 (=F. Millar); Georgi, *Opponents,* 83–84; Feldman, "Omnipresence," 59; "Jewish Proselytism."

20. On demographics, see the more cautious and historically reliable conclusions in Byatt, "Josephus and Population"; Rosenbloom, *Conversion,* 13–15. After approving M. Rostovtzeff's conclusion that we do not have even an approximate idea of the density of population of Jews in the Hellenistic world in Palestine, Rosenbloom states: "Considering the size of the land and the possible population per square mile, no ancient data available even approximate an accurate estimate" (p. 14). However, on pp. 38–39, Rosenbloom slips back into the old argument that "dramatic population changes among the Jews in Palestine and the diaspora are attributed partially to the great number of proselytes" (p. 38). It is far from clear to me how he harmonizes these divergent conclusions, because he is discussing, in both passages, Palestine, although he does include the Diaspora in the latter passage. For a more complete discussion of my views on this subject, see my essay "Jewish Missionary Activity: The Evidence of Demographics and Synagogues," in *Jewish Proselytism* (Perspectives in Ancient Judaism series, ed. A.-J. Levine, R. Pervo [Lanham, Md.: University Press of America, forthcoming]). See also the forthcoming nuanced view of P. Fredriksen in her essay "Judaism, the Circumcision of Gentiles, and Apocalyptic Hope: Another Look at Galatians 1 and 2."

21. See Dalbert, *Theologie,* 23; Bertholet, *Stellung,* 91–104, 110–22.

22. Bialoblocki, *Beziehungen,* 12–13; Hegermann, "Das hellenistische Judentum," 1:309–10; Siegfried, "Prophetische Missionsgedanke," 447; Hempel, "Wurzeln," 269–70; Derwacter, *Preparing,* 61–75. This is the majority position today, but, again, there is little evidence that can support such a conclusion.

23. Bertholet, *Stellung,* 228 (but cf. 318); Bousset, *Religion,* 77.

24. Hegermann, "Das hellenistische Judentum," 1:307–8 (translation mine);

see also Munck, who states that the Diaspora and homeland did not differ in this regard (*Paul and the Salvation*, 265).

25. See Lévi, *Hebrew Text*, 14 (on 10:21).

26. See Bertholet, *Stellung*, 204–5; *APOT* 1:351.

27. See Middendorp, *Stellung*, 127.

28. *T. Levi* 2:11 reads: "Through you and Judah the Lord will be seen by men [by himself saving every race of humankind]" (*OTP*): *kai dia sou kai Iouda ophthēsetai kyrios en anthrōpois, sōzōn en autois pan genos anthrōpōn.*

29. See Charles, *APOT* 2:358; H. C. Kee, *OTP*, note d; also de Jonge, *Study*, 46; Josephus *Ant.* 13.355; *J.W.* 1.88–89; *b. Sukk.* 48b.

30. Perhaps an interpolation, but see H. C. Kee, *OTP*, note b.

31. Although parts of 7:3 are undoubtedly later Christian interpolations, the clause pertaining to the salvation of the Gentiles seems to be traditional.

32. On the text, see de Jonge, *Studies*, 225.

33. Manuscript Θ puts this in the vocative, making it a confession.

34. Axenfeld, "Propaganda," 46–47, plays this down, arguing it to be an individual's reflection, not a corporate consciousness; it is a moment of "*Begeisterung*" ("inspiration"). See also Reese, *Hellenistic Influence*, 62, 154, 156.

35. See van der Horst, *Sentences*, 139–40.

36. K. G. Kuhn draws attention to the parallel of 41:4 with the rabbinic notion of a convert as one who is under the wings of the Shekinah; see *TWNT* 6:736.

37. See esp. the following studies by Murphy-O'Connor: "Critique"; "Demetrius I"; "Missionary Document"; "Literary Analysis"; "Original Text"; "Essenes and Their History"; see also Charlesworth, "Origin." I am aware that not all scholars take the Qumran scrolls as a reflection of the Essenes (though I disagree with them). Further, some scholars now argue that the scrolls are not the deposit of one religious community; rather, they are the deposit of a wide variety of Palestinian Jewish groups. For this view, see Golb, "Who Hid?" I am inclined to think that this latter view should be given more careful consideration.

38. Vermes, *Qumran in Perspective*, 103.

39. Bialoblocki, *Beziehungen*, 13; Belkin, *Oral Law*, 44–48; see also the ideas of Georgi (*Opponents*, 120–22).

40. See Wolfson, *Philo* 2:165–321, on Philo's transformation of virtue.

41. See esp. Goodenough, *By Light*.

42. The verb *methormizō* is a conversion term; see *Abr.* 24, 78; *Spec.* 1.51, 227; *Praem.* 15, 27, 116.

43. The Loeb translation "newly-joined" is an unnecessary redundancy, and "joined" is too weak. Thus, the proselyte is the one who approaches the community. The rendering of the Old Testament text behind this (Lev. 19:33) shows the Hellenistic transformation of the *gēr* to the religious convert; see Bertholet, *Stellung*, *passim*.

44. See Amir, *Die hellenistische Gestalt*, 23–24.

45. See van Unnik, "Critique of Paganism"; Wolfson, *Philo* 2:252–59.

46. See Georgi, *Opponents*, 84–118, esp. 109–11.

47. On mystery, see Goodenough, *By Light*, 235–64; Wolfson, *Philo* 1:43–55; Caragounis, *Ephesian Mysterion*, 1–34.

48. See Sanders, "Covenant," 29.

49. It is very unlikely that *J.W.* 7.191 refers to converts. For a negative view of proselytes by Gentiles, see Sevenster, *Roots*, 196–97; Smallwood, "Some Notes." On Josephus's own progressively positive attitude, see S. J. D. Cohen, "Respect," 416–30.

50. See S. J. D. Cohen, "Respect," 415.

51. Ibid., 430; Cohen prefers to see these women as "adherents," but I am not sure his description accounts for the verb *hypagō*. See also Stern, *GLAJJ* 1:524.

52. Georgi leans heavily on this piece of evidence for his theory that the synagogue was an evangelistic platform (*Opponents*, 85); see chap. 3 below.

53. In light of Josephus's clear nationalistic thrust, the phrase "not family ties alone" needs to be understood as boundary (in an exclusive sense), not unbounded universalism (in an inclusive sense).

54. It strikes me that S. J. D. Cohen overstates his case in seeing in the negative results of conversion a negative attitude on the part of Josephus (in *Antiquities*); see "Respect," 424. There is ample evidence that faithfulness may involve martyrdom and that martyrdom is seen positively. Moreover, in spite of Cohen's separation of the Izates story from the rest of the evidence and his explanation of it in politically acceptable (to Rome) terms, that story is nonetheless viewed positively by Josephus ("Respect," 424–25). However, it is accurate to say that *Ag. Ap.* is more positive in orientation.

55. See Neusner, *Politics*; S. J. D. Cohen, "Respect," 416–30.

56. Such is the theory of the polemically inspired writings: Bamberger, *Proselytism*; Braude, *Jewish Proselytizing*; Raisin, *Gentile Reactions*. In addition to the evidence cited below, see the macarism of the *Amidah*; see Braude, *Jewish Proselytizing*, 16–17; Graetz, "Proselyten," 10–11; Grünebaum, "Fremden," 49; Safrai, "Synagogue," *WHJP* 1.8: 80–81; for more, see Schürer, *History* 2:455–63.

57. As J. Neusner has pointed out, this story tells us as much about later rabbinic attitudes toward Shammai and Hillel as it does about proselytism. "No story is overtly hostile to Hillel" (Neusner, *Rabbinic Traditions* 1:294), but the same is not true of his rival (ibid., 2:212–302). The result of this tendency is the "quest for the historical Hillel" and the need to recognize that first-century Judaism was not entirely, perhaps not even predominantly, Hillelite (Neusner, *Rabbinic Traditions* 1:301; idem, *Politics*, 13–44; Meyer, "*pharisaioi*," *TDNT* 9:33, 35; Lauterbach, "Pharisees," 73; Büchler, "Levitical Impurity," 26 n. 60; G. F. Moore, *Judaism* 1:81; Bowker, *Pharisees*, 29–38.

58. Urbach, *Sages* 1:542–43.

59. See the comments of Braude (*Jewish Proselytizing*, 22–23); see also Urbach, *Sages* 1:549–50.

60. So Lerle, *Proselytenwerbung*, 132–35; Lübkert, "Proselyten," 700; Bousset, *Religion*, 84–85; Grünebaum, "Fremden," 49, 53.

61. So S. J. D. Cohen, "Conversion," 40.

62. On this unfavorable attitude, especially as found among the rabbis, see

Bialoblocki, *Beziehungen*, 23–28; Bertholet, *Stellung*, 339–48; Bamberger, *Proselytism*, 161–69; Braude, *Jewish Proselytizing*, 39–43; Grünebaum, "Fremden," 49–53; Urbach, *Sages* 1:541–54.

63. See Georgi, who relates these notions to the mysteries (*Opponents*, 117, 142–47); see also Wolfson, *Philo* 1:52–55.

64. This paragraph is based on my forthcoming article "*De Vita Mosis* 1:147—Lion Proselytes in Philo?" *Studia Philonica*, which contends that Philo's view is rooted in a targumic rendering seen also in *Tg. Neof.* Exod. 12:38.

65. He had a known antipathy to proselytes; see G. F. Moore, *Judaism* 1:341.

66. On the *minim/nazrim* of the *Shemoneh Esreh*, see Graetz, "Proselyten," 9–10 (first century) and Schürer, *History* 2:455–63 (healthy skepticism). There is no consensus, as far as I can tell, on the origin of this element, and so we have excluded it.

67. Cf. *b. 'Abod. Zar.* 24a; see Braude, *Jewish Proselytizing*, 45–46.

68. This is a play on *sph* in Isa. 14:1. See Braude, *Jewish Proselytizing*, 42.

69. I have seen no better treatment of this than Bamberger, *Proselytism*, 60–132; see also Axenfeld, "Propaganda," 68–69; Bialoblocki, *Beziehungen*, 23–27; Braude, *Jewish Proselytizing*, 79–135; Kuhn, "*prosēlytos*," *TDNT* 6:739–40; J. Jeremias, *Jerusalem*, 323–34; Derwacter, *Preparing*, 102–13.

70. This formulation is that of Rabbi Jose b. Halafta; see J. Jeremias, *Jerusalem*, 325; *contra* D. Daube, *Rabbinic Judaism*, 112.

71. See Bialoblocki, *Beziehungen*, 23–24; Zeitlin, "Proselytes," 417 (only among strict Jews); G. F. Moore, *Judaism* 1:334–35; J. Jeremias, *Jerusalem*, 320–34.

72. Neusner is perhaps too skeptical here (*Rabbinic Traditions* 1:145–46, 157–58). Hillel's refusal to admit the proselyte to the Passover meal has nothing to do with the status of a proselyte, and his ruling on intermarriage is late (*m. Qidd.* 3:12; 2:4; *b. Qidd.* 78ab; *b. Yeb.* 37a, 85ab; Neusner, *Rabbinic Traditions* 1:261).

73. See Segal, "Costs," 358–59; Schiffman, *Who?* 21; on the motives of Gentiles, see Feldman, "Jewish Proselytism," 11–13.

74. See Georgi, *Opponents*, 120 (see also pp. 118–20); Lerle, *Proselytenwerbung*, 9–11.

75. Segal, "Costs," 346.

76. See, e.g., G. F. Moore, *Judaism* 1:323.

77. This will be developed below. It ought to be noted here that although Jews buried proselytes alongside of Jews, "God-fearers" were buried with Gentiles. See Kuhn, "*prosēlytos*," *TDNT* 6:732–33; Bousset, *Religion*, 86–96; Gressmann, "Jüdische Mission," 169–83.

78. On future conversion, see J. Jeremias, *Jesus' Promise*, 56–73; Bosch, *Heidenmission*, 35–52; Lerle, *Proselytenwerbung*, 67–74; Staerk, "Ursprung," col. 36; Schürer, *History* 2:525–29; Donaldson, "Proselytes." Donaldson argues, cogently I think, that the restoration and pilgrimage eschatology is ambiguous about Gentiles. He argues further that the emphasis is on the sociological fact of Israelite vindication and its status. I would add that the absence of reflections

of a missionary nature in this motif probably reflects the absence of missionary activity in reality.

79. Goppelt, "Missionar," 138 n. 5 (translation mine); see also G. F. Moore, *Judaism* 1:324; Bosch, *Heidenmission*, 40–41; Hempel, "Wurzeln," *passim;* Segal, "Costs," 341; Vande Kappelle, "Evidence," 34–38. This is against the majority of scholars, who have followed Harnack and Jeremias; see, e.g., J. Jeremias, *Jesus' Promise*, 11–19; Derwacter, *Preparing*, 114–29; Bamberger, *Proselytism;* Braude, *Jewish Proselytizing.*

80. G. F. Moore, *Judaism* 1:342. The rabbinic views varied by rabbi, by time, and by circumstance—and by the point being scored. This is the conclusion of Urbach (*Sages* 1:549–53). At the least, rabbis were cautious about admitting proselytes; see Bialoblocki, *Beziehungen, passim;* Bamberger, *Proselytism*, 31–33; Bertholet, *Stellung*, 339–42.

Chapter 3

1. See Nock, *Conversion*, 77–98 (on how eastern cults traveled); Derwacter, *Preparing*, 41–60, 76–94; Georgi, *Opponents*, 83–228; interesting is also Gressmann, "Heidnische Mission."

2. See, e.g., Lerle, *Proselytenwerbung*, 18; Axenfeld, "Propaganda," *passim;* Dalbert, *Theologie, passim;* Hahn, *Mission*, 24–25; Gressmann, "Jüdische Mission," 176–78.

3. Derwacter, *Preparing*, 14.

4. See G. F. Moore, *Judaism* 1:230 n. 1; Axenfeld, "Propaganda," 50; Staerk, "Ursprung," col. 36.

5. See Wolfson, *Philo* 2:395–426; Goodenough, *Politics*, 115–19.

6. Dalbert, *Theologie*, 125–26, 131–36.

7. For some reason, H. St. J. Thackeray has translated the aorist third plural as a third singular reflexive; the text refers to Jewish preservation of Metilius because of his promise to convert. See *J.W.* 2.454: "he alone saved his life by entreaties and promises to turn Jew, and even to be circumcised" (LCL).

8. D. Georgi infers from the similarities of Josephus and Philo to the apologetic tradition, along with some evidence from Juvenal, that there was an unofficial exegetical tradition that had some traveling members (see *Opponents*, 90–117). This theory is without substantial evidence and will be excluded from our discussion. His anchoring of the banishment of four thousand Jews (to military service in Sardinia) to these exegetes is difficult to prove (see pp. 92–96). On wandering preachers, see the enlightening exposition of W. L. Liefeld ("Wandering Preacher").

9. Derwacter, *Preparing*, 86, 94; see also Georgi, *Opponents*, 101.

10. Derwacter, *Preparing*, 86–90.

11. Feldman, "Jewish Proselytism" (forthcoming; p. 8 of the MS).

12. Text of A. Rahlfs, *Septuaginta* (2 vols.; Stuttgart: Württembergische Bibelanstalt, 1965).

13. See Middendorp, *Stellung*, 170–73; Hengel, *Judaism* 1:31.

14. See Schlier, "*deiknymi*," *TDNT* 2:25-33; Bultmann, "*peithō*," *TDNT* 6:1-11; H. D. Betz, *Galatians: A Commentary on Paul's Letter to the Churches in Galatia,* Hermeneia (Philadelphia: Fortress, 1979), esp. 14-25; Murray, "Aristeas."

15. *T. Levi* 2:10-11 makes the declaration to humanity in an apocalyptic future and *Testament of Naphtali* is unclear here.

16. The classical idea of proclaiming good news (*biśśar*) plays no important role at Qumran; see Becker, *Heil,* 67; Schilling, "*baśar,*" *TDOT* 2:313-16.

17. The evidence is not altogether clear because there are directions against quarrelling with nonsectarians but also evidence that such quarrels took place; see, e.g., 1QS 9:16; 10:19; 1QH 2:7-8; 5:20-6:3; 4:17-18; 6:19-21; 8:16-26.

18. Trans. A. Dupont-Sommer, *The Essene Writings from Qumran* (Oxford: Blackwell, 1961).

19. Trans. G. Vermes, *The Dead Sea Scrolls in English,* 3d ed. (New York: Penguin, 1985).

20. Esotericism is plainly seen in Josephus, *J.W.* 2.141: "to conceal nothing from the members of the sect and to report none of their secrets to others." See, e.g., W. D. Davies, "Knowledge"; Wagner, "ידע," 250-51; O. Betz, *Offenbarung;* Sanders, *Paul and Palestinian Judaism,* 260-61.

21. See esp. G. Jeremias, *Lehrer,* 239-42; on the history of this sect reflected in this hymn, see Murphy-O'Connor, "Essenes and Their History," 233-38.

22. 1QS 10:24-25 has an interesting textual problem. Does 10:24b read *str* ("hide") or *spr* ("reveal")? The photograph of the scroll shows '*str* with a *p* written over the *t,* which changes the text from "hide" to "reveal." For a picture, see Trevor, *Scrolls,* 144-45. Contextually, both readings could fit, but *spr* is the better reading because *b'sr* makes more sense with "reveal." The bigger question is, To whom did the psalmist reveal such knowledge? I would suggest that this "revealed knowledge" best pertains to the level of information given to the initiate who is "suited to the discipline" (6:13). If the other reading be taken, the esotericism I am advocating would be strengthened. For a proponent of this latter view, see Leaney, *Rule of Qumran,* 250.

23. On the Testimonium Flavianum, see Thackeray, *Josephus,* 125-33; Brandon, *Jesus,* 359-64; Schürer, *History* 1:428-41 (by Paul Winter); Bammel, "Zum Testimonium Flavianum."

24. On *Ant.* 18:116-19, see Hoehner, *Herod Antipas,* 110-71.

25. See also *Ant.* 18:81-84; and Georgi, *Opponents,* 92-97. In spite of Georgi's claims, it is not clear how this "scoundrel" "enlisted three confederates." In fact, the text states that Fulvia came to the "scoundrel," not the reverse.

26. See Bowers, "Religious Propaganda," 318.

27. See Neusner, *Rabbinic Traditions* 1:142-59.

28. See Daube, *Rabbinic Judaism,* 336-46, using *t. Ber.* 2:24 as a tactic.

29. See Liefeld, "Wandering Preacher," 206-8.

30. It is particularly important here to avoid reading early (and even modern!) Christian missionary practices into the ancient texts. The evidence remaining to us suggests much more what we might now describe as "mission through vocation." This, interestingly, is how R. F. Hock has described Paul's work

(*Social Context*). His work is worthy of more careful reading in light of what we are arguing about the nature of Jewish missionary activity. In addition, R. MacMullen discounts the presence of (Pauline-type) evangelists in the early church ("Two Types," 191 n. 46).

31. Dalbert, *Theologie;* see also Hegermann, "Das hellenistische Judentum," 1:342–45; Georgi, *Opponents,* 118–51; Kramer, *Christ,* 94–99. G. F. Moore is probably not far from the mark when he sees the basic ideas as monotheism and ethics in the context of an authoritative demand to secure one's position before God (*Judaism* 1:324–25).

32. Dalbert, *Theologie,* 137–43. "In spite of the manifold attempts of hellenistic Jews to build bridges to the spiritual world of the environment, and in spite of their partially accurate monotheistic stance, the consciousness of the election of their people remains very strong and unbroken" (p. 137).

33. See Lauterbach, "Pharisees," 92–93. It is hard to imagine a Judaism at that time without temple, law, land, and nation. See more recently the diversity of Judaism as described by J. J. Collins, who delineates the view that identity existed in reliance on ancient traditions, however diverse their expression (*Between*).

34. See Schürer, *History* 3.1: 160 (but see the caution of M. Goodman at pp. 594, 609, which sees the primary audience in Jews and even questions if the literature was given to Gentiles); see also pp. 177–307, 470–704; Hegermann, "Das hellenistische Judentum," 1:314–42; Axenfeld, "Propaganda"; Dalbert, *Theologie,* 27–123; Bialoblocki, *Beziehungen,* 12–13; Bertholet, *Stellung,* 260–302; Hengel, *Judaism* 1:58–254; Siegfried, "Prophetische Missionsgedanke," 445ff.; Bousset, *Religion,* 76–81; Bosch, *Heidenmission,* 31–35; Munck, *Paul and the Salvation,* 267–68; De Ridder, *Dispersion,* 110–20; Derwacter, *Preparing,* 48–55; Feldman, "Jewish Proselytism" (forthcoming; MS pp. 8–11).

Looming large over this discussion also is the dark cloud of literacy percentage, an issue of crucial importance that is almost never discussed in this context. Recent study shows that reading was the domain of a significant minority. See esp. W. V. Harris, *Ancient Literacy.* However, this is not to suggest that the intended audience of this literature was not primarily hearers.

35. Georgi has a more complete listing (*Opponents,* 69 n. 80); Schürer provides summaries and bibliographies (*History* 3.1). See also G. E. Sterling, "Apologetic Historiography"; Attridge, "Jewish Historiography."

36. For a current survey of apologetics, see the lengthy note of Georgi (*Opponents,* 69–70 n. 80, 422–45); see also Conzelmann, *Heiden.*

37. See Tcherikover, "Jewish Apologetic"; Goodman in Schürer, *History* 3.1: 609; and now Fredriksen, "Judaism" (forthcoming). J. J. Collins seeks a *via media* by suggesting that the literature served both sides (*Between,* 8–10), but unfortunately he does not attempt a thorough defense of what may prove to be an accurate portrayal. See also his "Symbol," 164–70. At the 1988 meeting of the Society of Biblical Literature in Chicago, R. Chesnutt of Pepperdine University offered a challenge to the apologetical interpretation of *Joseph and Aseneth.* The paper was read in the Hellenistic Judaism section.

38. See, e.g., Schürer, *History* 3.1: 594–616, for a survey of the literature.

39. See Tcherikover, "Prolegomena," *CPJ* 1:42. See also Dalbert, *Theologie,* 92–102; Bertholet, *Stellung,* 261–65.

40. Dalbert, *Theologie,* 108 (translation mine); see also 20, 106–23; Bertholet, *Stellung,* 269–71.

41. This is the J text of *OTP*; readings enclosed in angle brackets ‹ › indicate the J text supplemented with R; readings enclosed in vertical rules indicate J supplemented with P. It ought also to be noted that the A text does not include "nations" at 48:7.

42. Derwacter, *Preparing,* 48–49.

43. Note the attempt of E. R. Goodenough to show that *De Vita Mosis* was propaganda ("Philo's Exposition"); his view is difficult to sustain and has not met with general approval.

44. For further bibliography, see Vande Kappelle, "Evidence."

45. See Simon, "Débuts," 512.

46. See Vande Kappelle, "Evidence," 118–20, 185–216.

47. Again, see Vande Kappelle, "Evidence," 147, 186 and 218–19.

48. This is the thesis of Vande Kappelle, "Evidence"; see also Simon, "Débuts."

49. For the text and versification of *Joseph and Aseneth,* see Burchard, "Vorläufiger"; idem, "Verbesserungen." The translation in the text is that of C. Burchard in *OTP* 2:202–47. His text is eclectic and superior to M. Philonenko's text (which is essentially *d*). For introductory matters, see Burchard, *OTP* 2:177–201; Chesnutt, "Conversion," 2–95; idem, "Social Setting"; Kee, "Socio-Cultural"; Schürer, *History* 3.1. 546–52. In my view, the dating of *Joseph and Aseneth* is still an open question, and one must account for what appear to be (at least possible) Christian interpolations (e.g., 8:11). If there are no Christian interpolations, then it is clear that this text contains some of the strongest parallels to New Testament material in any Jewish text. On the genre of *Joseph and Aseneth,* see Pervo, "Greek Novel"; West, "Greek Romance." On the purpose, see esp. Chesnutt, "Conversion," 119–29, 342–56. A useful (mini-) commentary on the text can be found in Delling, "Kunst."

50. See Chesnutt, "Conversion," 129–31.

51. See, e.g., J. Jeremias, *Jesus' Promise,* 12–13. R. D. Chesnutt agrees with the position taken here ("Conversion," 342–56). This view does not deny that the story had some gentile appeal (however one might intuit such a view); see Nickelsburg, "Stories," 69–70. But that the story fills a speculative need for Jewish legal justification of Joseph's purity (and therefore of problems with intermarriage at the time of its writing) is altogether clear. See Burchard, *OTP* 2:182–84, 194–95.

52. See also Chesnutt, "Conversion," 344–51. Chesnutt offers serious counter-evidence for the propaganda view of *Joseph and Aseneth.* The consensus of modern scholarship is noted here; see also pp. 2–58.

53. See Chesnutt, "Conversion," 99–117.

54. See West, "Greek Romance," 75–76.

55. It could be conjectured that a motive latent in *Joseph and Aseneth* is that

conversion is to take place prior to marriage so the marriage will not be defiling. See the comments here of Delling ("Kunst," 25–26).

56. See Burchard, *OTP* 2:192.

57. Ibid. 2:194–95.

58. See West, "Greek Romance," 78; see also Delling, "Kunst," 39; Chesnutt, "Conversion," 349–51.

59. Momigliano, *Alien Wisdom,* 91. See also Conzelmann, *Heiden,* 52–54; Tcherikover, "Jewish Apologetic," 177 and n. 19; Nock, *Conversion,* 78–80; Munck, *Paul and the Salvation,* 268. I suspect that the conviction, seen frequently in New Testament scholarship, that Jews regularly gave Gentiles copies of Jewish books, including the Tanach, is based heavily on the work of G. Rosen (*Juden und Phönizier,* 35–62); see Georgi, *Opponents,* 174–75 n. 1! The evidence cited by Rosen hardly justifies the conviction. I do not, however, intend to suggest that no Gentiles read the Septuagint (or Jewish literature). The occasional allusion to such mitigates this position; cf. Pseudo-Longinus (*De Sublimitate* 9.9). See Feldman, "Jewish Proselytism" (forthcoming; MS pp. 8–9 and esp. n. 3).

60. G. F. Moore, *Judaism* 1:324; see also Vande Kappelle, "Evidence," 210–16, in spite of the concession made on p. 213. On the wider context, see Hengel, *Judaism* 1:65–83; Riesner, *Jesus,* 97–206; Simon, "Débuts," 517–20.

61. Kraabel, "Roman," 458.

62. See esp. Hengel, "Proseuche."

63. On *Legum Allegoriae* as a collection of sermons, see Thyen, *Stil,* 7–11.

64. See Tcherikover, "Jewish Apologetic," 178; Wolfson, *Philo* 1:57–73.

65. Georgi, *Opponents,* 89.

66. Georgi, *Opponents,* 83–84; I cite from p. 84 (emphasis his). The *inclusio* on p. 87 draws the threads together, showing that he has proven his case: "These examples show in summary fashion (supported and complemented by many individual examples) that Judaism in the Hellenistic diaspora was held together most of all by the synagogue service, by its reading and exposition of the Pentateuch translated into Greek. *In this way Judaism acquired and maintained its ability to attract converts*" (p. 87; emphasis added). Further discussion (pp. 84–90) multiplies hypotheses and so decreases one's confidence in probability; the decisively weak link in the argument from Philo and Josephus to gentile attraction in the synagogue is the nature of the apologetic tradition.

67. See above, chap. 2 n. 20.

68. Harnack's influence can be seen in the recently published essay of Dietrich Bonhoeffer, who was then a student of Harnack, "The Jewish Element of 1 Clement" (in *Dietrich Bonhoeffer Werke* [Munich: Kaiser, 1986] 9:223–24).

69. See Nolland, "Proselytism or Politics." Approval of Nolland's view has recently been tendered in Kraabel, "Roman," 455.

70. *Ca.* A.D. 127. Trans. G. G. Ramsey (LCL) xii. But compare the ambiguous comment at *Satires* 3.296; Georgi draws little from this statement (*Opponents,* 98 and n. 100).

71. Georgi, *Opponents,* 85.

72. Ibid.

73. Partial support for this conclusion can be found in Tcherikover, "Jewish Apologetic," 178–79. Tcherikover says that interpretation of the Torah was for Jews. Further support is gained from my next point, "education."

74. Kraabel makes a similar point from archaeological and epigraphical evidence ("Disappearance," 115–17). On my response to his view of the "God-Fearers," see chap. 6 below, under "Lukan Writings."

75. On education, see chap. 1, nn. 32, 33.

76. See Kuhn, "prosēlytos," *TDNT* 6:733–34 n. 64.

77. Bialoblocki, *Beziehungen*, 13.

78. This explains *Mos.* 1.2 and the means of *Prob.* 62. Unfortunately for our study, the participle *anapimplantes* describes the fact, not the means, of this freedom.

79. See SB 4.1: 378–80; J. S. Raisin, *Gentile Reactions,* 168–69; S. J. D. Cohen, "Prohibition of Intermarriage"; idem, "Matrilineal Principle."

80. See Kuhn, "prosēlytos," *TDNT* 6:733–34; Puzicha, *Christus peregrinus,* 10–11. It is possible that *threptē of CIJ* 21 refers to an adopted child. At any rate, that Eirene is only three years old shows that some sort of household conversion is in mind. See the discussion of Kraemer ("Term 'Jew,'" 38–41).

81. See Neusner, *Babylonia* 1:65–67; idem, "Conversion."

82. See Bertholet, *Stellung,* 228–29, 238–41; Axenfeld, "Propaganda," 25–26; Bialoblocki, *Beziehungen,* 13–15; Bamberger, *Proselytism,* 20 n. 10.

83. G. F. Moore, *Judaism* 1:336. See also the helpful discussion of the social nature of this kind of conversion in S. J. D. Cohen, "Crossing the Boundary," 24–26.

84. Georgi, *Opponents,* 126; I disagree with Georgi's social framework but agree with the general description and apply it here to both Josephus and Philo.

85. See Goodenough, "Philo's Exposition," which attempts to show the propaganda technique of *De Vita Mosis.* Even though scholars constantly utilize Philo as evidence for Jewish propaganda, there is, to my knowledge, no single study on Philo's propaganda method. But cf. Conley, "Philo's Rhetoric."

86. See Mendelson, *Secular Education,* 7–11.

87. This is discussed often; see, e.g., Hamerton-Kelly, "Techniques"; Goodenough, *By Light,* 72–94; Wolfson, *Philo* 1:115–38.

88. There is a vast bibliography here; see, e.g., Tiede, *Charismatic Figures,* 101–206; Meeks, "Divine Agent"; idem, "Moses as God"; Gager, *Moses;* Holladay, *Theios Aner,* 103–98; Georgi, *Opponents,* 122–37.

89. See Georgi, *Opponents,* 126–37; Goodenough, *By Light,* 74.

90. See Mack, "Imitatio," 33.

91. See Meeks, "Divine Agent," 47; Holladay, *Theios Aner,* 108–29; Tiede, *Charismatic Figure,* 105, 123, 134–37; Georgi, *Opponents,* 126–37. For the implications of these attributions for New Testament Christology, see Hurtado, *One God,* esp. 59–63.

92. See Hermippus of Smyrna, *De Legislatoribus* in Stern, *GLAJJ* 1:96; Antonius Diogenes, in Porphyrius, *Vita Pythagorae* 11 in *GLAJJ* 1:537; see also

Pseudo-Eupolemus in Wacholder, "Pseudo-Eupolemus," 95–96; Feldman, "Orthodoxy," 220–21.

93. See Sevenster, *Roots;* Conzelmann, *Heiden,* 43–120, 127–218, esp. 171–88.

94. See, e.g., G. C. Field, "Sophists," *OCD,* 1000; Daube, "Hellenistic Rhetoric"; Feldman, "Orthodoxy," 229–30; Belkin, *Oral Law,* 11–18; Hamerton-Kelly, "Techniques"; Wolfson, *Philo* 1:57–66; Hay, "Philo's References."

95. Smallwood, *Jews,* 233–50; idem, "Some Notes," 322–29.

96. This is common in Greek and Latin authors: see Strabo *Geogr.* 16.2.34 (*apud* Augustine *De Civ. Dei* 4.31); Livy *Scholia* 2.593; idem, from Lydus *De Mensibus* 4–53 (in Stern, *GLAJJ* 1:330–31); Lucanus *Pharasalia* 2:592–93; Schürer, *History* 2:81–83.

97. See Diodorus, *Bibl. Hist.* 34–35.1.1; Strabo *Geogr.* 16.2.35–36; Gager, *Moses,* 113–61.

98. Stern, *GLAJJ* 1:323–24.

99. On his character, see Brandon, "Renegade." On his propagandistic and historiographical methods, see van Unnik, *Schriftssteller,* 19–20; Thackeray, *Josephus,* 19–22, 45–50; Mosley, "Historical Reporting"; Rajak, *Josephus;* idem, "Josephus"; Schürer, *History* 1:57–58; Blosser, "Sabbath Year Cycle"; Eisman, "Dio and Josephus"; Bilde, "Emperor Gaius"; Broshi, "Credibility"; S. J. D. Cohen, "Masada"; Georgi, *Opponents,* 118–20; Feldman, "Flavius Josephus Revisited"; idem, "Josephus as an Apologist to the Greco-Roman World: His Portrait of Solomon," in *Aspects of Religious Propaganda in Judaism and Early Christianity,* UNDCSJCA 2 (Notre Dame: University of Notre Dame Press, 1976) 69–98; idem, "Pro-Jewish"; *et passim.* The consensus today is that Josephus is essentially reliable but with not uncommon embellishments.

100. On these various terms, see Schlatter, *Wie Sprach Josephus?* 38, 49–55; idem, *Theologie,* 24; Langen, "Theologische Standpunkt," 20–22; van Unnik, *Schriftssteller,* 66; Tiede, *Charismatic Figure,* 207–40; Lindner, *Geschichtsauffassung,* 42–48; Montgomery, "Religion," 287–90; Sowers, "Reinterpretation," 19–20; Blenkinsopp, "Prophecy," 248–50; Wächter, "Unterschiedliche Haltung"; G. F. Moore, "Fate"; Martin, "Use."

101. Pompeius Trogus's statement shows that such an accusation was a contemporary issue (in Justin *Hist. Phil.* 36; *Epit.* 2.12–13); also Nicarchus in Photius (see Stern, *GLAJJ* 1:533; cf. Gager, *Moses,* 113–61).

102. See Revel, "Some Anti-Traditional Laws."

103. See 1 Kings 8:43, 60, which do not contain these ideas. This is again a defense against charges, like that found in Hecataeus of Abdera *Aeg.* 1.25; see Stern, *GLAJJ* 1:30; also in Diodorus, *Bibl. Hist.* 34–35.1.1, 1.2–4; Cicero *Pro Flacco* 28.68–69; Pompeius Trogus, in Justin *Hist. Phil.* 36; *Epit.* 2.15; Quintillian *Inst. Orat.* 3.7.21; cf. Wilken, "Judaism," 314–17.

104. See Lindner, *Geschichtsauffassung,* 49–68; Thackeray, *Josephus,* 23–27; Schalit, "Josephus and Justus"; Sevenster, *Do You Know Greek?* 61–76.

105. See further van Unnik, *Schriftssteller,* 26–40, esp. 28–29. Josephus's boasting moves also into his military, political, moral, and intellectual life (*J.W.*

3.135–37, 197–202, 345–91; *Vita* 6, 8, 80–81, 112–13).

106. On his sources, see Schürer, *History* 1:48–52; Thackeray, *Josephus*, 36–41.

107. See Georgi, *Opponents*, 122–37 (personalities); Feldman, "Helleniza-tions" (ideas); Tcherikover, "Polis" (institutions).

108. See Hermann, "Genossenschaft," *RAC* 10:83–155; Baumbach, "Saddu-zäerverständnis"; Schürer, *History* 2:404–14; Wächter, "Unterschiedliche Haltung"; Pines, "Platonistic Model"; Smith, "Palestinian Judaism"; Rasp, "Flavius Josephus"; G. F. Moore, "Fate." Martin argues that a non-Stoic use of "fate" is found in Josephus and renders it as determinism that has no power over the Jew who lives responsibly under the Torah ("Use").

109. On Abraham, see Wacholder, "Pseudo-Eupolemus," 101–3; Holladay, *Theios Aner*, 73–74; Mayer, "Aspekte"; Feldman, "Abraham"; Knox, "Abraham."

110. See Feldman, "Apologist."

111. See Thoma, "Weltanschauung," 41–48; Farmer, *Maccabees*, 11–23; Smith, "Palestinian Judaism"; Neusner, *Rabbinic Traditions* 3:241–44; idem, *Politics*, 45–66.

112. See Feldman, "Jewish Proselytism," ms pp. 5–7 (forthcoming); see also Schürer, *History* 3.1: 73–81.

113. See now Hodgson, "Valerius Maximus."

114. So Stern, *GLAJJ* 1:359. But see Lane, "Sabazius." In addition to the two texts of M. Stern, Lane cites another text (Vat. Lat. 4929), and this text does not connect the Jews with Jupiter Sabazius. See also Trebilco, "Studies," 148–51.

115. Interestingly, J. J. Collins concedes that "such active proselyting is not well attested elsewhere" ("Symbol," 170–71) and A. T. Kraabel pronounces the evidence from Rome to be unclear ("Roman," 451–52).

116. See Feldman, "Jewish Proselytism," ms pp. 6–7 (forthcoming).

117. Jeremias, *Jesus' Promise*, 56–73.

118. Momigliano; Tcherikover.

119. See Stern, *GLAJJ*.

120. Collins, "Symbol," 184.

Chapter 4

1. For this discussion, see Bialoblocki, *Beziehungen*, 16–21; Bamberger, *Proselytism*, 31–37, 42–52; Braude, *Jewish Proselytizing*, 74–78; Zeitlin, "Pros-elytes," 411–14; Klein, *Katechismus*, 244–46 (post-70 A.D. phenomenon); Lübkert, "Proselyten," 691–97; Meyer and Weiss, "*Pharisaioi*," *TDNT* 9:17–19; Kuhn, "*proselytos*," *TDNT* 6:738–39; Grünebaum, "Fremden," 49–52; Lake, "Proselytes," 77–80; De Ridder, *Dispersion*, 102–10; Derwacter, *Preparing*, 102–8; Schiffman, "Conversion," 304–6; Chesnutt, "Conversion," 183–98. Little has been written on this topic from a critical viewpoint.

2. See Snow and Machalek, "Sociology," 171–73. This small section casts some light on the requirements in the ancient world. The authors state: "These activities [demonstration events of conversion] are essentially public displays of conversion that function as status confirmation rituals" (p. 171). It is argued here

that sometimes this behavior is nothing more than "compliance behavior" that comes about as a result of "orchestration."

3. Schürer, *History* 3.1: 173–74; citation from p. 173; Hegermann, "Das hellenistische Judentum," 1:310; Lübkert, "Proselyten," 689–90; G. F. Moore, *Judaism* 1:331–35; J. Jeremias, *Jerusalem*, 320; Lesétre, "Prosélyte," cols. 762–63.

4. It ought also to be observed that the preponderance of evidence pertaining to requirements is found in rabbinic sources that are mostly later than the first century (A.D.), and naturally the discussion resorts to the antiquity of these traditions. Scholars continue to use third-century evidence, without critical inquiry, for determining first-century practices; e.g., Lohse, "Jüdische Mission," *RGG* 4:971; Kasting, *Anfänge*, 22.

5. It is well known that many converts also changed their names at times, but I am unaware that any text suggests this as a requirement and I know of no scholars who construe it as one. As an example, the inscription at Aphrodisias lists three proselytes with Hebrew names: Samouel (*a* l. 13), Ioses (*a* l. 17), and Eioseph son of Eusebios (*a* l. 22). See also *CIJ* nos. 462, 523; *Jos. Asen.* 15:7. See Horsely, "Name Change"; idem, *NewDocs* (1976) 89-96 (no. 55).

6. See Schüssler Fiorenza, "Called Father"; Kraemer, "Women"; idem, "Hellenistic Jewish Women."

7. Thus, Josephus's narrative about Queen Helena and Izates (*Ant.* 20.17–53) and Fulvia (*Ant.* 18.82). On the conversion of women, see Kraemer, *Maenads,* 247–89; idem, "Women"; Witherington, *Women*; Trebilco, "Studies," 110–35 (for a careful study of women in Asia Minor).

8. See de Vaux, *Ancient Israel,* 46–48; Bertholet, *Stellung,* 323, 335–38; Lerle, *Proselytenwerbung,* 43–51; Sigal, *Emergence* 1.1: 172–73 (and notes); Zeitlin, "Proselytes," 411–13; Lübkert, "Proselyten," 695–97; Graetz, "Proselyten," 12–13; Polster, "Talmudtraktat," 28–31; SB 4.1: 23–40; Eckert, *Urchristliche Verkündigung,* 53–58; McEleney, "Conversion," 328-34; Schmidt, *"akrobystia,"* *TDNT* 1:225–26; Meyer, *"peritemnō," TDNT* 6:72–84; Nolland, "Uncircumcised Proselytes"; Borgen, "Paul Preaches"; idem, "Observations" (a fuller article of the preceding); Vermes, *Scripture,* 178–92; Hecht, "Exegetical Contexts"; Collins, "Symbol"; Schiffman, *Who?* 23-25.

9. See, e.g., Herodotus *Historicae* 1.104.2–3; Diodorus *Bibl. Hist.* 1.28.3; 1.55.5; Artapanus (*apud* Eusebius *Praep. Ev.* 9.27); Josephus *J.W.* 1.34–35; *Ant.* 1.192, 214; 12.26; *Ag. Ap.* 1.168–71; Tacitus *Histories* 5.5; Petronius *Frag.* 37.

10. Hengel, *Judaism* 1:112; Axenfeld, "Propaganda," 25, 57; P. Dalbert suggests that Ezekiel the Tragedian dismissed circumcision as a requirement because of its offensiveness (*Theologie,* 65).

11. Trans. C. A. Moore, *Judith, A New Translation with Introduction and Commentary,* Anchor Bible 40 (Garden City, N.Y.: Doubleday, 1985). See also Esther 8:17 for a "forbidden nation convert." See further Bamberger, *Proselytism,* 16; Lerle, *Proselytenwerbung,* 25; C. A. Moore, *Judith,* 235–36.

12. See Borgen, "Observations," 87–88 (status not entrance); Finn, "Godfearers," 82–83.

13. Thus, circumcision (1) prevents carbuncle, (2) promotes cleanliness,

(3) assimilates body to heart, (4) generates fertility, (5) symbolizes excision of pleasures, and it (6) removes self-conceit of generative powers. See esp. Hecht, "Exegetical Contexts."

14. So Nolland, "Uncircumcised Proselytes," 175. See also J. J. Collins, who suggests that Philo's comments reveal at least some who did not see circumcision as necessary or important ("Symbol," 171-73). Further, he infers (*contra* Nolland) that Philo did not see circumcision as a requirement. *De Migratione Abrahami* 92 goes too much against Collins, regardless of how spiritual Philo wanted the rite to be in its deepest sense.

15. See Ptolemy the Historian *Historia Herodis,* in Ammonius *De Adfinium Vocabulorum Differentia* 243 (Stern, *GLAJJ* 1:356, lines 4–5).

16. See Nolland, "Uncircumcised Proselytes," 192–94; he relates Izates' predicament to socioeconomic and political conditions. See also Collins, "Symbol," 177–79; *Gen. Rab.* 46:11, however, is more explicit regarding the mandate of conversion.

17. See also Tacitus *Histories* 5.5.2 (Stern, *GLAJJ* 2: no. 281) and Juvenal *Satires* 14. 96-106 (Stern, *GLAJJ* 2: no. 301).

18. It is probable that this incident was not recorded until Rabbi Jose b. Halafta (fourth-generation Tanna); see Neusner, *Rabbinic Traditions* 2:142, 296; 3:212; Büchler, "Levitical Impurity," 30; Bamberger, *Proselytism,* 69–71.

19. See Neusner, *Rabbinic Traditions* 2:132-33.

20. See also *Sifra Tazria,* pereq 1:5; *t. Šabb.* 3.18; Neusner, *Rabbinic Traditions* 2:15–16; Bialoblocki, *Beziehungen,* 16–17.

21. This conflict is discussed in Bamberger, *Proselytism,* 42–52. He shows that the original dispute did not concern proselytes but the case of a Jewish child born without the foreskin.

22. Too much caution seems to be expressed by N. J. McEleney ("Conversion," 328-33). See Bertholet, *Stellung,* 335–36; Lerle, *Proselytenwerbung,* 24–39; Lübkert, "Proselyten," 696; Taylor, "Beginnings," 195; Schürer, *History* 3.1: 173-74; *contra* Felsenthal, "Proselytenfrage," 237.

23. See Ysebaert, *Greek Baptismal Terminology;* SB 1:102–13; Beasley-Murray, *Baptism,* 18–31; Bamberger, *Proselytism,* 43–44; Bertholet, *Stellung,* 324–25; Lerle, *Proselytenwerbung,* 52–60; Sigal, *Emergence* 1.1: 172–73; Lübkert, "Proselyten," 689–95; Torrance, "Proselyte Baptism"; Taylor, "Beginnings"; Polster, "Talmudtraktat"; Finkelstein, "Institution"; Rowley, "Baptism"; J. Jeremias, "Proselytentaufe"; Daube, *Rabbinic Judaism,* 106-40; Abrahams, *Studies* 1:36-46; Lake, "Proselytes," 18–19; Oepke, "*baptō,*" *TDNT* 1:529–46; O. Betz, "Proselytentaufe"; Pusey, "Baptism"; Werblowsky, "Purification"; Schiffman, *Who?* 25–30; S. J. D. Cohen, "Conversion," 37–39; idem, "Matrilineal Principle" (in this latter article Cohen suggests that the matrilineal principle [status is determined by the mother] assumes a rite [e.g., baptism]). See also now the important observations of W. A. Meeks about baptism in light of sociological theories (*First Urban,* 150–57).

24. See Rowley, "Baptism," 315–16, 326–30. W. Meeks is careful to point to the distinction between entrance rites and lustrations; he argues that Jewish

lustrations are not identical to Christian baptism in this regard, and I concur (Meeks, *First Urban*, 153 and n. 62).

25. Trans. J. J. Collins, *OTP*.

26. Lerle, *Proselytenwerbung*, 56; Rowley, "Baptism," 330; J. Jeremias, "Proselytentaufe," 426; SB 1:106 n. 1; Abrahams, *Studies*, 39–40; Schürer, *History* 3.1: 165, 174. On the other hand, K. Pusey rejects the association ("Baptism," 142). See also J. J. Collins, who dissociates it from proselyte baptism but sees it as a "symbol" (physical?) of repentance and therefore an analogy with John the Baptist ("Symbol," 168–69). Unclear, however, is how he understands the relationship of John's baptism to proselyte baptism—are they that different?

27. E.g., O. Eissfeldt, *The Old Testament: An Introduction*, trans. P. R. Ackroyd (New York: Harper & Row, 1965), 616; J. Jeremias, "Proselytentaufe," 426; Collins, *OTP* 1:381.

28. *Sib. Or.* 3:591–93 and *T. Levi* 14:6 do not refer to baptism as an initiation rite; the evidence from Qumran is also inconclusive. See Zeitlin, "A Note on Baptism"; Finkelstein, "Institution"; Beasley-Murray, *Baptism*, 22–23; Schürer, *History* 3.1: 174 n. 87 [F. Millar]. Similarly, the evidence from Juvenal *Satires* 14.104, is inconclusive because "fountain" (*fontes*) is probably also a metaphor.

29. So also S. J. D. Cohen, "Conversion," 37–38.

30. See, e.g., Abrahams, *Studies* 1:37, 40; Rowley, "Baptism," 317.

31. See Beasley-Murray, *Baptism*, 24–25. Further, it seems to me that the stronger one argues for circumcision as a requirement the less likely it is that this text refers to proselyte baptism.

32. See Taylor, "Beginnings," 195; J. Jeremias, "Proselytentaufe," 423–25; Daube, *Rabbinic Judaism*, 107–11; Alon, "Uncleanness," 150–52, 172–76; SB 1:102–5.

33. Neusner, *Rabbinic Traditions* 2:142.

34. Bialoblocki, *Beziehungen*, 19–20; Braude, *Jewish Proselytizing*, 74 n. 1; Lerle, *Proselytenwerbung*, 53–59; Sigal, *Emergence* 1.1: 173; Lübkert, "Proselyten," 695; Kuhn, "*prosēlytos*," *TDNT* 6:738–39; Alon, "Uncleanness," 148.

35. See also Rowley, "Baptism," 322–23; *contra* Abrahams, *Studies* 1:38.

36. So Lübkert, "Proselyten," 694; Taylor, "Beginnings," 195; Rowley, "Baptism," 316–17; Chesnutt, "Conversion," 185–88. J. Jeremias does not give this question the attention it deserves ("Proselytentaufe," 423). This passage raises these questions: Can a new proselyte simply be purified and then eat of the meal (not mentioning circumcision)? Or must he wait seven days to purify himself after his circumcision and then eat? It does not raise this question: Is circumcision (Hillel) or baptism (Shammai) the vital requirement? A failure to read the context has led a host of scholars to answer the wrong question. See also Büchler, "Levitical Impurity," 16–21; Neusner, *Rabbinic Traditions* 2:142; Alon, "Uncleanness," 151–52; SB 1:104; Meeks, *First Urban*, 238 n. 62.

37. See Bialoblocki, *Beziehungen*, 16–18; Alon, "Uncleanness," 173 n. 51; Felsenthal, "Proselytenfrage," 237–38 n. 1. H. H. Rowley uses this passage to date baptism by inferring that *m. 'Ed.* 5:2 is of the same view ("Baptism," 318–20). But his treatment is too uncritical and illogical (he uses the simple

deduction that Jews would not have borrowed the rite from Christians too often [which presupposes absolute dichotomies between Christianity and Judaism across the board]). He slides too quickly from lustrations to baptism. See also SB 1:105–8; Lake, "Proselytes," 78–79.

38. The decline of circumcision and the rise of baptism as a rite among Jews are traced to universalism, individualism, and spiritualization by M. Karnetzki ("Israel, die Taufe").

39. *M. Yoma* 3:3 probably refers to purification; see Finkelstein, "Institution," 205–7.

40. Schürer, *History* 3.1: 174 n. 89.

41. See, e.g., editorial note in Babli, *b. Yeb.*, 304 n. 14; Lübkert, "Proselyten," 692; S. J. D. Cohen, "Conversion," 37–39; Daube, *Rabbinic Judaism*, 106–7.

42. Esp. Zeitlin, "Note on Baptism"; Büchler, "Levitical Impurity," 16–21; cf., however, Beasley-Murray, *Baptism*, 21–22 n. 2.

43. E.g., Rowley, "Baptism," and many others. The problem here, as mentioned previously, is the sharp wedge driven between Judaism and nascent Jewish Christianity. See also now Pusey, "Baptism," 42.

44. See Daly, *Sacrifice*, 389–422.

45. G. F. Moore, *Judaism* 1:332.

46. See Graetz, "Proselyten," 11–12; Allerhand, "Hintergrund," 148 (on *m. Bik.* 2:2–6); Braude, *Jewish Proselytizing*, 41, 74–75; *contra* Zeitlin, "Proselytes," 413–14; Taylor, "Beginnings," 195.

47. We will not enter here into a discussion of initiation into the Qumran sect, because it does not apply, except indirectly, to "conversion to Judaism"; rather, it deals with "conversion to a particular interpretation of the Scriptures and history"; see Wernberg-Møller, "Yahad," 61–68; Rabin, *Qumran Studies*, 1–21; Vermes, *Qumran in Perspective*, 94–96; see also Josephus *J.W.* 2.137–42.

48. See Goodenough, *By Light*, 81–85.

49. See further *Abr.* 251; *Spec.* 1.51–53, 102–4; 2.44–48, 73; 4.176–78; *Virt.* 102–8, 175–76, 219–27; *Cher.* 31; *Praem.* 61, 152; *Migr.* 2, 184–95; *Som.* 2.273.

50. See Bialoblocki, *Beziehungen*, 21; Klein, *Katechismus*, 86–92, 137–43.

51. See further Bamberger, *Proselytism*, 38–41.

52. B. J. Bamberger states, "We need not doubt, however, that the rise of Christianity . . . led the Rabbis to stress the halakic requirements of Judaism and the Oral Law more explicitly" (*Proselytism*, 31). See also *Sifra* 91a (as cited in C. G. Montefiore and H. Loewe, *Rabbinic Anthology*, 570–71); *t. Dem.* 2.2–3, 10–14; Schiffman, *Who?* 21–23.

53. See Daube, *Rabbinic Judaism*, 113-38. The theory of Klaus Berger that almsgiving had an expiatory function in Judaism for the "God-fearers" is beyond the scope of our work; see Berger, "Almosen," esp. 182-92. Relating such a view to the collection of Paul, however, is fascinating. Comparison here with *Jos. Asen.* 10:11 is also interesting.

54. So Bamberger, *Proselytism*, 31–32; Siegfried, "Prophetische Missionsbedanke," 450; Sanders, *Paul and Palestinian Judaism*, 83–84, 206; Lake, "Proselytes," 77–78; see also Collins, "Symbol," 164–70 (conclusion from

propaganda literature from Diaspora); S. J. D. Cohen, "Crossing the Boundary," 26-30. Later discussions also revolved around the Noahide commandments; see, e.g., Segal, "Costs," 362-69.

55. See A.-M. Denis, *Introduction aux pseudépigraphes grecs d'Ancien Testament*, SVTP 1 (Leiden: E. J. Brill, 1970), 47.

56. See esp. Chesnutt, "Conversion," 133-77; idem, "Social Setting." Chesnutt accurately shows that the text betrays no ritual. Social factors are involved in this absence.

57. See Chesnutt, "Conversion," 138-43, 160-66.

58. But this meal seems to be more related to table fellowship than entry rites. See again Chesnutt, "Conversion," 150-58, 215-21, 332-35, 339-40. On clothes, see 145-47, 325-30.

59. See Chesnutt, "Conversion," 176-77. In my opinion, this is evidence for an early dating. The water of 18:9-10 is not in the end used for a cleansing; the water of 14:12-15 is potentially useful but ambiguous; see pp. 147-49.

60. The hymnic material about separation from family does not show up in the realia of the story. It is difficult, then, to know what to make of the data here; see Chesnutt, "Conversion," 199-202.

Chapter 5

1. On the various levels of adherence or "kinds" of proselytes, as they have been designated, see esp. Bamberger, *Proselytism*, 133-40; G. F. Moore, *Judaism* 1:35-38; Lübkert shows that scholars have differed little in amost a century and a half of study ("Proselyten," 686ff.); see also Graetz, "Proselyten," 13-14; Polster, "Talmudtraktat," 34-37; J. Jeremias, *Jerusalem*, 320-34; Schürer, *History* 2:150-76; Lake, "Proselytes," 80-88; S. J. D. Cohen, "Crossing the Boundary." I have profited also from Shaye Cohen's paper "Boundaries between Jew and Gentile: Conversion and Intermarriage," read before the Social History of Early Christianity Group of the Society of Biblical Literature, Dec. 7, 1987 (Boston).

2. See R. Kanter, *Commitment;* see also the summary of Segal, "Costs," 337-40.

3. For recent confirmation of this theory, even if unaware of Kanter, see Siegert, "Gottesfürchtige," 147-51; he distinguishes at times between "God-fearers" (e.g., sabbatarians) and "sympathizers" (political friends); see also S. J. D. Cohen, "Respect"; Segal, "Costs."

4. See esp. Segal, "Costs," 344-50.

5. S. J. D. Cohen, "Crossing the Boundary," 31. However, Cohen is not discussing the distinctions between various groups of Judaism but the various levels of adherence that could be made.

6. Methodologically, it is important to distinguish here between vocabulary generally used of people (i.e., those who "fear God") from vocabulary with a technical meaning (i.e., "God-fearers"). Too frequently scholars have not been sufficiently careful in this regard, thinking that every reference to "fearing" is a reference to "God-fearers."

7. On *Leg.* 211, see Smallwood, *Legatio,* 269–70; on *Mos.* 2.17–25, see Siegert, "Gottesfürchtige," 147–49.

8. See Mack, *"Imitatio,"* 34–41; Sanders, "Covenant," 33–36; Goodenough, *By Light,* 95–234.

9. H. J. Schoeps makes far too much of *Spec.* 1:51 in this regard; see *Paul,* 227.

10. Y. Amir is one of the few who sees the import of this text, although he does not explore it further (*Die hellenistische Gestalt,* 26).

11. This discussion is adapted from my forthcoming article "Lion Proselytes."

12. Manuscript M reads *ʿrbrwbyn,* "mixed multitudes."

13. For a survey that cannot be documented here, see L. Ginzberg, *The Legends of the Jews,* trans. H. Szold (Philadelphia: Jewish Publication Society of America, 1913), under "Mixed multitudes."

14. See M. Jastrow, *A Dictionary of the Targumim, the Talmud Babli and Yerushalmi, and the Midrashic Literature* (2 vols.; New York: Pardis, 1950) s.v. *giyyôr.*

15. My colleague John Sailhamer confirms that *Neofiti* on Exodus does indeed understand *gywryn* as "proselyte," a circumcised *gēr,* in light of the distinctions drawn between *gywr, dyyr,* and *br ʿmmin* in *Neofiti* Exod. 12:48–49. I am grateful for his observation and his reading of my article.

16. See S. J. D. Cohen, "Respect," 412–15; he states that such is not in effect conversion. Cohen also observes the lack of clarity in Josephus in the matters of adherence and conversion (pp. 416–30) and shows development, or change, or inconsistency (!). But see also Williams, "Tendencies," 108–9.

17. See Siegert, "Gottesfürchtige," 161.

18. See Smallwood, "Alleged"; Siegert, "Gottesfürchtige," 155–61.

19. See Feldman, "Omnipresence," 61; Schiffman, "Conversion," 302–4.

20. See Marcus, *"Sebomenoi"*; Siegert, "Gottesfürchtige," 126–29; Feldman, "Omnipresence," 61; Diffenderfer, "Conditions," 306–7; Simon, "Débuts," 514 (two groups).

21. See further Feldman, "Omnipresence," 61–62. On Poppaea Sabina as "disposed toward Judaism," perhaps as a religious eclectic, see Williams, "Tendencies."

22. Other terms arose later; see Schürer, *History* 3.1: 171–72; Siegert, "Gottesfürchtige," 110–26.

23. See, e.g., Schürer, *History* 2:459; Axenfeld, "Propaganda," 51; Klein, *Katechismus,* 246.

24. This expression, which derives from Old Testament usage, is discussed for later notions in Bamberger, *Proselytism,* 134–35; Kuhn, *"prosēlytos," TDNT* 6:740–42; Graetz, "Proselyten," 18–19; Grünebaum, "Fremden," 164–72; G. F. Moore, *Judaism* 1:339–40.

25. Bamberger, *Proselytism,* 135 (his emphasis); he uses the term "utopian." See Schürer, *History* 3.1: 172; Bertholet, *Stellung,* 328; note the uncritical use of this category in Lerle, *Proselytenwerbung,* 37–39.

26. This group will be discussed in chap. 6. For the rabbis, see Bamberger,

"Fear"; idem, *Proselytism*, 135–38; Kuhn, "*prosēlytos,*" *TDNT* 6:741–42; Wilcox, "God-Fearers," 115–17; Feldman, "Omnipresence," 62–63.

27. See Bamberger, *Proselytism*, 137–38; Wilcox, "God-Fearers," 115–17.
28. See also SB 4.1: 378–80.
29. On the latter, see Bammel, "Gerim Gerurim," 127–31.
30. See Horsely, *NewDocs* 2 (1983) 123–25 (no. 96).
31. S. J. D. Cohen, "Respect"; Kraemer, "Hellenistic Jewish Women."
32. See esp. S. J. D. Cohen, "Crossing the Boundary," 24–26.

Chapter 6

1. Bialoblocki, *Beziehungen*, 12 (translation mine). Bialoblocki conceives of the Pharisees as the major representative of Judaism, as many of his generation did. "Propaganda" here is larely synonymous with "missionary activity."
2. For the text of Q that is being assumed here, see Polag, *Fragmenta Q.* The texts will be referred to as Logion, number, and lines when necessary; hence, L36:27–35 means Logion 36, lines 27–35. The second set of signs refers the reader to the critical text of Kloppenborg, *Q Parallels.* The references are Saying number and Q reference; hence, Polag's L36 is Kloppenborg's S34, Q11:49–51. In Kloppenborg's numbering system, the Q numbers themselves (e.g., Q11:49–51) are also usually the chapter and verses of Luke's Gospel.
3. See J. A. Fitzmyer, *The Gospel according to St. Luke,* AB 28 (Garden City, N.Y.: Doubleday, 1981–1985), 1:641–42; I. H. Marshall, *The Gospel of Luke: A Commentary on the Greek Text* (Grand Rapids: Eerdmans, 1978), 268.
4. See SB 1:721; Schulz, *Q,* 473 n. 544.
5. H. Schürmann sees the Lukan intention concerned with intercommunity problems (*Das Lukasevangelium,* Erster Teil, *Kommentar zu Kap. 1,1–9,50,* HTKNT 3/1 [Freiburg/Basel/Vienna: Herder, 1969], 1:368), and R. H. Gundry seems to see a similar application by Matthew (*Matthew: A Commentary on His Literary and Theological Art* [Grand Rapids: Eerdmans, 1982], 307).
6. E. Schweizer comes close to this in connecting the logion with Rom. 2:19–20 (*The Good News according to Matthew* [Atlanta: John Knox, 1975] 326–27); for other views, see Schulz, *Q,* 473–74; Hare, *Persecution,* 142; Barth in Bornkamm et al., *Tradition,* 88 n. 2.
7. See J. Jeremias, *Jerusalem,* 233–45, esp. 235–43.
8. See Polag, *Fragmenta Q,* 57, citing only A. von Harnack and S. Schulz as contending that Pharisees were original.
9. So Schulz, *Q,* 111; Manson, *Sayings,* 103.
10. Scholars are agreed today that Paul's conversion made a decisive impact not only on his life but also on his theology, and certainly the largest factor in his theological conversion pertained to the place of the Gentiles in God's plan of salvation. See S. Kim, *Origin;* Schoeps, *Paul,* 219–58, though I demur from his exegesis of Gal. 5:11 (see below) and therefore from his conclusion that Paul was a missionary prior to conversion (219). See also Dunn, "Light."

11. This cannot be worked out in detail here. The concerns for table fellowship and purity (2:12), their guardianship role of the Torah (1:7, 10, 11-24; 4:17; 6:12)—expressing itself in concern for authority and opposition to those with "liberating" views of the law—point in the direction of the Pharisees. Most scholars identify these opponents with Jewish Christians who were at the same time Judaizers. We can probably identify the "wing" of Judaism from which they emerged. See the various viewpoints in Jewett, "Agitators"; H. D. Betz, *Galatians*, 5-9 (who, although he makes a strong connection with Acts 15:1, does not complete the observation that those Jews were of a Pharisaic stripe); F. Mussner, *Der Galaterbrief*, HTKNT 9, 4th ed. (Freiburg/Basel/Vienna: Herder, 1981), 11-29; Howard, *Paul*, 1-19. In addition, although their Pharisaic origins cannot be established, the so-called Jewish missionaries found in Justin Martyr are almost certainly Jews involved in *Gegenmission*, not evangelism. See Justin, *Dial. Trypho* 17, 108, 117.

12. See Beker, *Paul*, 37-58; Lerle, *Proselytenwerbung*, 111-31. For the complex interplay between social markers and religious issues (e.g., purity), see the discriminating analysis of J. D. G. Dunn ("Incident").

13. This observation works heavily against the view of E. P. Sanders that Paul is not opposing Judaism. If Paul is criticizing these opponents for the imposition of baggage from their previous persuasion, then, in effect, Paul is opposing Judaism—at least as he understood their understanding of Judaism. See Sanders, *Paul, the Law*, 17-20.

14. H. D. Betz shows the difficulties here and that any interpretation must be cautious (*Galatians*, 268-69). See also A. Oepke, *Der Brief des Paulus an die Galater*, THK 9, 5th ed. (Berlin: Evangelische Verlagsanstalt, 1984), 161: "A further, disconnected, difficult to understand and much-debated remark follows (translation mine)."

On the "unreal condition," see Oepke, *Galater*, 161; Burton, *Galatians*, 286-87; Mussner, *Galaterbrief*, 358 n. 106. H. Graetz, among others, suggested that Paul preached circumcision after his conversion but then changed his mind ("Zeit," 302). It is hard for me to see how Paul could escape a fatal accusation here if he in fact did compel circumcision after his conversion. Therefore, it is hard to see why Paul would have brought up the matter (especially in such an offhand way; see H. D. Betz, *Galatians*, 268) had he after his conversion been involved in circumcising converts. (I take Acts 16:3 to have occurred after Paul's letter to the Galatians and certainly after the Jerusalem Council, which most see in Gal. 2:1-10.) We must exercise restraint in equating "preaching circumcision" with "evangelizing Gentiles prior to conversion."

15. So also E. D. Burton, *The Epistle to the Galatians*, ICC (Edinburgh: T. & T. Clark, 1921), 287; Schoeps, *Paul*, 219; F. F. Bruce, *The Epistle to the Galatians: A Commentary on the Greek Text* (Grand Rapids: Eerdmans, 1982) 236, though I am unclear as to what he means by "Paul had engaged in proselytization among the Gentiles before his conversion." Does he mean that Paul evangelized Gentiles or that Paul sought total conversion from partial converts? Probably the former. "Preaching circumcision" is most likely metaphorical and

speaks for a ritual and sociological transfer. Observe how ethnic circumcision is in Galatians (e.g., 2:7, 8, 9, 12; 3:28; 5:6; 6:15). The emphatic element here is not *preaching* circumcision but rather circumcision (Paul the Jew) versus noncircumcision (Paul the Christian). On this social reading of Galatians, see esp. Dunn, "Works of the Law"; idem, "Theology"; see also his earlier "New Perspective."

16. See C. H. Dodd, *The Epistle of Paul to the Romans,* MNTC (London: Hodder & Stoughton, 1932), 42; C. K. Barrett, *A Commentary on the Epistle to the Romans,* HNTC (New York: Harper & Row, 1957), 55.

17. See Goppelt, "Missionar"; H. Schlier, *Der Römerbrief,* HTKNT 6 (Freiburg/Basel/Vienna: Herder, 1977) 81–90; E. Käsemann, *Commentary on Romans* (Grand Rapids: Eerdmans, 1980), 68–71; U. Wilckens, *Der Brief an die Römer.* 1. Teilband, Röm 1–5, Evangelisch-Katholischer Kommentar zum Neuen Testament 6.1 (Neukirchen-Vluyn: Neukirchener, 1978), 1:146–53; J. D. G. Dunn, *Romans,* WBC 38A, 38B (Dallas, Tex.: Word, 1988), 1:108–18; Zeller, *Juden und Heiden,* 155–57.

18. None of these is attached to the Pharisees prior to Paul, and the references in Matthew seem to be more on the level of Torah preservation. L. Goppelt sees Matt. 15:14 as the source of Rom. 2:19, not Matt. 23:16, 24 ("Missionar," 141 n. 19). M. Black is more cautious at this point (*Romans,* New Century Bible [London: Oliphants, 1973], 59).

19. See Schlier, *Römerbrief,* 84; Dunn, *Romans* 1:112; Zeller, *Juden und Heiden,* 156 (but he relies too heavily on later rabbis).

20. C. E. B. Cranfield takes *paideutēs* and *didaskalos* in the sense of the moral guidance offered by Jews to Gentiles (*The Epistle to the Romans,* ICC [2 vols.; Edinburgh: T. & T. Clark, 1975–1979], 1:66–67). See also Schlier, *Römerbrief,* 84–85; Dunn, *Romans* 1:112–13.

21. A case can be made for seeing these opponents as Pharisees: (1) Paul was a former Pharisee who is here lashing out against his past; (2) the expression *hodēgon . . . typhlōn* is applied elsewhere to Pharisees (Matt. 15:14; 23:16, 24); (3) the context suggests externalism (Rom. 2:1, 21–23, 25, 28–29), circumcision (2:25–29), adultery (2:22), and preoccupation with the Torah (2:17–18, 20, 23). These concerns are consistent with early Christian polemic with the Pharisees; in light of the first reason, I think the Pharisaic "wing" ought to be given first consideration. An identical or similar conclusion is found in Weiss, "Pharisäismus," 428–29; Lauterbach, "Pharisees," 137 n. 58; cf. Goppelt, "Missionar," 138, 142–43; Käsemann, *Romans,* 68–69; Dodd, *Romans,* 38–42; Wilckens, *Römer* 1:149–51; Garland, *Intention,* 130.

22. See esp. Dunn, *Romans* 1:109–11, 116–17; on p. 112, Dunn states: "None of these phrases necessarily implies an actively outgoing missionary concern . . . , more a sense of superior privilege and readiness to accept those who acknowledge their blindness and come for light and teaching." See also Hahn, *Mission,* 23; but K. Axenfeld describes these verses as "the picture of Jewish propagandists" ("Propaganda," 49).

23. See Schmithals, "False Teachers"; Käsemann, *Romans,* 416–18; Schlier,

Römerbrief, 448 (allies of Phil. 3:18–19; 2 Cor. 11:13–14; Gal. 6:11–13); Dodd, *Romans,* 243.

24. Cranfield, *Romans* 2:801–2.

25. See Munck, *Paul and the Salvation,* 264–71; Garland, *Intention,* 129–31; Flowers, "Matthew xxiii.15"; Hoad, "Matthew xxiii.15"; Lerle, *Proselytenwerbung,* 63–66; Goulder, *Midrash,* 424; Haenchen, "Matthäus 23"; Schweizer, *Matthew,* 440; J. Jeremias, *Jesus' Promise,* 17–19; SB 1:924–31; Graetz, "Der Vers"; De Ridder, *Dispersion,* 120–27; Derwacter, *Preparing,* 42–46.

26. Cf. 23:13, 15, 16, 23, 25, 27, 29. The expression is found also in Luke's accounts and therefore clearly stems from Q; however, it has been extended by Matthew (cf. 23:25). Its occurrence at 23:15 may then be due to Matthean redaction.

27. This is a Matthean formula (23:13, 15, 23, 25, 27, 29) with roots in Q (cf. 23:23, 25).

28. Cf. Matt. 8:12; 13:38; 23:31 and also Mark 2:19; 3:17; Luke 10:6; 16:8. See J. Jeremias, *Jesus' Promise,* 17–18 n. 4, for this and other Semitisms.

29. J. Jeremias, *Jesus' Promise,* 17–18 n. 4. Recently, A.-J. Levine (in a paper privately distributed) has argued that Matt. 23:15 is completely Matthean redaction, and she has further suggested that the verse reflects a particular development with respect to Jewish missionary activity in a post-70 Antiochene setting in which Matthew is battling Judaism. But (1) the evidence does not permit such a confident conclusion regarding redaction and tradition (and her work requires confidence here), and (2) external evidence does not support the inference that post-70 Judaism (in Antioch!) was involved in missionary activity. Whereas Levine infers plausible historical circumstances from a conclusion regarding redaction, I have tried to explain 23:15 in light of known historical circumstances.

30. "The sea and the land" is very probably an idiom (cf. Septuagint Jon. 1:9; Hag. 2:21; 1 Macc. 8:23, 32; Josephus *Ant.* 4.190; 11.53; Philo *Flacc.* 104, 123; *Spec.* 1.69) and not a precise "geographical description."

31. H. Graetz (unsuccessfully) reduced the "one" proselyte to Flavius Clemens ("Der Vers"). If my observations about the traditional nature of this logion are accurate, his view is wrong because he requires a date around A.D. 95. The tradition would precede this date considerably. Cf. the Semitic nature of "one" (*hena*) as exposed by J. Jeremias (*Jesus' Promise,* 17–18 n. 4 [e]). The emphasis here is not on the number of proselytes but on the fact of zeal and results of that zeal.

32. Bialoblocki, *Beziehungen,* 12.

33. See Flowers, "Matthew xxiii.15," 68–69.

34. Garland, *Intention,* 129: "The term proselyte denotes one who has fully accepted circumcision and the requisite submission to the Torah in its entirety." J. Jeremias rightly contests the view of J. Munck, which contends that the term refers to "party proselytizing"; see *Jesus' Promise,* 18 n. 1.

35. E.g., E. Klostermann, *Das Matthäusevangelium,* HNT 4 (4th ed.; Tübingen: J. C. B. Mohr [Paul Siebeck], 1971), 185.

36. So also Segal, "Costs," 358.

37. See Lerle, *Proselytenwerbung,* 63–65; Kuhn, "*prosēlytos,*" *TDNT* 6:742

n. 160; Garland, *Intention*, 129–31, for an emphasis on this element of the logion. See also Justin, *Dial. Trypho* 122.

38. See Garland, *Intention*, 130–31. Zeal per se is not condemned; rather, it is zeal for a (Pharisaic) view of the law and history, which excludes Jesus as the Messiah and his ethic as the condition for entry into the kingdom of God.

39. Axenfeld, "Propaganda," 43; cf. pp. 57–59; see also Bertholet, *Stellung*, 255. W. C. Allen, although he sees Matt. 23:15 as an attempt to proselytize into Pharisaism, shows that he understands such in terms of full conversion to the Torah (*The Gospel according to S. Matthew*, ICC [3d ed.; Edinburgh: T. & T. Clark, 1912], 246). See also similar (but not identical) views in Hahn, *Mission*, 21–25; Kuhn, *"prosēlytos,"* *TDNT* 6:742; Flowers, "Matthew xxiii.15"; Munck, *Paul and the Salvation*, 267; Garland, *Intention*, 129–31.

40. On this list, see E. Haenchen, *The Acts of the Apostles: A Commentary* (Oxford: Basil Blackwell, 1971), 196 n. 55; G. Schneider, *Die Apostelgeschichte*, HTKNT 5 (Freiburg/Basel/Vienna: Herder, 1980–1982), 1:239–56; Lüdemann, *Frühe Christentum*, 46–47.

41. This epexegetic expression, "both Jews and proselytes" (*Ioudaioi te kai prosēlytoi*), most probably refers to Jews and proselytes from Parthia to Rome, not just from Rome. See Bauernfeind, *Kommentar und Studien*, 41.

42. On the seven, see Haenchen, *Acts*, 259–69; on the Hellenists, see Moule, "Once More"; Windisch, *"Hellēn,"* *TDNT* 2:511–12; Schneider, *Apostelgeschichte* 1:406–10; Hengel, *Between*, 1–29; Cadbury, "The Hellenists."

43. The adjectival participle *sebomenoi* with the noun *prosēlytoi* is rather odd, because the terms are normally understood to designate two different groups. See Kuhn, *"prosēlytos,"* *TDNT* 6:743 (a gloss or a misuse of *prosēlytoi*); Lake, "Proselytes," 88 ("the proselytes who were worshipping"); Haenchen, *Acts*, 413 n. 5 (suggests that a possible later glossator added *prosēlytoi*); Lüdemann, *Frühe Christentum*, 162 (perhaps an irregular, weakened sense of *prosēlytoi*). See n. 61 below.

The most recent scholarship suggests that "proselyte" here has a "weakened" (nontechnical) sense of "resident alien associated loosely with Judaism."See, e.g., Overman, "God-Fearers," 20. But Overman is clearly mistaken in thinking that all proselytes are equivalent to Jews (p. 20). There is abundant evidence for Jewish classification of converts, and Acts 13:43, in fact, separates "devout proselytes" from the Jews. See, e.g., S. J. D. Cohen, "Conversion," 32–33.

44. From 6:5 we might infer that the other men, though having graecized names, were native Jews; this best explains why Nicolaus has a singular description. See Tcherikover, *CPJ* 1:29–30; H. Conzelmann, *Die Apostelgeschichte*, HNT 7 (2d ed.; Tübingen: J. C. B. Mohr [Paul Siebeck], 1972), 44; Haenchen, *Acts*, 264.

45. See J. Schneider, *"eunouchos,"* *TDNT* 2:765–68; Blinzler, *"Eisin eunouchoi"*; Nock, "Eunuchs," esp. 27–28; Haenchen, *Acts*, 309–17. Some contend that this was a castrated person; if so, Luke may see the inclusion of eunuchs as an eschatologically realized promise (Deut. 23:1; Isa. 56:3–4; Josephus *Ant.*

4.290–91; J. Schneider, *"eunouchos," TDNT* 2:768). For the place of Acts 8 in the theology of Luke, see G. Schneider, *Apostelgeschichte* 1:496–509.

46. On pilgrimages and worship, see J. Jeremias, *Jerusalem,* 73–84; Safrai, "Relations," 1.1: 186, 191–204.

47. The customs reflected here have not been investigated sufficiently; see Axenfeld, who points to Josephus (*Ant.* 20.44) to contend that this was a customary procedure ("Propaganda," 32); S. Safrai states that Torah reading was done only in public synagogue services, pointing to *m. Meg.* 4:3 ("Synagogue," in *WHJP* 1.8: 74–75); E. Schürer concludes that private ownership of the Torah was not uncommon (*History* 2:420), but J. Schneider notes that it was difficult for a non-Jew to obtain Jewish sacred books (*"eunouchos," TDNT* 2:768 n. 26). In my view, there is insufficient evidence to conclude that copies of the Torah were commonly given to non-Jews; rather, the two cases from our time period of which I am aware, the Ethiopian eunuch and Izates, may very well be exceptions because of their social status.

48. Undoubtedly, 8:26–40 is juxtaposed with 10:1–11:18 and creates "narrative tension" over the matter of which Gentiles first believed. See G. Schneider, *Apostelgeschichte* 1:499–500 (he deemphasizes the gentile aspect); Conzelmann, *Apostelgeschichte,* 55; J. Munck, *The Acts of the Apostles,* AB 31 (Garden City, N.Y.: Doubleday, 1967), 78; Haenchen, *Acts,* 314–17.

49. There has been intense discussion on the God-fearers. See Lake, "Proselytes"; Bamberger, *Proselytism,* 135–38; Wilcox, "God-Fearers"; Siegert, "Gottesfürchtige"; Romaniuk, "Gottesfürchtigen" (contains a complete linguistic discussion); Feldman, "Sympathizers"; idem, "Jewish Proselytism" (forthcoming; has the most complete compilation of the data); Kuhn, *"prosēlytos," TDNT* 6:743–44; Kraabel, "Disappearance"; Finn, "God-fearers"; Schürer, *History* 3.1: 166–76; Lüdemann, *Frühe Christentum,* 161–62; B. Lifschitz, "De nouveau sur les 'Sympathisants,'" *JSJ* 1 (1970): 77–84; Collins, "Symbol," 179–85; Diffenderfer, "Conditions," 291–308; S. J. D. Cohen, "Crossing the Boundary," 31–33; Segal, "Costs," 350–53. An interesting discussion can be seen in MacLennan and Kraabel, "Invention"; Tannenbaum, "God-Fearers"; Feldman, "Omnipresence." See also van der Horst, "Aphrodisias"; Simon, "Débuts," 512–17; Trebilco, "Studies," 154–77.

50. It is a fact that not all "sympathizers" had religious motives; so Kraabel, "Christian Evidence," 649. But on the presence of this social group, see esp. Feldman, "Jewish Proselytism," (forthcoming); S. J. D. Cohen, "Crossing the Boundary," 31–33; Trebilco, "Studies," 154–55. Kraabel is known for his famous essay "Disappearance," but it is now clear that he means (I'm not sure he meant so at the time of "Disappearance") disappearance from the narrative of Acts; see his forthcoming essay "Beloved." I detect somewhat of a concession on his part: perhaps from Luke the falsifier (as theologian) to Luke the magnifier (as theologian).

51. This has been established by Feldman, "Sympathizers"; Kraabel, "Christian Evidence," 647; Diffenderfer, "Conditions," 305, 308; Wilcox, "God-Fearers."

52. Lake, "Proselytes," 84; see also esp. Feldman, "Sympathizers." For

instance, the Miletus inscription, reading *tēs synagō/gēs tōn Ioudaiōn kai theon/ sebōn*, has been interpreted as referring to either pious Jews or Jews and pious Gentiles. See Bellen, "Aussage"; Wilcox, "God-Fearers," 112–13. Furthermore, we must not make the error of equating a group of people (gentile sympathizers) with the presence of a specific term (God-fearers) in some text or inscription. See Kraabel, who seems to make this mistake ("Christian Evidence," 640). More accurately, see Siegert, "Gottesfürchtige."

53. This methodological point is significant and seemingly overlooked by Kraabel in his various attempts to expunge false ideas about Judaism from Christian scholarship; more accurately, see Romaniuk, "Gottesfürchtige," 71.

54. See Haenchen, *Acts*, 357–60; Wilcox, "God-Fearers," 104 ("presumably"); on the Roman army, see Lundgreen, "Palästinische Heerwesen."

55. See Berger, "Almosen."

56. The expression of 10:28, *hōs athemiton estin andri Ioudaiō kollasthai ē proserchesthai allophylō*, accurately describes Judaism's practice only in a general sense (cf. e.g., 16:1, though note the probable interrogative of Matt. 8:7). Peter's view probably expresses the view and practice of a subgroup of Judaism (perhaps Pharisaism; cf. Gal. 2:11–14). See Haenchen, *Acts*, 350; K. Lake and H. J. Cadbury, *The Acts of the Apostles*, vol. 4, *English Translation and Commentary* 4:117–18, 125; a more traditional view is that of Bruce, *Acts*, 222–23. See also Dunn, "Incident"; Büchler, "Levitical Impurity"; Alon, "Uncleanness."

57. So Kraabel, "Disappearance," 119; for example, see Romaniuk, "Gottesfürchtige," 72–73. But M. R. Diffenderfer appropriately appeals to narrative order to suggest that the Cornelius episode does (and would) function definitionally for the readers of Acts ("Conditions," 305–6).

58. *Contra* Kraabel ("Disappearance," 118–21), I doubt that this pattern of Luke can be proved to be entirely fictional. J. J. Collins, after marshaling evidence for the existence of this group, said: "Moreover, even if one regards the account of Paul's missionary activity in Acts as largely fictional, the fiction requires verisimilitude to establish plausibility. Luke would scarcely have given such prominence to a category that was not known to exist at all" ("Symbol," 183). In debate with this view of Kraabel, see Finn, "God-fearers," 78–83; Overman, "God-Fearers"; Gager, "Jews, Gentiles."

59. Wilcox, "God-fearers," 107–9; cf. Haenchen, *Acts*, 409 n. 6; Romaniuk, "Gottesfürchtige," 72; Lifschitz, "Les Sympathisants," 79–80.

60. See Lake and Cadbury, *Beginnings* 4:159; Bruce, *Acts*, 282–83; Wilson, *Gentiles*, 222–24; Diffenderfer, "Conditions," 298–99.

61. See *CIJ* 2:748. So Bertholet, *Stellung*, 331; Feldman, "Omnipresence," 59; S. J. D. Cohen, "Respect," 419 (in Josephus); Overman, "God-Fearers," 18–20. See also Wilcox, "God-fearers," 108–9. But I see no grammatical warrant for Wilcox's suggested translation of 13:43a as "the Jews, both native-born and devout converts." The "both native-born" is a clear mistranslation of the simple conjunction *kai* and the repetition of the article. Furthermore, Wilcox assumes too much for the meaning of *prosēlytoi*, arguing as he does from the "correct" definition (Jew by adoption) of the term in 2:10 and 6:5 to the probable correct

usage in 13:43. The former two references contain no heuristic clues whatso-ever; perhaps we should move from 13:43 back to 2:10 and 6:5 and speak of a looser attachment to Judaism in the case of the *prosēlytoi* at 2:10 and 6:5! M. R. Diffenderfer suggests "pious proselytes" ("Conditions," 300).

62. For discussion of the textual problems, see Wilcox, "God-Fearers," 111-12; and see the textual and contextual observations (13:43; 17:17) of K. Romaniuk ("Gottesfürchtige," 75-77).

63. Official publication is now available: Reynolds and Tannenbaum, *Jews*; see also Schürer, *History* 3.1: 25-26, 166 (= F. Millar); Tannenbaum, "God-Fearers." I have also benefited from the 1989 Society of Biblical Literature Hellenistic Judaism Seminar, under the direction of Bill Adler and Shaye Cohen. Presentations were made by L. M. White, D. Edwards, R. Kraemer, and S. Cohen. For the inscriptional data, see Trebilco, "Studies," 154-77.

64. R. F. Tannenbaum plausibly suggests a "soup kitchen for the poor" ("God-Fearers," 55; see also Reynolds and Tannenbaum, *Jews*, 26-28), but the growing consensus of the Hellenistic Judaism Seminar—and the discussions I had there-after—is that *dekanias* refers more probably to a "burial society."

65. Further inscriptional evidence is summarized by F. Millar in Schürer, *History* 3.1: 166-69.

66. I agree with A. T. Kraabel ("Synagoga," 230-32) that this inscription does not imply any kind of religious connection with Judaism; these "God-fearers" may be nothing more than "donors" to a burial society. But I part with him over the distinction that the term can have. Here we have an official designation of an apparently gentile group distinct from Jews and Gentiles. Other scholars have seen a deeper religious connection; see Feldman, "Omnipresence," 63; Trebilco, "Studies," 161-64.

67. *Contra* Kraabel, "Disappearance," 120. This is in agreement, with varia-tions, with the following scholars: Tannenbaum, "God-Fearers," 57; Feldman, "Omnipresence," 63; S. J. D. Cohen, "Respect," 419 n. 30; Overman, "God-Fearers"; Segal, "Costs," 351-52; Gager, "Jews, Gentiles," 97-99; Trebilco, "Studies," 154-77.

68. R. F. Tannenbaum takes this false step ("God-Fearers," 56-57).

69. See Goldenberg, "Jewish Sabbath," 430-42.

70. For further discussion of the evidence about Jewish sympathizers in Magna Graecia and Greece, Egypt, Syria, Adiabene, Persia, and especially Rome and Aphrodisias, see Feldman, "Jewish Proselytism," section 8 (forthcoming essay). These texts have been known in scholarship for many years and need not be cited here because of the decisive importance of the Aphrodisias inscrip-tion and the Juvenal text. In my view, there is an abundance of evidence for Jewish sympathizers, and I prefer that these be classed as "God-fearers."

71. On the synagogue, see Krauss, *Synagogale Altertümer*; Schürer, *History* 2:87-149 (general context), 423-54; G. F. Moore, *Judaism* 1:281-307; Safrai, "Synagogue," in *WHJF* 1.8: 65-98; SB 4:115-88, 293-333, 353-414; Hengel, "Proseuche."

See also Abrahams, *Studies,* 1–17; *t. Meg.* 3.7; Philo *Prob.* 82; Matt. 4:23; Mark 1:21; 6:2; Luke 4:15; 6:6; 13:10.

72. So Georgi, *Opponents,* 101; Safrai, "Synagogue," 89; Bruce, *Acts,* 268 n. 4. As far as I can see, the evidence for this practice is limited virtually to this one record in Acts.

73. Harnack, *Mission* 1:1; De Ridder, *Dispersion,* 77–87; G. F. Moore, *Judaism* 1:324; SB 1:924–31.

Select Bibliography

With a few exceptions, the following bibliography lists only those works that are cited in the text. The publication data of original sources are cited only when appropriate. Standard reference works (e.g., articles in G. Kittel, G. Friedrich) and commentaries are omitted from the general bibliography.

Abrahams, I. *Studies in Pharisaism and the Gospels.* 2 vols. Cambridge: Cambridge University Press, 1917, 1924.

Adler, E. N. "Aristotle and the Jews." *REJ* 82 (1926): 91–102.

Allen, W. C. "On the Meaning of ΠΡΟΣΗΛΥΤΟΣ in the Septuagint." *The Expositor,* 4th series, 10 (1894): 264–75.

Allerhand, J. "Der historische Hintergrund der 'Sprüche der Vater' und ihre Ethik." *Kairos* 21 (1979): 133–80.

Alon, G. "The Bounds of the Laws of Levitical Cleanness." In *Jews, Judaism and the Classical World,* edited by G. Alon, 190–234. Jerusalem: Magnes, 1977.

———. "The Levitical Uncleanness of Gentiles." In *Jews, Judaism and the Classical World,* edited by G. Alon, 146–89. Jerusalem: Magnes, 1977.

———, ed. *Jews, Judaism and the Classical World: Studies in Jewish History in the Times of the Second Temple and Talmud.* Jerusalem: Magnes, 1977.

Amir, Y. *Die hellenistische Gestalt des Judentums bei Philon von Alexandrien.* Forschungen zum Jüdisch-Christlichen Dialog 5. Neukirchen-Vluyn: Neukirchener, 1983.

Applebaum, S. "The Legal Status of the Jewish Communities in the Diaspora." In *The Jewish People in the First Century,* edited by S. Safrai and M. Stern, 1.1: 420–63. Philadelphia: Fortress Press, 1974.

Atkinson, K. M. T. "The Historical Setting of the Habakkuk Commentary." *JSS* 4 (1959): 238–63.

Attridge, H. W. "Jewish Historiography." In *Early Judaism and Its Modern Interpreters*, edited by R. A. Kraft and G. W. E. Nickelsburg, 311–43. Philadelphia: Fortress Press; Atlanta: Scholars Press, 1986. [=*EJMI*]

Aune, D. E. "Orthodoxy in First Century Judaism? A Response to N. J. McEleney." *JSJ* 7 (1976): 1–10.

Axenfeld, K. "Die jüdische Propaganda als Vorläuferin und Wegbereiterin der urchristlichen Mission." In *Missionswissenschaftliche Studien: Festschrift zum 70. Geburtstag des Herrn Prof. D. Dr. Gustav Warneck*, 1–80. Berlin: Martin Warneck, 1904.

Bamberger, B. J. "Fear and Love of God in the Old Testament." *HUCA* 6 (1929): 39–53.

――――. *Proselytism in the Talmudic Period*. 2d ed. New York: Ktav, 1968.

Bammel, E. "Gerim Gerurim." *ASTI* 7 (1968–69): 127–31.

――――. "Die Rechtstellung des Herodes." *Zeitschrift des Deutschen Palästina-Vereins* 84 (1968): 73–79.

――――. "Zum Testimonium Flavianum (Jos *Ant.* 18, 63-64)." In *Josephus-Studien: Untersuchungen zu Josephus, dem antiken Judentum und dem Neuen Testament: Otto Michel zum 70. Geburtstag gewidmet*, edited by O. Betz, 9–22. Göttingen: Vandenhoeck & Ruprecht, 1974.

Barclay, W. *Educational Ideals in the Ancient World*. 1959. Reprint. Grand Rapids: Baker Book House, 1974.

Bauernfeind, O. *Kommentar und Studien zur Apostelgeschichte*. Edited by V. Metelmann. WUNT 22. Tübingen: J. C. B. Mohr, 1980.

Baumbach, G. "Das Sadduzäerverständnis bei Josephus Flavius und im Neuen Testament." *Kairos* 13 (1971): 17–37.

――――. "'Volk Gottes' im Frühjudentum: Eine Untersuchung der 'ekklesiologischen' Typen des Frühjudentums." *Kairos* 21 (1979): 30–47.

Baumgarten, J. M. "The Exclusion of 'Netinim' and proselytes in 4QFlor." *RevQ* 8 (1972): 87–96.

――――. "Exclusions from the Temple: Proselytes and Agrippa I." *JJS* 33 (1982): 215–25.

Beasley-Murray, G. R. *Baptism in the New Testament*. Grand Rapids: Eerdmans, 1973.

Becker, J. *Das Heil Gottes: Heils- und Sündenbegriffe in den Qumrantexten und im Neuen Testament*. SUNT 3. Göttingen: Vandenhoeck & Ruprecht, 1964.

Beker, J. C. *Paul the Apostle: The Triumph of God in Life and Thought*. Philadelphia: Fortress Press, 1980.

Belkin, S. *Philo and the Oral Law: The Philonic Interpretation of Biblical Law in Relation to Palestinian Halakah.* HSS 11. Cambridge, Mass.: Harvard University Press, 1940.

Bell, H. I. *Jews and Christians in Egypt: The Jewish Troubles in Alexandria and the Athanasian Controversy.* Oxford: Oxford University Press, 1924.

Bellen, H. "*Synagoge ton Ioudion kai theosebon:* Die Aussage einer bosporanischen Freilassungsinschrift (CIRB 71) zum Problem der 'Gottesfürchtigen.'" *JAC* 8 (1965): 171–76.

Berger, K. "Almosen für Israel: Zum historischen Kontext der Paulinischen Kollekte." *NTS* 23 (1977): 180–204.

Bertholet, A. *Die Stellung der Israeliten und der Juden zu den Fremden.* Freiburg i. B./Leipzig: J. C. B. Mohr, 1896.

Betz, O. *Offenbarung und Schriftforschung in der Qumransekte.* WUNT 6. Tübingen: J. C. B. Mohr, 1960.

———. "Die Proselytentaufe der Qumransekte und die Taufe im Neuen Testament." *RevQ* 1 (1958–59): 213–34.

———, ed. *Josephus-Studien: Untersuchungen zu Josephus, dem antiken Judentum und dem Neuen Testament: Otto Michel zum 70. Geburtstag gewidmet.* Göttingen: Vandenhoeck & Ruprecht, 1974.

Bialoblocki, S. *Die Beziehungen des Judentums zu Proselyten und Proselytentum.* Vortrag gehalten bei dem wissenschaftlichen Kursus der Rabbiner der süddeutschen Landesverbände in Mainz am 17. XII. 1929. Berlin: n.p., 1930.

Bickermann, E. J. "The Altars of the Gentiles: A Note on the Jewish 'ius sacrum.'" *Revue Internationale des Droits et de l'Antiquité* (Brussels) 3, 5 (1958): 137–64.

———. *Der Gott der Makkabäer: Untersuchungen über Sinn und Ursprung der makkabäischen Erhebung.* Berlin: Schocken, 1937.

———. "The Historical Foundations of Postbiblical Judaism." In *The Jews, Their History,* edited by L. Finkelstein, 72–118. New York: Schocken, 1970.

———. "The Warning Inscriptions of Herod's Temple." *JQR* 37 (1946–47): 387–405.

Bilde, P. "The Roman Emperor Gaius (Caligula)'s Attempt to Erect His Statue in the Temple of Jerusalem." *ST* 32 (1978): 67–93.

Blenkinsopp, J. "Interpretation and the Tendency to Sectarianism: An Aspect of Second Temple History." In *Jewish and Christian Self-Definition,* edited by E. P. Sanders and A. I. Baumgarten, 2:1–26. London: SCM, 1981.

———. "Prophecy and Priesthood in Josephus." *JJS* 25 (1974): 239–62.

Blidstein, G. "4QFlorilegium and Rabbinic Sources on Bastard and Proselyte." *RevQ* 8 (1974): 431–35.

Blinzler, J. "Εἰσὶν εὐνοῦχοι: Zur Auslegung von Mt 19,12." *ZNW* 28 (1957): 254–70.

Blosser, D. "The Sabbath Year Cycle in Josephus." *HUCA* 52 (1981): 129–39.

Bonsirven, J. *Le Judaïsme Palestiniens au temps de Jesus-Christ: Sa Theologie. 1 La Théologique Dogmatique.* 2d ed. BTH. Paris: Beauchesne, 1934.

Borgen, P. "Observations on the Theme 'Paul and Philo': Paul's Preaching of Circumcision in Galatia (Gal. 5:1) and Debates on Circumcision in Philo." In *Die Paulinische Literatur und Theologie,* edited by S. Pedersen, 85–102. Göttingen: Vandenhoeck & Ruprecht, 1980.

———. "Paul Preaches Circumcision and Pleases Men." In *Paul and Paulinism: Essays in honour of C. K. Barrett,* edited by M. D. Hooker and S. G. Wilson, 37–46. London: SPCK, 1982.

Bornkamm, G., G. Barth., and H. J. Held. *Tradition and Interpretation in Matthew.* NTL. Philadelphia: Westminster Press, 1963.

Bosch, D. *Die Heidenmission in der Zukunftsschau Jesu: Eine Untersuchung zur Eschatologie der synoptischen Evangelien.* ATANT 36. Zurich: Zwingli, 1959.

Bousset, W. *Die Religion des Judentums im Späthellenistischen Zeitalter.* Edited by H. Gressmann. 3d ed. HNT 21. Tübingen: J. C. B. Mohr, 1966.

Bowers, P. "Paul and Religious Propaganda in the First Century." *NovT* 22 (1980): 316–23.

Bowker, J. *Jesus and the Pharisees.* Cambridge: Cambridge University Press, 1973.

Brandon, S. G. F. *Jesus and the Zealots: A Study of the Political Factor in Primitive Christianity.* Manchester: Manchester University Press, 1967.

———. "Josephus: Renegade or Patriot?" *History Today* 8 (1958): 830–36.

Braude, W. G. *Jewish Proselytizing in the First Five Centuries of the Common Era, the Age of the Tannaim and Amoraim.* BUS 6. Providence: Brown University Press, 1940.

Broshi, M. "The Credibility of Josephus." *JJS* 33 (1982): 379–84.

Buchanan, G. W. "The Role of Purity in the Structure of the Essene Sect." *RevQ* 4 (1963–64): 397–406.

Büchler, A. "The Levitical Impurity of the Gentiles in Palestine before the Year 70." *JQR* 17 (1927): 1–81.

Burchard, C. "Verbesserungen zum vorläufigen Text von Joseph und Aseneth." *Dielheimer Blätter zum Alten Testament* 16 (1982): 37–39.

———. "Ein vorläufiger griechischer Text von Joseph und Aseneth." *Dielheimer Blätter zum Alten Testament* 14 (1979): 2–53.

Byatt, A. "Josephus and Population Numbers in First Century Palestine." *PEQ* 105 (1973): 51–60.

Cadbury, H. J. "The Hellenists." In *The Beginnings of Christianity.* Edited by F. J. Foakes Jackson and K. Lake, 5:59–74. 5 vols. 1922–33. Reprint. Grand Rapids: Baker Book House, 1979.

Caragounis, C. C. *The Ephesian Mysterion: Meaning and Content.* ConBNTS 8. Lund: C. W. K. Gleerup, 1977.

Cardauns, B. "Juden und Spartaner: Zur hellenistisch-judischen Literatur." *Hermes* 95 (1967): 317–24.

Charlesworth, J. H. "The Origin and Subsequent History of the Authors of the Dead Sea Scrolls: Four Transitional Phases Among the Qumran Essenes." *RevQ* 10 (1980): 213–34.

Chernick, M. "Some Talmudic Responses to Christianity, Third and Fourth Centuries." *JES* 17 (1980): 393–406.

Chesnutt, R. D. "Conversion in Joseph and Aseneth: Its Nature, Function, and Relation to Contemporaneous Paradigms of Conversion and Initiation." Ph.D. diss., Duke University, 1986.

———. "The Social Setting and Purpose of Joseph and Aseneth." *JSP* 2 (1988): 21–48.

Cohen, S. J. D. "Conversion to Judaism in Historical Perspective: From Biblical Israel to Post-Biblical Judaism." *ConsJud* 36 (1983): 31–45.

———. "Crossing the Boundary and Becoming a Jew." *HTR* 82 (1989): 14–33.

———. "From the Bible to the Talmud: The Prohibition of Intermarriage." *HAR* 7 (1983): 23–39.

———. *From the Maccabees to the Mishnah.* LEC 7. Philadelphia: Westminster Press, 1987.

———. "Masada: Literary Tradition, Archaeological Remains, and the Credibility of Josephus." *JJS* 33 (1982): 385–405.

———. "The Origins of the Matrilineal Principle in Rabbinic Law." *AJSReview* 10 (1985): 19–53.

———. "Respect for Judaism by Gentiles according to Josephus." *HTR* 80 (1987): 409–30.

Cohen, Y. "The Attitude to the Gentile in the Halakah and in Reality in the Tannaitic Period." *Immanuel* 9 (1979): 32–41.

Collins, J. J. *Between Athens and Jerusalem: Jewish Identity in the Hellenistic Diaspora.* New York: Crossroad, 1983.

———. "A Symbol of Otherness: Circumcision and Salvation in the First Century." In *"To See Ourselves as Others See Us": Christians, Jews,*

"Others" in Late Antiquity, edited by J. Neusner and E. S. Frerichs, 163–86. Chico, Calif.: Scholars Press, 1985.

Conley, T. M. "Philo's Rhetoric: Argumentation and Style." *ANRW* 2.21.1: 343–71.

Conzelmann, H. *Heiden-Juden-Christen: Auseinandersetzungen in der Literatur der hellenistisch-römischen Zeit.* BHT 62. Tübingen: J. C. B. Mohr, 1981.

Dalbert, P. *Die Theologie der hellenistisch-jüdischen Missionsliteratur unter Ausschluss von Philo u. Josephus.* TF 4. Hamburg-Volksdorf: Herbert Reich, 1954.

Daly, R. J. *Christian Sacrifice: The Judaeo-Christian Background Before Origen.* CUASCA 18. Washington, D.C.: Catholic University Press, 1978.

Daube, D. *The New Testament and Rabbinic Judaism.* London: Athlone, 1956.

———. "Rabbinic Methods of Interpretation and Hellenistic Rhetoric." *HUCA* 22 (1949): 239–64.

Davies, P. "Hasidim in the Maccabean Period." *JJS* 28 (1977): 127–40.

Davies, W. D. "'Knowledge' in the DSS and Matthew 11:25–30." *HTR* 46 (1953): 113–39.

———. *Paul and Rabbinic Judaism: Some Rabbinic Elements in Pauline Theology.* 4th ed. Philadelphia: Fortress Press, 1980.

de Jonge, M. *Studies on the Testaments of the Twelve Patriarchs: Text and Interpretation.* SVTP 3. Leiden: Brill, 1975.

———. *The Testaments of the Twelve Patriarchs: A Study of Their Text, Composition, and Origin.* Assen: van Gorcum, 1953.

Delling, G. "Josephus und die heidnische Religionen." *Klio* 43–45 (1965): 263–69.

———. "Die Kunst des Gestaltens in 'Joseph und Aseneth.'" *NovT* 26 (1984): 1–42.

De Ridder, R. *The Dispersion of the People of God.* 1971. Reprinted as *Discipling the Nations.* Grand Rapids: Baker Book House, 1975. [Cited as *Dispersion*]

Derwacter, F. M. *Preparing the Way for Paul: The Proselyte Movement in Later Judaism.* New York: Macmillan, 1930.

de Vaux, R. *Ancient Israel: Its Life and Institutions.* London: Darton, Longman, & Todd, 1966.

Dexinger, F. "Die Sektenproblematik im Judentum." *Kairos* 21 (1979): 273–87.

Diffenderfer, M. R. "Conditions of Membership in the People of God: A Study Based on Acts 15 and Other Relevant Passages in Acts." Ph.D. diss., University of Durham, 1987.

Dix, G. *Jew and Gentile: A Study in the Primitive Church.* New York: Harper & Bros., n.d.

Donaldson, T. L. "Preaching Circumcision: Gal. 5:11 and the Origin of Paul's Gentile Mission." Paper presented at the annual meeting of the Society of Biblical Literature in Chicago. 1988.

———. "Proselytes or 'Righteous Gentiles'? The Status of Gentiles in Eschatological Pilgrimage Patterns of Thought." Paper delivered before the Torah-Nomos Seminar in the Canadian Society of Biblical Literature. 1986. Forthcoming in *Torah and Nomos in Post-Biblical Judaism.* Waterloo: Wilfrid Laurier Press.

Douglas, M. T. *Purity and Danger: An Analysis of the Concepts of Pollution and Taboo.* London: Routledge & Kegan Paul, 1966.

Drazin, N. *History of Jewish Education From 515 B.C.E. to 220 C.E.* JHUSE 29. Baltimore: Johns Hopkins University Press, 1940.

Drummond, J. *Philo Judaeus: Or, The Jewish-Alexandrian Philosophy in Its Development and Completion.* 2 vols. London: Williams & Norgate, 1888.

Dunn, J. D. G. "The Incident at Antioch (Gal. 2:11-18)." *JSNT* 18 (1983): 3-57.

———. "'A Light to the Gentiles': The Significance of the Damascus Road Christophany for Paul." In *The Glory of Christ in the New Testament: Studies in Christology in Memory of George Bradford Caird,* edited by L. D. Hurst and N. T. Wright, 251-66. Oxford: Clarendon, 1987.

———. "The New Perspective on Paul." *BJRLUM* 65 (1983): 95-122.

———. "The Theology of Galatians." In *Society of Biblical Literature 1986 Seminar Papers,* edited by K. H. Richards, 1-16. Atlanta: Scholars Press, 1986.

———. *Unity and Diversity in the New Testament: An Inquiry into the Character of Earliest Christianity.* Philadelphia: Westminster Press, 1977.

———. "Works of the Law and the Curse of the Law (Galatians 3.10-14)." *NTS* 31 (1985): 523-42.

Eckert, J. *Die urchristliche Verkündigung im Streit zwischen Paulus und seinen Gegnern nach dem Galaterbrief.* MUS. Regensburg: Pustet, 1971.

Eisman, M. M. "Dio and Josephus: Parallel Analyses." *Latomus* 36 (1977): 657-73.

Ericksen, R. P., *Theologians under Hitler: Gerhard Kittel, Paul Althaus, and Emanuel Hirsch.* New Haven/London: Yale University Press, 1985.

Farmer, W. R. *Maccabees, Zealots, and Josephus: An Inquiry into Jewish Nationalism in the Greco-Roman Period.* New York: Columbia University Press, 1956.

Feldman, L. H. "Abraham the Greek Philosopher in Josephus." *TAPA* 99 (1968): 143–56.

———. "Flavius Josephus Revisted: The Man, His Writings, and His Significance." *ANRW* 2.21.2: 763–862.

———. "Hellenizations in Josephus' Portrayal of Man's 'Decline.'" In *Religions in Antiquity: Essays in Memory of Erwin Ramsdell Goodenough,* edited by J. Neusner, 336–53. SHR 14. Leiden: Brill, 1968.

———. "Jewish Proselytism." In *Eusebius, Christianity, and Judaism,* edited by H. W. Attridge and G. Hata. Detroit: Wayne State University Press. Forthcoming.

———. "Jewish 'Sympathizers' in Classical Literature and Inscriptions." *TAPA* 81 (1950): 200–8.

———. "The Omnipresence of the God-Fearers." *BAR* 12 (1986): 58–69.

———. "The Orthodoxy of the Jews in Hellenistic Egypt." *Jewish Social Studies* 22 (1960): 215–37.

———. "Pro-Jewish Intimations in Anti-Jewish Remarks Cited in Josephus' *Against Apion.*" *JQR* 78 (1988): 187–251.

Felsenthal, B. "Zur Proselytenfrage im Judenthum." *MGWJ* 27 (1879): 236–40.

Ferguson, E. F. *Backgrounds of Early Christianity.* Grand Rapids: Eerdmans, 1987.

Finkelstein, L. "The Institution of Baptism for Proselytes." *JBL* 52 (1933): 302–11.

Finn, T. M. "The God-fearers Reconsidered." *CBQ* 47 (1985): 75–84.

Fischer, T., "Zu den Beziehungen zwischen Rom und den Juden im 2. Jahrhundert v. Chr." *ZAW* 86 (1974): 90–93.

Flowers, H. J. "Matthew xxiii.15." *ExpTim* 73 (1961): 67–69.

Flusser, D. "Paganism in Palestine." In *The Jewish People in the First Century,* edited by S. Safrai and M. Stern, 1.2: 1065–1100. Philadelphia: Fortress Press, 1976.

Freyne, S. *Galilee from Alexander the Great to Hadrian, 323 B.C.E. to 135 C.E.: A Study of Second Temple Judaism.* Notre Dame: University of Notre Dame Press, 1980.

Fry, V. R. L. "The Warning Inscriptions from the Herodian Temple." Ph.D. diss., Southern Baptist Theological Seminary, 1974.

Gager, J. G.. "Jews, Gentiles, and Synagogues in the Book of Acts." In *Christians among Jews and Greeks,* edited by G. W. E. Nickelsburg and G. MacRae, 91–99. Philadelphia: Fortress Press, 1986.

———. "Judaism as Seen by Outsiders." In *Early Judaism and Its Modern Interpreters,* edited by R. A. Kraft and G. W. E. Nickelsburg, 99–116. Philadelphia: Fortress Press; Atlanta: Scholars Press, 1986. [= *EJMI*]

———. *Moses in Graeco-Roman Religion.* SBLMS 16. Nashville: Abingdon, 1972.

———. *The Origins of Anti-Semitism: Attitudes Toward Judaism in Pagan and Christian Antiquity.* New York/Oxford: Oxford University Press, 1983.

Garland, D. E. *The Intention of Matthew 23.* SNovT 52. Leiden: Brill, 1979.

Gaventa, B. R. *From Darkness to Light: Aspects of Conversion in the New Testament.* OBT 20. Philadelphia: Fortress Press, 1986.

Georgi, D. *The Opponents of Paul in Second Corinthians.* Philadelphia: Fortress Press, 1986.

Gilbert, G. H. "The Hellenization of the Jews between 334 B.C. and 70 A.D." *AJTh* 13 (1909): 520–40.

Ginsburg, M. S. "Fiscus Judaicus." *JQR* 21 (1930–31): 281–91.

———. "Sparta and Judaea." *Classical Philology* 29 (1934): 117–22.

Giovannini, A., and H. Müller. "Die Beziehungen zwischen Rom und den Juden im 2. Jh. v. Chr." *Mus. Helv.* 28 (1971): 156–71.

Golb, N. "Who Hid the Dead Sea Scrolls?" *BA* 48 (1985): 68–82.

Goldenberg, R. "The Jewish Sabbath in the Roman World up to the Time of Constantine the Great." *ANRW* 2.19.1: 414–47.

Goldstein, J. A. "Jewish Acceptance and Rejection of Hellenism." In *Jewish and Christian Self-Definition,* edited by E. P. Sanders and A. I. Baumgarten, 2:64–87. London: SCM, 1981.

Goodenough, E. R. *By Light, Light: The Mystic Gospel of Hellenistic Judaism.* New Haven: Yale University Press, 1935.

———. *Jewish Symbols in the Greco-Roman Period.* 13 vols. New York: Bollingen Foundation, 1953–68.

———. "Philo's Exposition of the Law and his De vita Mosis." *HTR* 26 (1933): 109–25.

———. *The Politics of Philo Judaeus: Practice and Theory.* New Haven: Yale University Press, 1938.

Goppelt, L. "Der Missionar des Gesetzes: Zu Röm. 2,21f." In *Christologie und Ethik: Aufsätze zum Neuen Testament,* 137–47. Göttingen: Vandenhoeck & Ruprecht, 1968.

Goulder, M. *Midrash and Lection in Matthew.* London: SPCK, 1974.

Grabbe, L. L. "Orthodoxy in First Century Judaism: What are the Issues?" *JSJ* 8 (1977): 149–53.

Graetz, H. "Die jüdische Proselyten im Römerreiche unter den Kaisern Domitian, Nerva, Trajan und Hadrian." *Jahresbericht des jüdisch-theologischen Seminars 'Fraenckl'sche Stiftung'* (1884): 1–38.

———. "Der Vers im Matthäus-Evangelium: eines Proselyten machen." *MGWJ* 18 (1869): 169–70.

———. "Zeit der Anwesenheit der adiabenischen Königin in Jerusalem und der Apostel Paulus." *MGWJ* 26 (1877): 241–55, 289–306.

Greenewalt, C. H., Jr., M. L. Rautman, and R. Meriç. "The Sardis Campaign of 1983." In *Preliminary Reports of ASOR-Sponsored Excavations 1980-84,* edited by W. E. Rast, 1–30. BASORS 24. Winona Lake: Eisenbrauns, 1986.

Greenewalt, C. H., Jr., N. D. Cahill, and M. L. Rautman. "The Sardis Campaign of 1984," and "The Sardis Campaign of 1985." In *Preliminary Reports of ASOR-Sponsored Excavations 1982-1985,* edited by W. E. Rast, 13–54, 55–92. BASORS 25. Baltimore: Johns Hopkins University Press, 1988.

Gressmann, H. "Heidnische Mission in der Werdezeit des Christentums." *ZMR* 39 (1924): 10–24.

———. "Jüdische Mission in der Werdezeit des Christentums." *ZMR* 39 (1924): 169–83.

Grünebaum, E. "Der Fremde (Ger) nach rabbinischer Begriffen." *Jüdische Zeitschrift für Wissenschaft und Leben* (1871): 164–72.

———. "Die Fremden (Gerim) nach rabbinischer Gesetzen: Ein Beitrag zur weiteren Kenntnis der rabbinischen Sittenlehre." *Jüdische Zeitschrift für Wissenschaft und Leben* (1870): 43–57.

Gutmann, J. "The 'Second Commandment' and the Image in Judaism." *HUCA* 32 (1961): 161–74.

Haenchen, E. "Matthäus 23." *ZTK* 48 (1951): 38–63.

Hahn, F. *Mission in the New Testament.* SBT 47. London: SCM, 1981.

Hamerton-Kelly, R. G. "Some Techniques of Composition in Philo's Allegorical Commentary with Special Reference to *De Agricultura:* A Study in Hellenistic Midrash." In *Jews, Greeks and Christians: Religious Cultures in Late Antiquity: Essays in Honor of William David Davies,* 45–56. SJLA 21. Leiden: Brill, 1976.

Hanfmann, G. M., and W. E. Mierse, eds. *Sardis from Prehistoric to Roman Times: Results of the Archaeological Exploration of Sardis, 1958-1975.* Cambridge, Mass.: Harvard University Press, 1983.

Hare, D. R. A. *The Theme of Jewish Persecution of Christians in the Gospel according to St Matthew.* SNTSMS 6. Cambridge: Cambridge University Press, 1967.

von Harnack, A. *The Mission and Expansion of Christianity in the First Three Centuries.* 2 vols. London: Williams & Norgate, 1904–5.

Harrington, D. J. "Joseph in the Testament of Joseph, Pseudo-Philo, and Philo." In *Studies on the Testament of Joseph*, edited by G. W. E. Nickelsburg, 127–31. SBLSCS 5. Missoula, Mont.: Scholars Press, 1975.

Harris, H. A. *Greek Athletics and the Jews*. Trivium Special Publications 3. Cardiff: University of Wales Press, 1976.

Harris, W. V. *Ancient Literacy*. Cambridge, Mass.: Harvard University Press, 1989.

Hasenclever, Dr. "Christliche Proselyten der höheren Stände im ersten Jahrhundert." *Jahrbuch für Protestantische Theologie* 8 (1882): 34–78.

Hay, D. M. "Philo's References to Other Allegorists." *StPhilonica* 6 (1979–80): 41–75.

Hecht, R. D. "The Exegetical Contexts of Philo's Interpretation of Circumcision." In *Nourished with Peace: Studies in Hellenistic Judaism in Memory of Samuel Sandmel*, edited by F. E. Greenspahn, E. Hilgert, and B. L. Mack, 51–79. Chico, Calif.: Scholars Press, 1984.

Hegermann, H. "Das hellenistische Judentum." In *Umwelt des Urchristentums: I, Darstellung des neutestamentlichen Zeitalters*, edited by J. Leipoldt and W. Grundmann, 1:292–345. 2 vols. Berlin: Evangelische Verlagsanstalt, 1971.

Heinemann, I. *Die griechische Weltanschauung bei Juden und Römern*. Berlin: Philo-Verlag, 1932.

Hempel, J. "Die Wurzeln des Missionswillens im Glauben des AT." *ZAW* 66 (1954): 244–72.

Hengel, M. "Between Jesus and Paul: The 'Hellenists,' the 'Seven' and Stephen (Acts 6:1–15)." In *Between Jesus and Paul*, by M. Hengel, 1–29. Philadelphia: Fortress Press, 1983.

———. *Between Jesus and Paul: Studies in the Earliest History of Christianity*. Philadelphia: Fortress Press, 1983.

———. *Jews, Greeks and Barbarians: Aspects of the Hellenization of Judaism in the pre-Christian Period*. Philadelphia: Fortress Press, 1980.

———. *Judaism and Hellenism: Studies in their Encounter in Palestine during the Early Hellenistic Period*. 2 vols. Philadelphia: Fortress Press, 1974.

———. "The Origins of the Christian Mission." In *Between Jesus and Paul*, by M. Hengel, 48–64. Philadelphia: Fortress Press, 1983.

———. "Proseuche and Synagoge: Jüdische Gemeinde, Gotteshaus und Gottesdienst in der Diaspora und in Palästina." In *Tradition und Glaube: Das Frühe Christentum in seiner Umwelt: Festgabe für Karl Georg Kuhn zum 65. Geburtstag*, edited by G. Jeremias, 157–84. Göttingen: Vandenhoeck & Ruprecht, 1971.

Hoad, J. "On Matthew xxiii.15: A Rejoinder." *ExpTim* 73 (1962): 211–12.

Hock, R. F. *The Social Context of Paul's Ministry: Tentmaking and Apostleship.* Philadelphia: Fortress Press, 1980.

Hodgson, R., Jr. "Valerius Maximus and the Social World of the New Testament." *CBQ* 51 (1989): 683–93.

Hoehner, H. *Herod Antipas.* SNTSMS 17. Cambridge: Cambridge University Press, 1972.

Hoenig, S. B. "Oil and Pagan Defilement." *JQR* 61 (1970): 63–75.

Holladay, C. R. *Theios Aner in Hellenistic Judaism: A Critique of the Use of This Category in New Testament Christology.* SBLDS 40. Missoula, Mont.: Scholars Press, 1977.

Howard, G. *Paul: Crisis in Galatia.* SNTSMS 35. Cambridge: Cambridge University Press, 1979.

Hurtado, L. W. *One God, One Lord: Early Christian Devotion and Ancient Jewish Monotheism.* Philadelphia: Fortress Press, 1988.

Jaeger, W. "Greeks and Jews: The First Greek Records of Jewish Religion and Civilization." *JR* 18 (1938): 127–43.

Jellicoe, S. "The Occasion and Purpose of the Letter of Aristeas: A Reexamination." *NTS* 12 (1965–66): 144–50.

Jeremias, G. *Der Lehrer der Gerechtigkeit.* SUNT 2. Göttingen: Vandenhoeck & Ruprecht, 1963.

Jeremias, J. "The Gentile World in the Thought of Jesus." *BSNTS* 3 (1952): 18–28.

———. "Die Heidenwelt in der Sicht Jesu." *Wissenschaftliche Zeitschrift der Martin-Luther-Universität Halle-Wittenberg, gesellschafts- und sprachwissenschaftliche Reihe* 3 (1954): 483–84.

———. *Jerusalem in the Time of Jesus: An Investigation into Economic and Social Conditions during the New Testament Period.* Philadelphia: Fortress Press, 1969.

———. *Jesus' Promise to the Nations.* Franz Delitzsch Lectures for 1953. SBT 24. London: SCM, 1958.

———. "Proselytentaufe und Neues Testament." *TZ* 5 (1949): 418–28.

Jervell, J. "Imagines und Imago Dei: Aus der Genesis-Exegese des Josephus." In *Josephus-Studien,* edited by O. Betz, 197–204. Göttingen: Vandenhoeck & Ruprecht, 1974.

Jewett, R. "The Agitators and the Galatian Congregation." *NTS* 17 (1970–71): 198–212.

Johnson, L. T. "The New Testament's Anti-Jewish Slander and the Conventions of Ancient Polemic." *JBL* 108 (1989): 419–41.

Jones, H. S. "Claudius and the Jewish Question at Alexandria." *JRS* 16 (1926): 17–35.

Juster, J. *Les Juifs dans l'empire romain.* 2 vols. Paris: Geuthner, 1914.

Kanter, R. *Commitment and Community.* Cambridge, Mass.: Harvard University Press, 1972.

Kanter, S. *Rabban Gamaliel II: The Legal Traditions.* BJS 8. Chico, Calif.: Scholars Press, 1980.

Karnetzki, M. "Israel, die Taufe und die Proselyten." *Quatember* 23 (1958–59): 137–41.

Kasting, H. *Die Anfänge der Urchistlichen Mission: Eine historische Untersuchung.* BEvT 55. Munich: Kaiser, 1969.

Kee, H. C. "The Socio-Cultural Setting of *Joseph and Aseneth.*" *NTS* 29 (1983): 394–413.

Kertelge, K., ed. *Mission im Neuen Testament.* QD 93. Freiburg/Basel/ Vienna: Herder, 1982.

Kim, S. *The Origin of Paul's Gospel.* Grand Rapids: Eerdmans, 1981.

Kittel, G. "Das kleinasiatische Judentum in der hellenistisch-römischen Zeit: Ein Bericht zur Epigraphik Kleinasiens." *TLZ* 69 (1944): 9–20.

———— "Das Konnubium mit den Nicht-Juden im antiken Judentum." *Forschungen zur Judenfrage* 2 (1937): 30–62.

Klein, G. *Der älteste christliche Katechismus und die jüdische Propagandaliteratur.* Berlin: n.p., 1909.

Kloppenborg, J. S. *Q Parallels: Synopsis, Critical Notes & Concordance.* FFNT. Philadelphia: Fortress Press, 1988.

Knox, W. L. "Abraham and the Quest for God." *HTR* 28 (1935): 55–60.

Koester, H. "ΝΟΜΟΣ ΦΥΣΕΩΣ: The Concept of Natural Law in Greek Thought." In *Religions in Antiquity: Essays in Memory of Erwin Ramsdell Goodenough,* edited by J. Neusner, 521–41. SHR 14. Leiden: Brill, 1968.

Kraabel, A. T. "The Diaspora Synagogue: Archaeological and Epigraphic Evidence since Sukenik." *ANRW* 2.19.1: 477–510.

————. "The Disappearance of the God-fearers." *Numen* 28 (1981): 113–26.

————. "The God-fearers meet the Beloved Disciple." Helmut Koester Festschrift. Forthcoming.

————. "Greeks, Jews, and Lutherans in the Middle Half of Acts." In *Christians Among Jews and Gentiles,* edited by G. W. E. Nickelsburg and G. MacRae, 147–57. Philadelphia: Fortress Press, 1986.

————. "*Hypsistos* and the Synagogue at Sardis." *GRBS* 10 (1969): 81–93.

————. "The Impact of the Discovery of the Sardis Synagogue." In *Sardis from Prehistoric to Roman Times: Results of the Archaeological Exploration of Sardis, 1958–1975,* edited by G. M. Hanfmann and W. E. Mierse, 178–90. Cambridge, Mass.: Harvard University Press, 1983.

———. "Paganism and Judaism: The Sardis Evidence." In *Paganisme, Judaïsme, Christianisme: Influences et affrontements dans le monde antique. Mélanges offerts à Marcel Simon*, edited by A. Benoit et al., 13-33. Paris: Boccard, 1978.

———. "The Roman Diaspora: Six Questionable Assumptions." *JJS* 33 (1982): 445-64.

———. "Social Systems of Six Diaspora Synagogues." In *Ancient Synagogues: The State of Research*, edited by J. Gutmann, 79-91. Chico, Calif.: Scholars Press, 1981.

———. "Synagoga Caeca: Systematic Distortion in Gentile Interpretations of Evidence for Judaism in the Early Christian Period." In *"To See Ourselves as Others See Us": Christians, Jews, "Others" in Late Antiquity*, edited by J. Neusner and E. S. Frerichs, 219-46. Chico, Calif.: Scholars Press, 1985.

———. "Traditional Christian Evidence for Diaspora Judaism: The Book of Acts." In *Society of Biblical Literature 1986 Seminar Papers*, edited by K. H. Richards, 644-51. Atlanta: Scholars Press, 1986.

Kraeling, C. H. "The Episode of the Roman Standards at Jerusalem." *HTR* 35 (1942): 263-89.

———. "The Jewish Community at Antioch." *JBL* 51 (1932): 130-60.

Kraemer, R. S. "Hellenistic Jewish Women: The Epigraphical Evidence." In *Society of Biblical Literature 1986 Seminar Papers*, edited by K. H. Richards, 183-200. Atlanta: Scholars Press, 1986.

———. *Maenads, Martyrs, Matrons, Monastics: A Sourcebook on Women's Religions in the Greco-Roman World*. Philadelphia: Fortress Press, 1988.

———. "On the Meaning of the Term 'Jew' in Greco-Roman Inscriptions." *HTR* 82 (1989): 35-53.

———. "Women in the Religions of the Greco-Roman World." *RelSRev* 9 (1983): 127-39.

Kraft, R. A., and G. W. E. Nickelsburg, eds. *Early Judaism and Its Modern Interpreters*. Philadelphia: Fortress Press; Atlanta: Scholars Press, 1986. [=*EJMI*]

Kramer, W. *Christ, Lord, Son of God*. SBT 50. London: SCM, 1963.

Krauss, S. *Synagogale Altertümer*. Berlin: Benjamin Harz, 1922.

Kuhn, K. G., and H. Stegemann. "Proselyten." In *Pauly's Realencyclopädie der classischen Altertumswissenschaft*, edited by G. Wissowa, W. Kroll, K. Mittelhaus, and K. Ziegler, 1248-83. Supplementary volume no. 9. 1962.

Lake, K. "Proselytes and God-fearers." In *The Beginnings of Christianity*, edited by F. J. Foakes Jackson and K. Lake, 5:74-96. 5 vols. 1922-1933. Reprint. Grand Rapids: Baker Book House, 1979.

Lane, E. N. "Sabazius and the Jews in Valerius Maximus: A Reexamination." *JRS* 69 (1979): 35–38.

Langen, J. "Der theologische Standpunkt des Flavius Josephus." *TQ* 47 (1865): 3–59.

La Piana, G. "Foreign Groups in Rome During the First Centuries of the Empire." *HTR* 20 (1927): 183–403.

Laporte, J. "Philo in the Tradition of Biblical Wisdom Literature." In *Aspects of Wisdom in Judaism and Early Christianity*, edited by R. L. Wilken, 103–41. UNDCSJCA 1. Notre Dame: University of Notre Dame Press, 1975.

Lauterbach, J. Z. "The Pharisees and Their Teaching." *HUCA* 6 (1929): 69–135.

Leaney, A. R. C. *The Rule of Qumran and Its Meaning*. NTL. London: SCM, 1966.

Lerle, E. *Proselytenwerbung und Christentum*. Berlin: Evangelische Verlagsanstalt, 1960.

Lesétre, H. "Prosélyte." *DB* 5: cols. 758–64.

Lévi, J. "Le prosélytisme juif." *REJ* 50 (1905): 1–9; 51 (1906): 1–31; 53 (1907): 56–61.

Lévy, I. *The Hebrew Text of the Book of Ecclesiasticus*. SSS 3. Leiden: Brill, 1909.

Liefeld, W. "The Wandering Preacher as a Social Figure in the Roman Empire." Ph.D. diss., Columbia University, 1967.

Lifshitz, B. *Donateurs et Fondateurs dans les Synagogues Juives*. Cahiers de la Revue Biblique 7. Paris: Gabalda, 1967.

Lindner, H. *Die Geschichtsauffassung des Flavius Josephus im Bellum Judaicum: Gleichzeitig ein Beitrag zur Quellenfrage*. AGAJU 12. Leiden: Brill, 1972.

Lübkert, J. H. B. "Die Proselyten der Juden." *TSK* 8 (1835): 681–700.

Lüdemann, G. *Das frühe Christentum nach den Traditionen der Apostelgeschichte: Ein Kommentar*. Göttingen: Vandenhoeck & Ruprecht, 1987.

Lundgreen, F. "Das palästinische Heerwesen in der neutestamentlichen Zeit." *Palästinajahrbuch* 17 (1921): 46–63.

Mack, B. L. "*Imitatio Mosis:* Patterns of Cosmology and Soteriology in the Hellenistic Synagogue." *StPhilonica* 1 (1972): 27–55.

MacLennan, R. S., and A. T. Kraabel. "The God-Fearers: A Literary and Theological Invention." *BAR* 12 (1986): 46–53, 64.

MacMullen, R. "Conversion: A Historian's View." *SecCent* 5 (1985–86): 67–81.

———. *Paganism in the Roman Empire*. New Haven: Yale University Press, 1981.

———. "Two Types of Conversion to Early Christianity." *VC* 37 (1983): 174–92.

Maier, P. L. "The Episode of the Golden Roman Shields at Jerusalem." *HTR* 62 (1969): 109–21.

Malinowski, F. X. "Torah Tendencies in Galilean Judaism according to Flavius Josephus with Gospel Connotations." *BTB* 10 (1980): 30–36.

Manson, T. W. *The Sayings of Jesus.* London: SCM, 1949.

Marcus, R. "The *Sebomenoi* in Josephus." *Jewish Social Studies* 14 (1952): 247–50.

Martin, L. H. "Josephus' Use of *Heimarmene* in the *Jewish Antiquities* XIII, 171–3." *Numen* 28 (1981): 127–35.

Mayer, G. "Aspekte des Abrahambildes in der hellenistisch-jüdischen Literatur." *EvT* 32 (1972): 118–27.

McEleney, N. J. "Conversion, Circumcision, and the Law." *NTS* 20 (1973–74): 319–41.

———. "Orthodoxy in Judaism of the First Christian Century." *JSJ* 4 (1973): 19–42.

———. "Orthodoxy in Judaism of the First Christian Century: Replies to David E. Aune and Lester L. Grabbe." *JSJ* 9 (1978): 83–88.

McKnight, S. "*De Vita Mosis* 1.147: Lion Proselytes in Philo?" In *The Studia Philonica Annual: Studies in Hellenistic Judaism,* edited by D. T. Runia, 1:58–62. Atlanta: Scholars Press, 1989.

Meek, T. J. "The Translation of *Ger* in the Hexateuch and Its Bearing on the Documentary Hypothesis." *JBL* 49 (1930): 172–80.

Meeks, W. A. "The Divine Agent and His Counterfeit in Philo and the Fourth Gospel." In *Aspects of Religious Propaganda in Judaism and Early Christianity,* edited by E. S. Fiorenza, 43–67. UNDCSJCA 2. Notre Dame: University of Notre Dame Press, 1976.

———. *The First Urban Christians: The Social World of the Apostle Paul.* New Haven: Yale University Press, 1983.

———. "Moses as God and King." In *Religions in Antiquity: Essays in Memory of Erwin Ramsdell Goodenough,* edited by J. Neusner, 354–71. SHR 14. Leiden: Brill, 1968.

Mendelson, A. *Secular Education in Philo of Alexandria.* MHUC 3. Cincinnati: Hebrew Union College Press, 1982.

Meyer, R. "Die Figurendarstellung in der Kunst des späthellenistischen Judentums." *Judaica* 5 (1949): 1–40.

Meyers, E. M., and L. M. White. "Jews and Christians in a Roman World." *Archaeology* 42 (1989): 26–33.

Michel, O. "Freudenbotschaft und Völkerwelt." *Deutsche Theologie* 6 (1939): 45–68.

——. "Studien zu Josephus: Simon bar Giora." *NTS* 14 (1967–68): 402–8.

Middendorp, T. *Die Stellung Jesu Ben Siras zwischen Judentum und Hellenismus.* Leiden: Brill, 1973.

Momigliano, A. *Alien Wisdom: The Limits of Hellenization.* Cambridge: Cambridge University Press, 1975.

Montefiore, C. G., and H. Loewe. *A Rabbinic Anthology.* New York: Schocken, 1938.

Montgomery, J. A. "The Religion of Flavius Josephus." *JQR* 11 (1920–21): 277–305.

Moore, G. F. "Fate and Free Will in the Jewish Philosophies According to Josephus." *HTR* 22 (1929): 371–89.

——. *Judaism in the First Centuries of the Christian Era: The Age of the Tannaim.* 3 vols. Cambridge, Mass.: Harvard University Press, 1927–30.

——. "The Rise of Normative Judaism." *HTR* 17 (1924): 307–73; 18 (1925) 1–38.

Mosley, A. W. "Historical Reporting in the Ancient World." *NTS* 12 (1965–66): 10–26.

Moule, C. F. D. *The Birth of the New Testament.* 3d ed. San Francisco: Harper & Row, 1981.

——. "Once More, Who Were the Hellenists?" *ExpTim* 70 (1958–59): 100–102.

Munck, J. *Paul and the Salvation of Mankind.* London: SCM, 1959.

Murphy-O'Connor, J. "The Critique of the Princes of Judah." *RB* 79 (1972): 200–216.

——. "Demetrius I and the Teacher of Righteousness." *RB* 83 (1976): 400–420.

——. "The Essenes and Their History." *RB* 81 (1974): 215–44.

——. "An Essene Missionary Document? CD 2:14–6:1." *RB* 77 (1970): 201–29.

——. "A Literary Analysis of Damuscus Document XIX, 33–XX, 34." *RB* 79 (1972): 544–64.

——. "The Original Text of CD 7:9–8:2=19:5–14." *HTR* 64 (1971): 379–86.

Murray, O. "Aristeas and Ptolemaic Kingship." *JTS* 18 (1967): 337–71.

Neusner, J. "The Conversion of Adiabene to Judaism: A New Perspective." *JBL* 83 (1964): 60–66.

——. "From Moore to Urbach and Sanders: Fifty Years of 'Judaism.'" *RelStuTheol* 6 (1986): 7–26.

——. *From Politics to Piety: The Emergence of Pharisaic Judaism.* Englewood Cliffs: Prentice-Hall, 1973.

——. *A History of the Jews in Babylonia*. SPB 9, 11, 12, 14, 15. Leiden: Brill, 1965–70.

——. *The Idea of Purity in Ancient Judaism*. SJLA 1. Leiden: Brill, 1973.

——. "'Judaism' after Moore: A Programmatic Statement." *JJS* 31 (1980): 141–56.

——. "Judaism in a Time of Crisis: Four Responses to the Destruction of the Second Temple." *Judaism* 21 (1972): 313–27.

——. *Rabbinic Traditions about the Pharisees before 70*. 3 vols. Leiden: Brill, 1971.

Nickelsburg, G. W. E. "Stories of Biblical and Early Post-Biblical Times." In *Jewish Writings of the Second Temple Period: Apocrypha, Pseudepigrapha, Qumran Sectarian Writings, Philo, Josephus*, edited by M. E. Stone, 2.2: 33–87. Philadelphia: Fortress Press, 1984.

Nock, A. D. *Conversion: The Old and the New in Religion from Alexander the Great to Augustine of Hippo*. New York: Oxford University Press, 1933.

——. "Eunuchs in Ancient Religions." *ARW* 23 (1925): 25–33.

Nolland, J. "Proselytism or Politics in Horace *Satires* 1,4, 138–43?" *VC* 33 (1979): 347–55.

——. "Uncircumcised Proselytes." *JSJ* 12 (1981): 173–94.

Oepke, A. "Internationalismus, Rasse und Weltmission im Lichte Jesu." *ZST* 10 (1933): 278–300.

Overman, J. A. "The God-Fearers: Some Neglected Features." *JSNT* 32 (1988): 17–26.

Paul, A. "Prosélyte, Prosélytisme." *DBSup* 8: cols. 1353–56.

Pervo, R. I. "Joseph and Aseneth and the Greek Novel." In *Society of Biblical Literature 1976 Seminar Papers*, edited by G. W. MacRae, 171–81. Missoula, Mont.: Scholars Press, 1976.

Pesch, R. "Voraussetzungen und Anfänge der urchristlichen Mission." In *Mission im Neuen Testament*, edited by K. Kertelge, 11–70. QD 93. Freiburg/Basel/Vienna: Herder, 1982.

Pick, B. "Jewish Propaganda in the Time of Christ." *Quarterly Review of the Evangelical Lutheran Church (=Lutheran Quarterly)* 23 (1893): 149–72; 24 (1894): 115–31.

Pines, S. "A Platonistic Model for Two of Josephus' Accounts of the Doctrine of the Pharisees Concerning Providence and Man's Freedom of Action." *Immanuel* 7 (1977): 38–43.

Polag, A. *Fragmenta Q: Textheft zur Logienquelle*. 2d ed. Neukirchen-Vluyn: Neukirchener, 1979.

Polster, G. "Der kleine Talmudtraktat über die Proselyten." *Angelos* 2 (1926): 1–38.

Porton, G. G. "Diversity in Postbiblical Judaism." In *Early Judaism and Its Modern Interpreters*, edited by R. A. Kraft and G. W. E. Nickelsburg, 57-80. Philadelphia: Fortress Press; Atlanta: Scholars Press, 1986. [=*EJMI*]

——. *GOYIM: Gentiles and Israelites in Mishnah-Tosefta.* BJS 155. Atlanta: Scholars Press, 1988.

Priest, J. F. "Mebaqqer, Paqid, and the Messiah." *JBL* 81 (1962): 55-61.

Pusey, K. "Jewish Proselyte Baptism." *ExpTim* 95 (1984): 141-45.

Puzicha, M. *Christus peregrinus: Die Fremdenaufnahme (Mt 25,35) als Werke der privaten Wohltätigkeit im Urteil der Alten Kirche.* MBT 47. Münster: Aschendorff, 1980.

Rabello, A. M. "L'observance des fêtes juives dan l'Empire romain." *ANRW* 2.21.2: 1288-1312.

Rabin, C. *Qumran Studies.* Scripta Judaica 2. Oxford: Oxford University Press, 1957.

Raisin, J. S. *Gentile Reactions to Jewish Ideals, with Special Reference to Proselytes,* edited by H. Hailperin. New York: Philosophical Library, 1953.

Rajak, T. "Jews and Christians as Groups in a Pagan World." In *"To See Ourselves as Others See Us": Christians, Jews, "Others" in Late Antiquity,* edited by J. Neusner and E. S. Frerichs, 247-62. Chico, Calif.: Scholars Press, 1985.

——. "Josephus and the 'Archaeology' of the Jews." *JJS* 33 (1982): 465-77.

——. *Josephus: The Historian and His Society.* Philadelphia: Fortress Press, 1983.

Rambo, L. R. "Current Research on Religious Conversion." *RelSRev* 8 (1982): 146-59.

Rasp, H. "Flavius Josephus und die jüdischen Religionsparteien." *ZNW* 23 (1924): 27-47.

Reese, J. M. *Hellenistic Influence on the Book of Wisdom and Its Consequences.* AnBib 41. Rome: Biblical Institute Press, 1970.

Revel, B. "Some Anti-Traditional Laws of Josephus." *JQR* 14 (1923-24): 293-301.

Reynolds, J., and R. F. Tannenbaum. *Jews and Godfearers at Aphrodisias: Greek Inscriptions with Commentary.* CPSSV 12. Cambridge: Cambridge Philological Society, 1987.

Riesner, R. *Jesus als Lehrer: Eine Untersuchung zum Ursprung der Evangelien-Überlieferung.* WUNT 2:7. Tübingen: J. C. B. Mohr, 1981.

Romaniuk, K. "Die 'Gottesfürchtigen' im Neuen Testament: Beitrag zur neutestamentlichen Theologie der Gottesfrucht [sic])." *Aegyptus* 44 (1964): 66-91.

Rosen, G. *Juden und Phönizier: Das antike Judentum als Missionsreligion und die Entstehung der jüdischen Diaspora*. Revised by F. Rosen and D. G. Bertram. Tübingen: J. C. B. Mohr, 1929.

Rosenbloom, J. R. *Conversion to Judaism: From the Biblical Period to the Present*. HUCAS. Cincinnati: Hebrew Union College Press, 1978.

Roth, C. "An Ordinance against Images in Jerusalem, A.D. 66." *HTR* 49 (1956): 169–77.

Rowley, H. H. "Jewish Proselyte Baptism and the Baptism of John." *HUCA* 15 (1940): 313–34.

Ruppel, W. "*Politeuma*: Bedeutungsgeschichte eines staatsrechtlichen Terminus." *Philologus* 82 (1927): 268–312, 433–54.

Safrai, S. "Relations between the Diaspora and the Land of Israel." In *The Jewish People in the First Century*, edited by S. Safrai and M. Stern, 1.1: 184–215. Philadelphia: Fortress Press, 1974.

———. "The Synagogue and Its Worship." In *The World History of the Jewish People. First Series: Ancient Times. Volume 8: Society and Religion in the Second Temple Period*, 1:65–98. London: W. H. Allen, 1977. [= *WHJP*]

Safrai, S., and M. Stern, eds. *The Jewish People in the First Century*. Multivolume. Philadelphia: Fortress Press, 1974–.

Sanders, E. P. "The Covenant as a Soteriological Category and the Nature of Salvation in Palestinian and Hellenistic Judaism." In *Jews, Greeks, and Christians: Studies in Honor of W.D. Davies*, edited by R. Hamerton-Kelly and R. Scroggs, 11–44. SJLA 21. Leiden: Brill, 1976.

———. *Jesus and Judaism*. Philadelphia: Fortress Press, 1985.

———. *Paul and Palestinian Judaism: A Comparison of Patterns of Religion*. Philadelphia: Fortress Press, 1977.

———. *Paul, the Law, and the Jewish People*. Philadelphia: Fortress Press, 1983.

Sanders, E. P., A. I. Baumgarten, et al. *Jewish and Christian Self-Definition*. Volume 2. London: SCM, 1981.

Schalit, A. "Josephus und Justus: Studien zur Vita des Josephus." *Klio* 26 (1933): 67–95.

Schiffman, L. H. "The Conversion of the Royal House of Adiabene in Josephus and Rabbinic Sources." In *Josephus, Judaism, and Christianity*, edited by L. H. Feldman and G. Hata, 293–312. Detroit: Wayne State University Press, 1987.

———. "Jewish Sectarianism in Second Temple Times." In *Great Schisms in Jewish History*, edited by R. Jospe and S. Wagner, 1–46. New York: Ktav, 1981.

——. *Who Was a Jew? Rabbinic and Halakhic Perspectives on the Jewish-Christian Schism.* Hoboken: Ktav, 1985.

Schlatter, A. *Die Theologie des Judentums nach dem Bericht des Josephus.* Gütersloh: n.p., 1932.

——. *Wie Sprach Josephus von Gott?* BFCT 14/1. Gütersloh: C. Bertelsmann, 1910.

Schmidt, K. L. "Israel's Stellung zu den Fremden und Beisassenen und Israel's Wissen um seine Fremdling- und Beisassenheit." *Judaica* 1 (1945–46): 269–96.

Schmithals, W. "The False Teachers of Romans 16:17-20." In *Paul and the Gnostics,* 219–38. Nashville: Abingdon, 1972.

Schoeps, H. J. *Paul: The Theology of the Apostle in the Light of Jewish Religious History.* London: Lutterworth, 1961.

Schubert, K. *The Dead Sea Community: Its Origin and Teachings.* London: A. & C. Black, 1959.

Schulz, S. *Q: Die Spruchquelle der Evangelien.* Zurich: Theologischer Verlag, 1972.

Schüpphaus, J. *Die Psalmen Salomos: Ein Zeugnis Jerusalemer Theologie und Frömmigkeit in der Mitte der vorchristlichen Jahrhunderts.* ALGHJ 7. Leiden: Brill, 1977.

Schürer, E. *The History of the Jewish People in the Age of Jesus Christ (175 B.C.–A.D. 135).* Revised and edited by G. Vermes, M. Black, F. Millar, M. Goodman, and P. Vermes. 3 vols. Edinburgh: T. & T. Clark, 1973–87.

Schüssler Fiorenza, E. "You are not to be Called Father: Early Christian History in a Feminist Perspective." *Cross Currents* 30 (1979): 301–23.

——, ed. *Aspects of Religious Propaganda in Judaism and Early Christianity.* UNDCSCJA 2. Notre Dame: University of Notre Dame Press, 1976.

Schweitzer, A. *The Mysticism of Paul the Apostle.* London: A. & C. Black, 1931.

Segal, A. F. "The Costs of Proselytism and Conversion." In *Society of Biblical Literature 1988 Seminar Papers,* edited by D. Lull, 336–49. Atlanta: Scholars Press, 1988.

Senior, D., and C. Stuhlmueller. *The Biblical Foundations for Mission.* Maryknoll, N.Y.: Orbis, 1983.

Sevenster, J. N. *Do You Know Greek? How Much Greek Could the First Jewish Christians Have Known?* SNovT 19. Leiden: Brill, 1968.

——. *The Roots of Pagan Anti-Semitism in the Ancient World.* SNovT 41. Leiden: Brill, 1975.

Siegert, F. "Gottesfürchtige und Sympathisanten." *JSJ* 4 (1973): 109–64.

Siegfried, C. F. "Prophetische Missionsgedanke und jüdische Missionsbestrebungen." *JPT* 16 (1890): 435–53.

Sigal, P. *The Emergence of Contemporary Judaism.* Volume 1: *The Foundations of Judaism.* Part 1: *From the Origins to the Separation of Christianity.* PTMS 29. Pittsburgh: Pickwick, 1980.

Simon, M. "Sur les débuts du proselytisme juif." In *Hommages à André Dupont-Sommer*, edited by A. Caquot and M. Philonenko, 509–20. Paris: Librairie d'Amerique et d'Orient Adrien-Maisonnueve, 1971.

Smallwood, E. M. "The Alleged Jewish Tendencies of Poppaea Sabina." *JTS* 10 (1959): 329–35.

———. "The Chronology of Gaius' Attempt to Desecrate the Temple." *Latomus* 16 (1957): 3–17.

———. *The Jews under Roman Rule: From Pompey to Diocletian.* SJLA 20. Leiden: Brill, 1976.

———. *Philonis Alexandrini: Legatio ad Gaium.* Edited with an Introduction, Translation and Commentary. Leiden: Brill, 1961.

———. "Some Notes on the Jews under Tiberius." *Latomus* 15 (1956): 314–29.

Smith, M. "The Image of God: Notes on the Hellenization of Judaism, with especial Reference to Goodenough's Work on Jewish Symbols." *BJRLUM* 40 (1957–58): 473–512.

———. "Palestinian Judaism in the First Century." In *Israel: Its Role in Civilization*, edited by M. Davis, 67–81. New York: Harper & Row, 1956.

———. "Rome and the Maccabean Conversions: Notes on 1 Mac. 8." In *Donum Gentilicium: New Testament Studies in Honour of David Daube*, edited by E. Bammel et al., 1–7. Oxford: Clarendon, 1978.

Snow, D. A., and R. Machalek. "The Convert as a Social Type." In *Sociological Theory 1983*, edited by R. Collins, 259–89. San Francisco: Jossey-Bass, 1983.

———. "The Sociology of Conversion." *AnnRev of Soc* 10 (1984): 167–90.

Sowers, S. "On the Reinterpretation of History in Hellenistic Judaism." In *Oikonomia: Heilsgeschichte als Thema der Theologie. Oscar Cullmann z. 65. Geburtstag gewidmet*, edited by F. Christ, 18–27. Hamburg-Bergstedt: Herbert Reich, 1967.

Staerk, W. "Ursprung und Grenzen der Missionskraft der alttestamentlichen Religion." *TBl* 4 (1925): 25–37.

Staples, C. L., and A. L. Mauss. "Conversion or Commitment? A Reassessment of the Snow and Machalek Approach to the Study of Conversion." *JSSR* 26 (1987): 133–47.

Steiner, A. "Warum lebten die Essener asketisch?" *BZ* 15 (1971): 1–28.

Sterling, G. E. "Luke-Acts and Apologetic Historiography." In *Society of Biblical Literature 1989 Seminar Papers*, edited by D. Lull, 326–42. Atlanta: Scholars Press, 1989.

Stern, M. *Greek and Latin Authors on Jews and Judaism*, edited with Introductions, Translations and Commentary. 3 vols. Jerusalem: The Israel Academy of Sciences and Humanities, 1974–84. [= *GLAJJ*]

——. "The Jewish Diaspora." In *The Jewish People in the First Century*, edited by S. Safrai and M. Stern, 1:117–83. Philadelphia: Fortress Press, 1974.

——. "Zealots." *Encyclopedia Judaica Yearbook* (1973): 135–52.

Sundkler, B. "Jésus et les païens." *RHPhR* 16 (1936): 462–99; also in *Arbeiten und Mitteilungen aus dem neutestamentlichen Seminar zu Uppsala* 6 (1937): 1–38.

Sutcliffe, E. F. "Hatred at Qumran." *RevQ* 2 (1959–60): 345–56.

Swain, J. W. "Gamaliel's Speech and Caligula's Statue." *HTR* 37 (1944): 341–49.

Tannenbaum, R. F. "Jews and God-Fearers in the Holy City of Aphrodite." *BAR* 12 (1986): 54–57.

Taylor, T. M. "The Beginnings of Jewish Proselyte Baptism." *NTS* 2 (1955–56): 193–98.

Tcherikover, V. "The Decline and Fall of the Jewish Diaspora in Egypt in the Roman Period." *JJS* 14 (1963): 1–32.

——. *Hellenistic Civilization and the Jews*. New York: Atheneum, 1977.

——. "Jewish Apologetic Literature Reconsidered." *Eos* 48 (1956): 169–93.

——. "Was Jerusalem a 'Polis'?" *IEJ* 14 (1964): 61–78.

Teixidor, J. "The Kingdom of Adiabene and Hatra." *Berytus* 17 (1967–68): 1–11.

Thackeray, H. St. J. *Josephus: The Man and the Historian*. New York: Jewish Institute of Religion Press, 1929.

Thoma, C. "Die Weltanschauung des Josephus Flavius: Dargestellt anhand seiner Schilderung des jüdischen Aufstandes gegen Rom (66–73 n. Chr.)." *Kairos* 11 (1969): 39–52.

Thyen, H. *Der Stil der jüdisch-hellenistischen Homilie*. FRLANT N.F. 47. Göttingen: Vandenhoeck & Ruprecht, 1955.

Tiede, D. *The Charismatic Figure as Miracle Worker*. SBLDS 1. Missoula, Mont.: Society of Biblical Literature, 1973.

Timpe, D. "Der römische Vertrag mit den Juden von 161 v. Chr." *Chiron* 4 (1974): 133–52.

Torrance, T. F. "Proselyte Baptism." *NTS* 1 (1954–55): 150–54.

Trebilco, P. R. "Studies on Jewish Communities in Asia Minor." Ph.D. diss., University of Durham, 1987.

Trevor, J. C. *Scrolls from Qumran Cave One.* Jerusalem: Albright Institute of Archaeological Research, 1972.

Urbach, E. E. *The Sages: Their Concepts and Beliefs.* 2 vols. Jerusalem: Magnes, 1979.

———. "Self-Isolation or Self-Affirmation in Judaism in the First Three Centuries: Theory and Practice." In *Jewish and Christian Self-Definition,* edited by E. P. Sanders and A. I. Baumgarten, 2:269–98, 413–17. London: SCM, 1981.

Vande Kappelle, R. P. "Evidence of a Jewish Proselytizing Tendency in the Old Greek (Septuagint) Version of the Book of Isaiah: A Contribution to the Study of Jewish Proselytism in the Period of the Second Commonwealth." Ph.D. diss., Princeton Theological Seminary, 1977.

van der Horst, P. W. "Jews and Christians in Aphrodisias in the Light of their Relations in Other Cities of Asia Minor." *NedTTs* 43 (1989): 106–21.

———. *The Sentences of Pseudo-Phocylides: With Introduction and Commentary.* SVTP 4. Leiden: Brill, 1978.

van Unnik, W. C. "The Critique of Paganism in 1 Peter 1:18." In *Neotestamentica et Semitica: Studies in Honour of Matthew Black,* edited by E. E. Ellis and M. Wilcox, 129–42. Edinburgh: T. & T. Clark, 1969.

———. *Flavius Josephus als historische Schriftsteller.* Heidelberg: Lambert Schneider, 1978.

Vermes, G. *The Dead Sea Scrolls: Qumran in Perspective.* London: Collins, 1977.

———. *Scripture and Tradition in Judaism: Haggadic Studies.* 2d ed. SPB 4. Leiden: Brill, 1973.

Vlastos, G. "*Anamnesis* in the *Meno.*" *Dialogue* 4 (1965): 143–67.

Wacholder, B. Z. "Greek Authors in Herod's Library." *Studies in Bibliography and Booklore* 5 (1961): 102–9.

———. "Pseudo-Eupolemus' Two Greek Fragments on the Life of Abraham." *HUCA* 34 (1963): 83–113.

Wächter, L. "Die unterschiedliche Haltung der Pharisäer, Sadduzäer und Essener zur Heimarmene nach dem Bericht des Josephus." *ZRGG* 21 (1969): 97–114.

Wagner, S. "ידע in den Lobliedern von Qumran." In *Bibel und Qumran: Beiträge zur Erforschung der Beziehungen zwischen Bibel- und Qumranwissenschaft: Hans Bardtke zum 22.9.1966,* edited by S. Wagner, 232–52. Berlin: Evangelische Haupt-Bibelgesellschaft, 1968.

Weiss, H.-F. "Pharisäismus und Hellenismus: Zur Darstellung des Judentums im Geschichtswerk des jüdischen Historikers Flavius Josephus." *OLZ* 74 (1979): 421–33.

Werblowsky, R. J. Z. "A Note on Purification and Proselyte Baptism." In *Christianity, Judaism and Other Greco-Roman Cults: Studies for Morton Smith at Sixty.* Part Three, edited by J. Neusner, 200–205. SJLA 12. Leiden: Brill, 1975.

Wernberg-Møller, P. "The Nature of the YAHAD according to the *Manual of Discipline* and Related Documents." *ALUOS* 6 (1966–69): 56–81.

West, S. "*Joseph and Aseneth:* A Neglected Greek Romance." *ClassQuart* 24 (1974): 70–81.

Wilcox, M. "The 'God-Fearers' in Acts: A Reconsideration." *JSNT* 13 (1981): 102–22.

Wilken, R. L. "Judaism in Roman and Christian Society." *JR* 47 (1967): 313–30.

Williams, M. H. "'*Theosebes gar en*': The Jewish Tendencies of Poppaea Sabina." *JTS* 39 (1988): 97–111.

Wilson, S. G. *The Gentiles and the Gentile Mission in Luke-Acts.* SNTSMS 23. Cambridge: Cambridge University Press, 1973.

Wirgin, W. "Judah Maccabee's Embassy to Rome and the Jewish-Roman Treaty." *PEQ* 101 (1969): 15–20.

———. "Simon Maccabaeus' Embassy to Rome: Its Purpose and Outcome." *PEQ* 106 (1974): 141–46.

Witherington, B. *Women in the Ministry of Jesus.* SNTSMS 51. Cambridge: Cambridge University Press, 1984.

Wolfson, H. A. *Philo: Foundations of Religious Philosophy in Judaism, Christianity, and Islam.* 2 vols. Cambridge, Mass.: Harvard University Press, 1947.

———. "Philo on Jewish Citizenship in Alexandria." *JBL* 63 (1944): 165–68.

Ysebaert, J. *Greek Baptismal Terminology: Its Origin and Early Development.* Nijmegen: Dekker & Van de Vegt, 1962.

Zeitlin, S. "A Note on Baptism for Proselytes." *JBL* 52 (1933): 78–79.

———. "Proselytes and Proselytism during the Second Commonwealth and the Early Tannaitic Period." In *Solomon Zeitlin's Studies in the Early History of Judaism* 2:407–17. New York: Ktav, 1974.

Zeller, D. *Juden und Heiden in der Mission des Paulus: Studien zum Römerbrief.* Stuttgart: Katholisches Bibelwerk, 1976.

Index

SUBJECTS

AUTHORS

PASSAGES